Study on the Auditing Theory of Socialism with Chinese Characteristics

The Wiley Corporate F&A series provides information, tools, and insights to corporate professionals responsible for issues affecting the profitability of their company, from accounting and finance to internal controls and performance management.

Founded in 1807, John Wiley & Sons is the oldest independent publishing company in the United States. With offices in North America, Europe, Asia, and Australia, Wiley is globally committed to developing and marketing print and electronic products and services for our customers' professional and personal knowledge and understanding.

Study on the Auditing Theory of Socialism with Chinese Characteristics
Revised Edition

JIAYI LIU

WILEY

Library of Congress Cataloging-in-Publication Data:

Liu, Jiayi, 1956-
   Study on the auditing theory of socialism with Chinese characteristics/Jiayi Liu. — Revised edition.
      pages cm. — (Wiley corporate F&A series)
   Includes bibliographical references and index.
   ISBN 978-1-119-10781-1 (cloth); ISBN 978-1-119-10782-8 (ePub); ISBN 978-1-119-10786-6 (ePDF)
   1. Auditing—China.   2. Auditing, Internal—China.   I. Title.
   HF5616.C5L585 2015
   657′.450951—dc23
                                                                        2015007709

Contents

Prologue

A UDIT THEORY WITH CHINESE SOCIALIST characteristics is a part of the theory of socialism with Chinese characteristics. As an endogenous "immune system" of the general national governance system, featuring such functions as prevention, exposure, and resistance, government auditing serves as the cornerstone and surest guarantee of national governance. Government auditing emerged as demanded by governing activities; the aim of governance of a country determines the orientation of development of its audit system, and the mode of governance in a country determines the mode of its audit system. In a certain sense, the history of auditing is also a history of the rise and fall of a nation, and of the evolution of national governance. It is also a history that manifests conflicts between different interests, different ideologies, the collision of different cultures, and the evolution of different systems. Deeply rooted in the theoretical system featuring distinct Chinese characteristics, this book is closely linked to the national political system, economic operations, democracy and the rule of law, the market, history and culture, and the distinct characteristics of the times.

Audit theory with Chinese socialist characteristics is a theory based on auditing practices. Coming from auditing practices, audit theory is the enrichment and sublimation of practices and experience. Auditing in China has a history of more than 3,000 years, the auditing system under the leadership of the Chinese Communist Party dates back more than 80 years, and the modern auditing system in China was established over 30 years ago. With the continuous evolution of auditing in China, rich practical experience was accumulated. The audit theory with Chinese socialist characteristics was developed by summarizing the growth path and laws on the basis of deep analysis of various audit practices. Many viewpoints of the theory have strong Chinese features, imply China's vein of civilization, and are deeply rooted in Chinese history. The theory will be guiding China's audit practices for now and the future.

Audit theory with Chinese socialist characteristics is open and inclusive. It not only absorbed the essence of what was achieved by previous generations through their practice, research, and cognition efforts, but also drew on the experiences and practices of other fields and of the auditing profession of foreign countries. On the one hand, this book refers to both ancient and modern, Chinese and foreign knowledge in fields of politics, economics, law, and history, as an effort to seek the law of evolution of government auditing from the historical context of social-economic development. On the other hand, it also summarizes, inducts, and refines the practices, advanced audit theories, and cutting-edge methodologies from all countries that suit the Chinese reality to form an audit theory system with Chinese socialist characteristics.

Audit theory with Chinese socialist characteristics means advancing with the times. Government auditing in China has been developing for more than 30 years since government audit institutions were established in 1983. While developing this process, auditors nationwide endured great hardship in starting a new initiative; worked selflessly, fearlessly, and perseveringly; and showed great loyalty in performing their duties. They independently conducted audit supervision in accordance with the law and played a positive role in ensuring the fundamental interests of the people, promoting democracy and the rule of law, maintaining fiscal and economic order, increasing performance of funds, safeguarding national economic security, combating corruption, and promoting deepening of reform. These results would not have been achieved without our efforts of continuous exploration and understanding of government audit work and the effective guidance of audit theory with Chinese socialist characteristics. As Friedrich Engels (1820–1895) once said, "Our theory is a theory of development, rather than dogma that has to be learned and mechanically repeated." This is certainly the case with China's audit theory, which is still in the process of being enriched and improved.

There is no end to the development of practice and to the innovation of audit theory with Chinese socialist characteristics. Out of this understanding, we worked to summarize our national audit theory in order to meet the growing demands of a new reality and thus have undertaken a revision of the book entitled *Study on the Auditing Theory of Socialism with Chinese Characteristics*. The revision work features the following three aspects. First, we worked to suit the new demands of the modernization of the national governance system and governance ability and promotion of rule of law in an all-inclusive manner. Since the 18th CPC National Congress in November 2012, a series of measures have been taken. There have been new developments with regard to guiding theories and governance strategies. In particular, the 2nd, 3rd, and 4th Plenum of the 18th CPC Central Committee and the circular issued by the State Council—*Opinions on Strengthening Audit Work*—raised new requirements for government auditing. The latest version of the book aimed primarily at reflecting how government audit theory has been continuously innovated and upgraded to suit the new reality and to better promote and guide audit practices. Second, we analyzed the changes that have taken place in government auditing practices. We focused on combining theoretical analysis with practical exploration based on enhanced efforts in refinement of audit practices. We presented some new developments of government auditing in China with a view to matching theoretical development with practical development. In this process, new developments in auditing methods, management, standardization, and computerization were summarized. Third, we aimed to deepen understanding of the law that governs government auditing. During the revision of the book, while keeping pace with the times, efforts were made to summarize the fruits of past research, explain the essence of government auditing and the role it plays as a guarantee of national governance on the basis of the "immune system" theory, provide a deepened understanding of the nature and functions of government auditing, and achieve the modernization of a national governance system.

This book consists of nine chapters; each is an independent study on a specific topic. In order to thoroughly expound each chapter and achieve coherence between them, we provided certain theoretical perspectives and practical case studies from different viewpoints to present our readers with qualitative, accurate, and profound content.

Moving from practice to theory is a process in which cognition keeps deepening. Theories also require that practice is accurately understood, systematically summarized, and continuously refined. Based on in-depth research over a long period, we strived to expound practical experience, common approaches, and the knowledge of our audit practitioners formed in the past years through understandable language. Although we have done our best, we may have omitted some details. We sincerely welcome comments from auditors, experts, scholars, and readers so that the theory of government auditing with Chinese socialist characteristics can be continuously enriched, improved, and developed.

December 2014

Acknowledgments

SINCE 2009 THE NATIONAL AUDIT OFFICE has been carrying out a thorough study of the audit theory with Chinese socialist characteristics in order to better promote the scientific development of China's audit cause. A research working group was established under the chairmanship of Auditor General Mr. Liu Jiayi. Former deputy auditor generals Mr. Linghu An, Mr. Dong Dasheng, Ms. Yu Xiaoming, and Mr. Hou Kai as well as Deputy Auditor Generals Mr. Sun Baohou, Mr. Chen Chenzhao, and Mr. Yuan Ye and President Mr. Zhai Xigui of the China Audit Society worked as vice chairs and members of the research working group. Other members of the working group include those from the departments of the National Audit Office of China and those from local audit institutions, as well as professors from institutes of higher learning. They include Mr. Liu Dazhu, Mr. Yin Ping, Mr. Wang Xiaolong, Ms. Zuo Min, Mr. Zhang Limin, Mr. Wang Zhiyu, Mr. Hu Limin, Mr. Wang Xiuming, Mr. Chen Taihui, Mr. Cui Zhenlong, Mr. Wang Benqiang, Ms. Guo Caiyun, Mr. Liu Shaotong, and Ms. Liu Liyun. Those involved in writing research reports and carrying out relevant organization work include Mr. Ma Xiaofang, Mr. Lei Da, Mr. Xiao Zhendong, Mr. Zeng Jun, Mr. Niu Hongbin, Mr. Wang Changyou, Mr. Wang Gang, and Mr. Wang Biaohua. The results of their research were used to compile the book titled *Audit Theory with Chinese Socialist Characteristics*, published by the China Modern Economic Publishing House in May 2013.

As a profession with a strong practical feature, facing a rapidly changing external situation and requirements, the government auditing profession is experiencing never-ending changes and improvements, and audit techniques and methodologies are also developing at a very fast speed. In particular, the 2nd, 3rd, and 4th Plenum of 18th CPC Central Committee and the circular issued by the State Council—*Opinions on Strengthening Audit Work*—raised new requirements for government auditing, and our understanding about the nature, function, and role of government auditing has deepened. Therefore, we have reviewed and revised the book *Audit Theory with Chinese Socialist Characteristics*. The revision was led by Auditor General Mr. Liu Jiayi, and other leaders of the National Audit Office of China, Mr. Shi Aizhong, Mr. Sun Baohou, Ms. Chen Qiang, Mr. Chen Chenzhao, Mr. Zhang Tong, Mr. Yuan Ye, and Mr. Li Xiaozhong, provided valuable advice and comments in the revision process. Ms. Guo Caiyun, Mr. Shang Rui, Mr. Liu Junmin, Mr. Huang Wenbing, Mr. Chen Xiangjie, Mr. Xu Jun, Mr. Gao Zhan, Ms. Zou Xiaoping, Mr. Zhang Long, Mr. Wang Zhong, Mr. Hao Jingmin, Mr. Wang Gang, Mr. Peng Xinlin, Mr. Liu Dazhu, Mr. Cui Zhenlong, Mr. Wang Biaohua, and Mr. Wang Changyou also contributed important input. We wish to thank all of them.

CHAPTER ONE

The Nature of Auditing

NATURE IS THE FUNDAMENTAL PROPERTY and essence of a thing that makes it different. From the perspective of intrinsic property, the nature of auditing provides an understanding of what auditing is. It is the inherent and relatively stable fundamental property that decides the appearance and evolution of auditing, and is the basic feature that distinguishes it from other things. From the perspective of extrinsic correlations, the nature of auditing provides an understanding of why auditing is necessary, which sets the starting point of auditing, including its duties, functions, roles, and methods to achieve them.

I. SEVERAL VIEWPOINTS ON THE NATURE OF AUDITING

People's cognition of things, phenomena, and processes is an infinite process of understanding leading from phenomena to nature, and from a superficial to a profound degree.[1] The cognition of the nature of auditing deepens with the development of audit practice, the further exploration of laws of auditing, and the rising awareness of auditing. Only through in-depth analysis and research of existing cognitions, and by conscientiously summing up and refining audit experience and rules, can we accurately summarize the nature of socialist government auditing with Chinese characteristics.

Government auditing as an institutional arrangement was created and developed to meet certain objectives. Due to differing needs, countries have different audit system arrangements at different stages of their socioeconomic development, and the contents, responsibilities, and roles of auditing are also very different. In the early years after the founding of the People's Republic of China (PRC), independent auditing departments were not set up, and finance, banking, and taxation departments supervised their own revenues and expenditures according to their business management situation. The PRC Constitution promulgated in 1982 stipulated a government auditing system, and the establishment of audit offices by the State Council and local people's governments at county level and above. Over 30 years of development, the government audit system has been improved continuously, and audit guidelines, central tasks, priorities, and roles amid socioeconomic changes have undergone significant change. Based on different presentations of auditing in different historical periods, thinking on government auditing nature emerged from different perspectives and levels with distinctive characteristics of the times. They can be mainly divided into the following five categories.

(1) Theory of Accounts Checking

According to the Theory of Accounts Checking, auditing simply means the checking of accounts. This theory is viewed from the perspective of audit methods/means, with a simple or preliminary conclusion, and an accepted view on the nature of social auditing. This traditional theory is intuitional, visual, easy to understand, and still has great influence. The reasons for the emergence of this theory include: In early periods, most audits focused on checking accounts, and audit means and functions were relatively simple, encouraging a relatively intuitive approach. In 1953, the Committee on Terminology of the American Institute of Certified Public Accountants (AICPA) offered this definition in Accounting Terminology Announcement No. 1: "Auditing is an inspection means aiming to express views on fairness and consistency of the financial statements provided by a company or other entity to the public and the parties concerned in accordance with generally accepted accounting principles." *Encyclopedia Britannica* (1974) recorded that "Audit refers to the inspection of business activities, account books and financial statements by accounting experts excluding the accounting personnel originally responsible for preparing the accounts and statements."

The Theory of Accounts Checking interprets auditing from the perspective of audit means, but can only explain the characteristics of traditional financial auditing and social auditing, and cannot conform to the requirements of government auditing. For example, performance auditing, accountability auditing, resources and environmental auditing, and real-time auditing on policy implementation cannot be described as "checking accounts." Due to the long-term influence of the Theory of Accounts Checking, government auditing was positioned as "detecting errors and correcting disadvantages." The Theory of Accounts Checking advocated that government auditing institutions mainly function to rectify financial accounting and economic activities, while ignoring the roles of government auditing in socioeconomic development, the nation's political and legal system construction, and national governance.

(2) Economic Supervision Theory

According to the Economic Supervision Theory, the main idea of government auditing is as follows:

> The trusted economic responsibility relationship generated by the separation of ownership from the right of operation and management is the basis of auditing. It was developed for the owners to supervise the trusted economic responsibility performance situation of operators and managers. Auditing is an economic supervision activity carried out to evaluate, confirm and prove whether trusted operators and managers have properly performed their assigned economic responsibilities.[2]

Economic Supervision Theory was widely recognized by Chinese auditors in the 1980s–1990s. A national seminar on basic audit theories in 1989 proposed that auditing was the independent economic supervision activity carried out by a professional agency and its personnel in accordance with the laws to review the truthfulness, compliance, and performance in regard to financial status, financial revenue and expenditure, and relevant economic activities of audited units, and evaluate economic responsibilities, so as to maintain the financial laws and discipline, improve management and economic returns, and strengthen macrocontrol. The National Seminar on Audit Definition in 1995 further clarified: Auditing is an act of independently checking accounting records and supervising truthfulness, compliance, and performance of financial revenues. The two definitions, with profound impact on auditing theory and practice, were proposed from the viewpoint that economic supervision is the nature of auditing.

Defining the nature of government auditing as economic supervision and stressing its important role in the economic field, its supervision functions, the focus on specific economic behavior, and the detection of major violations of laws and regulations fulfilled the audit environment requirements and actual conditions of auditing offices in the early years, and played an active role in helping people understand and accept auditing. However, with economic and social development, Chinese audit practice has undergone significant change. Especially in recent years, government auditing has played an active and constructive role in political, economic, cultural, social, and ecological construction, as well as all other socioeconomic aspects. However, the Economic Supervision Theory cannot be used to explain changes of audit practices and their constructive role any longer.

(3) Economic Cybernetics

According to Economic Cybernetics, government auditing is an economic control activity.[3] Its main idea is as follows: Auditing was developed based on the trusted economic responsibility relationship. Upon starting a project for a client, auditors directly seek audit problems and determine any punishment, and report the accountability performance situation back to the client with judgment on the necessity of "correction," which brings into play the important role of information in system operation control. Therefore, auditing, especially government auditing, is a control mechanism ensuring accountability performance.

Economic Cybernetics stresses that auditing is part of the control mechanism for ensuring effective accountability performance. Its abstract description of direct correction by the audit office is in line with the actual situation of government auditing. There is widespread belief that control includes supervision. Supervision, in fact, is only an element of control. Although the objects of control and supervision are both information, the actors differ in attitude. Control is positive, while supervision is relatively passive and serves the overall control purpose. Therefore, compared to Economic Supervision Theory, Economic Cybernetics has richer content.[4]

Economic Cybernetics was proposed on the basis of recognizing that auditing is supervisory behavior, and summarizes the nature of auditing from the perspective of its direct role. Both it and Economic Supervision Theory emphasize the important role of government auditing in economics, and the focus on specific economic activities and economic matters, while ignoring its important role in the political, cultural, social, and environmental construction, as well as the macrofield.

(4) Power Restriction Theory

The Power Restriction Theory derives from a concept in *The Spirit of Law*, written by French thinker Montesquieu in the eighteenth century: "All powerful men are likely to abuse the power and will not stop until being restricted . . . To prevent the abuse, power must be restricted by power."[5] According to this viewpoint, we can conclude that government auditing, through supervision of management and use of public resources during the exercise of government powers, ultimately aims to control government power and prevent corruption and power abuse. After auditing the responsibility performance of administrative organs, government audit offices report the results to legislative bodies for possible further investigation. In fact, government auditing is the means and the mechanism for checks and balances between legislative and executive power. If audit supervision is regarded as a power, auditing by government audit offices is a process of restricting one power with another.

The Power Restriction Theory breaks the limitations of the Economic Supervision Theory and Economic Cybernetics concerning positioning in the economics field, and summarizes the nature of government auditing from the perspective of political science. It determines the nature of government auditing as power restriction, and stresses that auditing, as a power restriction tool, is a political system arrangement mainly used to restrict and prevent power abuse and corruption. This theory plays an active role in establishing the government audit theory from a political perspective, and guiding auditors to widen audit work to the political and social perspectives rather than merely the economic perspective.

However, the Power Restriction Theory was not unanimously accepted. Some scholars argued that it stressed the restrictive role of auditing, while giving insufficient attention to the constructive role of government auditing in promoting more effective exercise of powers. Others believed it still could not reasonably explain the design and implementation of the government audit system of administrative organs.

(5) Theory of Democracy and Rule of Law

According to this, modern government auditing is a product of democracy and rule of law, and also a tool for promoting these concepts.[6] Democracy and the rule of law are the basis of national governance. From the perspective of audit origin and development, an independent government audit system cannot operate well without sound rule of law. Of major importance is the safeguarding of independence, providing audit evidence and standards, and maintaining the efficiency and authority of audit results. The theory stresses that modern auditing is a means of promoting democracy and the rule of law mainly due to three aspects: Government auditing comes from and acts on behalf of the laws. In many countries, audit status is established constitutionally. Modern government auditing plays an active role in advancing the rule of law and safeguarding its dignity: (1) supervising the enforcement of financial laws and regulations, to maintain the solemnity of the law; (2) urging administration by law; and (3) revealing problems through auditing to improve laws and regulations. Furthermore, government auditing is derived from and serves people's democracy. Upon entrustment by the power organs, government audit agencies, on behalf of the masses and taxpayers, supervise government responsibility performance and report to the people. Therefore, government auditing is a tool for promoting democracy. Finally, as a tool for democracy and the rule of law, it is fully constructive. Democracy and the rule of law are complementary and inseparable. We should balance the interests of individuals, groups, and the whole society and build a harmonious society and avoid overly rigid law enforcement. Otherwise, true democracy cannot be achieved. Therefore, government audit offices should conduct regular financial auditing, supervise government departments and state-owned enterprises, broaden their horizons, reflect more public appeal, and pay more attention to people's fundamental interests. From this perspective, government auditing as a tool for promoting democracy and rule of law is active, creative, and constructive.

Compared to the Power Restriction Theory, the Theory of Democracy and Rule of Law expounds the relationship between government auditing and democracy from the political perspective, and also the relationship between government auditing and the rule of law from the perspective of establishing a law-based country. It emphasizes the supervisory and restrictive role of government auditing, and also the promotional aspect. Therefore, this theory is an abstraction and generalization of government auditing as an institutional arrangement from a higher level and a wider range.

II. UNDERSTANDING THE NATURE OF GOVERNMENT AUDITING FROM THE PERSPECTIVE OF NATIONAL GOVERNANCE

The foregoing analysis shows that recognition of the nature of government auditing is a gradual process, with certain characteristics of the times and history. But most fundamentally, we should constantly and promptly adapt to social changes and try to reveal the laws behind social phenomena, to maintain the vitality and creativity of government auditing. Engels said, "The theoretical thinking of every era, including the present, has historic characteristics. In different ages, it has completely different forms and contents."[7] Currently, to address a series of challenges including economic globalization, technology development, and diversification of public demands, all countries highlight improvement of national governance to seize opportunities and meet challenges. Against such a background, an important requirement for government audit theory and practice was to understand the nature and positioning of government auditing based on national governance needs so as to guide scientific development of the government audit cause.

The word "governance" is derived from Latin and ancient Greek, originally meaning control, guidance, and manipulation.[8] For a long time, "governance" and "government" were used interchangeably for management and political activities in regard to national public affairs. In the late 1970s, with major economic and social transformation underway, governance theories attracted extensive attention from social scientists, and countries everywhere launched governance-based reforms. Governance extensively involves "each social organization and institution including the family and the State," and stresses "three important governance departments directly related to sustainable human development, namely the State (governmental organizations and institutions), civil social organizations and private sectors."[9] Western and Chinese scholars and research institutions have different understandings about the governance concept and connotation, however. After studies, we define governance as the process of controlling and managing state affairs and social affairs and providing services by configuring and exercising state powers, so as to ensure national security, safeguard national interests and people's interests, maintain social stability, and promote scientific development. The core idea about the nature of government auditing from the perspective of national governance can be summarized as follows: Government auditing was generated and improved to meet national governance needs, and serves as an "immune system" for national governance, as well as the cornerstone of national governance and an important assurance for promoting modernization of national governance.

(1) Government Auditing Improved to Meet National Governance Needs

This cognition is mainly based on the Marxist theory of state in political science. It expounds the definition and nature of the state mainly from three aspects:

1. **Theory on the Origin and Nature of the State.** The first is the tool theory. In the *Critique of Hegel's Philosophy of Right*, Marx revealed the origin of the state from the perspective of the relationship between the state and civil society. He proposed that: "The State did not exist intrinsically . . . As the economy developed to a certain stage, society inevitably became fragmented into classes, thus contributing to the establishment of States."[10] That is to say, conflicts among various interest groups contributed to the emergence of the state, which became a tool of maintaining class rule. The second is the arbitrator role theory. Engels commented on Marx's view on the origin and nature of state as follows: "The origin of the State is as follows: society was trapped in unsolvable self-contradictions. . . To avoid the elimination of the opposite classes and society in the meaningless conflicts, a force superficially superior to the society should be generated. This force should be able to ease conflicts and keep conflicts within an orderly range. This force, that comes from society but is superior to society, and increasingly separate from it, is called 'the State.'"[11] That is to say, the state as a superficial mediator can help mutually conflicting classes achieve a temporary balance in special periods and becomes the basis for avoiding social breakdown or disintegration.

2. **Theory on the Relationship between Economic Base and Superstructure.** In *The German Ideology*, Marx said that "civil society always marks the social organization developed directly from production and communication. Such social organization always constitutes the basis of the State and any other conceptual superstructure."[12] Marx also believed that "a personal material life that does not change with personal will, i.e., a mutually restricted production mode and communication mode, are the realistic basis of the State, and does not change with personal will on the basis of division of labor and private ownership. These realistic relationships are not created by State power, but are the forces of creating State power."[13] That is to say, the state as part of the superstructure is decided by economic fundamentals.

3. **Theory on State Functions and Alienation.** Marx believed that the state functions "cover all kinds of social public affairs, and also include all special functions to address the contradictions between the government and the people."[14] That is to say, the state functions to maintain the ruling authority and force opponents to surrender, and also undertakes the public mission of social management and cultural education. According to the social development process, national governance functions will gradually shrink, while public affairs management functions gradually expand.

However, state functions, especially public affairs management functions, are often alienated because some ruling classes pursue their own interests. In that case, the state becomes a tool for some classes to pursue their own interests rather than the inherent general interests of a civil society. "For some bureaucrats, the State becomes a tool to achieve their own purpose, win promotion and get rich."[15] Marx criticized Hegel's view that an "internal hierarchy supervision system of bureaucracy can prevent the abuse of State power," thinking that depending solely on internal supervision is a self-deception. To prevent this situation, we must break the mystique and monopoly of state power based on the principle of political openness, and conduct effective external supervision on the basis of democracy.

According to the State Theory of Marx, during the evolution and development of the state, various state powers must be balanced and restrained mutually, healthy running of the state must be supported in finance, policy, and law, and so on; to avoid alienation of the state into a tool for some classes to seek their own interests and prevent abuse of state powers, we must create a state power configuration of mutual checks and balances through effective national governance. In the power allocation process, the state, on behalf of people, authorizes some public authorities and persons in power to allocate, manage, and use the public resources, public finances, and public assets, and also legally authorizes some independent organs to supervise the exercise of public power through various ways, especially government auditing. In terms of the origin and significance of auditing, "the government only cared about accounting revenues and expenditures and collecting taxes in the beginning. To this end, the government adopted control means including auditing, to reduce errors and malpractices caused by the incompetence or fraud of officials."[16] This can be fully verified by the origin of the state.

In the beginning, the state developed from the clan society had a small scale and single functions, and was established on the basis of original democracy; government officials were elected by the citizens, mainly to safeguard national territorial security, social order, and stability. Because of low productivity, the fiscal revenue from citizens had to be kept at a relatively low level as much as possible, and government officials received more direct supervision. Government officials' compliance with the social and moral standards is a decisive factor of judging the law enforcement legitimacy of government (officials). As a result, systems like the property audit system of Athenian society were established. Under such systems, any officer whose embezzlement was established after auditing of his properties when he came into office and when he left office would be severely punished.[17] At that time, each citizen could be elected as a government official, so everyone might be audited. The implementation of the official property audit system meant total lack of public tolerance for the embezzlement of public properties. This system helped prevent the abuse of limited government revenues, improved national governance, and eased contradictions between government officials and resource providers.

With the development of social productive forces, the state gradually expanded in scale. The further social division of labor resulted in the further differentiation of social class, government bureaucracy gradually formed, and government officials gradually became independent interest groups. Social classes providing financial sources, through financial auditing as a control tool, minimized the economic costs to maintain the running of state apparatus, and urged government officials and even the rulers to perform their responsibilities in accordance with certain code of conduct. Auditing became a necessity for the government to win the trust of the ruling class and obtain needed financial sources.

With the further expansion of the state scale, the highly centralized feudal bureaucracy system was formed. Conceptually, the emperor had the supreme power in every aspect. More complex principal-agent relationships existed between the royal family and government bureaucrats at all levels. To maintain the normal running of the state apparatus, the emperor effectively restricted government bureaucracy behavior at all levels through auditing, and required them to provide real data on payable taxes, so as to obtain necessary revenues and safeguard financial security.

With the success of capitalist revolution and the continuous improvement of productivity due to scientific and technological development, democracy became an increasingly important basis for the legitimacy of governance. Meanwhile, two world wars and the continuing economic crisis meant state scope and functions expanded continuously, and public resources obtained, dominated, and used by the state increased continuously. Although taxpaying is the obligation of every citizen, an ever-increasing tax burden created a public demand for government to control expenditures. In this period, government auditing became a direct means to control government expenditures and ensure reasonable exercise of power, and played a crucial role in ensuring the normal running of the state apparatus.

The process of state development shows that generation and improvement of government auditing derived from national governance, national governance needs determine the generation of government auditing, and national governance objectives determine the direction of government auditing. Under specific historical conditions, government auditing followed its own internal law, and its objectives, tasks, priorities, and methods changed with those of national governance. Government auditing always plays an irreplaceable role in national governance.

(2) Government Auditing as an "Immune System" for National Governance

This is mainly based on the system theory. "System" came from ancient Greek, with the connotation of "being combined, integrated, and orderly." Ludwig von Bertalanffy (1901–1972), the founder of modern system theory, thought that "system is the whole of various components correlated and related to the environment"; the *Modern Chinese Dictionary* explains that "system is the whole of similar things with certain correlation." The *Encyclopedia of China* defines system as "the organic whole of interactional elements"; American system management master Fremont E. Kast argued that "system is an organic and entire unit which is clearly different from other systems and composed of at least two interdependent parts, components or subsystems."[18] According to these definitions, system should have four basic meanings: It consists of several interrelated elements, it has a common goal, it is an organic whole made up of several elements, and it always has a certain relationship with the environment.

According to the requirements of system theory, the state is a large system. Regardless of any difference in national governance system and mode, the core of governance always lies in the effective allocation and exercise of public power, and different organs should respectively undertake the duties of decision making, execution, and supervision, mutually communicate, interact, and depend on each other to jointly maintain the healthy development of the economy and society. Among them, the decision-making organs mainly function to analyze and process information according to national governance goals, make, optimize, and assess feasible plans, coordinate and control the decision-making process, and make final decisions; the executive organs mainly function to accurately execute decisions and achieve decision-making goals and tasks; and supervision and control organs mainly function to supervise the executive system in decision execution, feedback the assessment situation to the decision-making system, urge the timely decision amendment, and put forward the suggestions on reward and punishment. Government auditing belongs to the scope of supervision and control, serves the decision-making organs of national governance, and plays the role of supervising and restraining the organs of executing national governance. If national governance is compared to the life system, government auditing can be called an "immune system" because the role and action mechanism of government auditing are highly similar to those of a body's "immune system." In other words, government auditing can help to detect the risks of affecting economic and social development, reveal potential hazards, prevent such risks with statutory powers, coordinate various forces in a timely way, and suggest to governments or appropriate authorities ways to avoid risks with a variety of resources, so as to improve the "immunity" of the whole national system, promote the harmonious development of society as a whole, and achieve and maintain balance.

From the perspective of auditing functions and role, and economic and social development needs, the cognition of government auditing as an "immune system" expounds the definition, reasons, functions, and role of auditing. The operational mechanism and functions of auditing as the "immune system" will be discussed later.

(3) Government Auditing Is a Cornerstone and Important Assurance of National Governance

Based on the previous two judgments, this cognition reflects in-depth thinking on the nature and functions of government auditing from the perspective of national governance modernization, government audit institutional property, legal status, functions, and role. Generally speaking, "cornerstone" refers to the stone that plays a vital role in a building's foundation, and is often compared to the support base or backbone. It has such basic characteristics as stability, sufficient bearing capacity, and deformation and variation resistance. As the cornerstone and important assurance of national governance, government auditing can be interpreted from the following aspects:

- Fundamental institutional arrangement
- Important force to enhance national governance capacity
- Important assurance of governance modernization

(a) Government Auditing: Fundamental Institutional Arrangement[19]

The national governance system consists of a range of institutional arrangements to standardize the exercise of power and maintain public order. Managing economic and social affairs through systemic application is an important feature and essential requirement for modern governance. Government auditing is also a system of national governance, and an institutional property; the role of government auditing determines its status as the cornerstone and important assurance for national governance.

First, government auditing is an important link in the governance mechanism of checks and balances contributing to basic national stability. Political science studies show that the relationship between power and right is a fundamental issue concerning national governance.[20] To better deal with the relationship, we should follow Chinese Premier Li Keqiang's requirement: "Power cannot be exercised without legal authorization; a right not prohibited by law can be exercised." That is to say, we should protect and maintain "rights," while restricting and supervising "power." National activities and governance are inseparable from allocation and exercise of public powers. Generally speaking, for better power allocation, we should follow the basic principle of checks and balances, matching powers to responsibilities, democracy, and the rule of law, in order to form a power structure and operating mechanism under which powers of decision making, execution, and supervision interact and become coordinated, and ensure a match between powers and responsibilities, and power supervision. Government auditing belongs to the scope of supervision and control, serving the decision-making organs and playing a role of supervising and restraining the executive organs. Government auditing is an important aspect of the power checks and balances, mainly in that it ensures the good running of the state through supervision and control, and information feedback. In history, national supervision activities, including government auditing, were first carried out almost simultaneously with the emergence of the state, laying an important foundation for it to function. The functions and role of government auditing, and the government audit system established on this basis, are decided by the national political system. In other words, the government audit system will always adapt to the national political system, and have obvious high stability.

Second, government auditing is an institutional arrangement made in accordance with the fundamental Constitution, which reflects its stability, coerciveness, and authority. "A country will be governed well if decrees can be enforced well; otherwise, a country will fall into chaos."[21] Rule of law is national governance conducted in accordance with the law, and is the important assurance for its continuous development. Government auditing is the cornerstone of national governance judged from three main aspects: Functions and status of government auditing are determined by the Constitution. Most countries endow government auditing with transcendent constitutional status. Furthermore, government auditing is an important embodiment of the spirit of the rule of law, and an important carrier of governance and administration by law. It is an integral part of the national legal system. Power to supervise through auditing is determined in the Constitution, and the basis, procedures, and standards for auditing are mandatory. We must adhere to objective and impartial auditing according to law; audit law construction is an important part of the national legal system construction. In history, countries whose audit activities played a strong role produced a relatively high degree of rule of law and governance. Finally, government auditing should play its due role for maintaining and promoting the rule of law. By supervising enforcement of laws and regulations, audit offices strictly investigate and deal with financial violations, safeguarding the authority and dignity of the laws and ensuring law-based socioeconomic development; through in-depth analysis of vulnerabilities and problems concerning the implementation of existing laws and regulations, audit offices seek to improve the legal system. Therefore, government auditing is a basic system with a solid legal basis—statutory, stable, and long-term.

Third, government auditing is an endogenous "immune system" for the healthy operation of national governance,[22] and can prevent abuse of power and governance failure, which reflects its features of resistance to variation and deformation. First, it is the result of endogenous evolution of national governance. "National governance demands determine the generation of government audit, national governance objectives determine the direction of government audit, and the national governance mode determines the system and form of government audit."[23] Government auditing exists in all national governance systems and mechanisms, and provides an important basis for establishing complete, scientific, standard, and effective systems and mechanisms. Second, government audit offices, through tracking and supervision to ensure no overuse of public funds and public powers, can prevent abuse of power, detect anomalies in policy and decision implementation in a timely manner, provide objective, detailed, and reliable information for decision-making departments, ensure decisions and deployment interact in policy orientation, implementation, and actual effect, and maximize the integrated role and effect of governance. Third, government auditing can enhance the "immunity" of the national governance system. With unique functions of "prevention, revealing, and resisting," government auditing can detect and prevent economic and social risks, reflect the real situation and reveal existing problems, and protect against various kinds of economic and social "diseases" by standardizing and improving systems, mechanisms, and institutions that promote the all-round, coordinated, and sustainable development of economy and society.[24]

Therefore, government auditing is a basic system for national governance, and one of the cornerstones for ensuring normal operation. Government auditing is also an important and indispensable "institutional infrastructure" of national governance.[25]

(b) Government Auditing: Important Force to Enhance National Governance Capacity

National governance capacity is the capability to manage all social affairs by using national institutional systems and other elements. Social affairs include reform, development and stability, domestic and foreign affairs, national defense, and the affairs of the Party, the state, and the military.[26] National governance capacity reflects the operational performance of national governance systems, is the external representation of measuring the national governance level, and is also an important way of testing whether the system is scientific and rational. Government auditing is an important force to enhance national governance capacity, which has two connotations: Government audit capacity is an element of national governance capacity; and national governance capacity determines government audit capacity, which, in turn, is an important force to improve national governance capacity. It is mainly decided by the characteristics of audit supervision such as independence, comprehensiveness, and specialization. The budget expert Naomi Caiden has stressed that an important symbol of change from "prebudget era" to the "budget era" is the establishment of the comprehensive, professional, and independent finance audit system.[27]

First is the independence of government auditing. Public powers tend towards self-aggrandizement. Power expansion is mainly embodied in "selfish departmentalism" of various entities, the tendency to expand their powers and increase budgetary outlays, and undesirable phenomena such as "departmentalization of government authorities, interest-orientation of departmental powers, and individualization of departmental interests," as well as lack of coordination, raising barriers, impeding information flow, and even being closed up. All these inevitably will harm national governance functions, weaken governance capacity, and influence the governance effect. To realize the modernization of national governance systems and governance capacity, we must "overcome 'chronic diseases' of systems and institutions, and break through the interest barriers."[28] Among national governance organs, government audit offices enjoy high independence. For example, in accordance with the laws including the Constitution and the Audit Law of the People's Republic of China, audit offices are entitled to exercise their power of supervision without interference by any other administrative organ, social organization, or individual. Meanwhile, audit offices do not have any decision-making power or any specific administrative function, so there is no departmental benefit to be protected. The unique role and status mean audit offices as defenders of public interests have the responsibility to break the fetters of vested interests, exercise audit supervisory power legally and independently, understand the status quo from the macro-, global, and overall perspectives, reveal problems in systems, mechanisms, and individual institutions, and suggest improvements to laws and systems and ways to control risk. Audit offices become an important force in promoting good governance.

Second is the comprehensiveness of government auditing, which is stipulated by the Constitution and Audit Law, and is also an objective demand for governance modernization. Anything involving the use and management of public funds, public assets, and public resources, as well as public interests, is subject to audit supervision. It thus basically covers all areas of economic, political, cultural, social, and ecological governance, as well as reform, development, and stability. National governance involves elements such as labor, financial, and material resources (assets). Governance refers to the integrated use, management, and control of these elements, while powers and responsibilities are reflected by them all. Therefore, the comprehensiveness of audit supervision refers to not only the universality of audit objects (running through the whole process of national governance) but also the comprehensiveness of the audit role. That is to say, by exercising audit supervision power legally and independently, government audit offices function to reflect the situation regarding use of public funds, the exercise of public powers, and the duty performance of public sectors, and improve wealth management, power usage, and duty performance, as well as the mechanisms for power control, accountability, and personnel employment. The comprehensiveness of government auditing also lies in the change from traditional compliance auditing to performance auditing covering all public resource management elements of "input-process-output-outcome-impact." The comprehensiveness also ensures government auditing becomes an important force of national governance.

Third is the specialization of government auditing. It involves full-time and professional supervision behavior: Different from the economic supervision duties of related departments deriving from their administration functions, auditing involves full-time supervision. Based on laws and facts, audit offices supervise public sectors and individual units, and seek to reveal problems objectively and fairly. Furthermore, specialization of audit supervision also lies in the principle of "grasping two key links at the same time." On the one hand, audit offices should reveal and investigate major violations of laws and regulations and economic crimes, always paying attention to corruption and fraudulent behavior closely related to funds, assets, and resources, reveal major violations of laws and regulations in a timely and effective manner, and transfer cases to the relevant sectors for further investigation. On the other hand, audit offices should promote improvement of laws, systems, mechanisms, and institutions. Finally, auditors should have adequate professional knowledge, rich practical experience, and good organizational and coordination skills, including mastery in checking accounts and familiarity with financial affairs and business management knowledge. By checking audited units in regard to capital, business, material, and information flows, audit offices can understand the situation, detect problems, and put forward highly targeted audit suggestions.

Especially against the current background of advancing national governance updates in China, people increasingly hope to build a law-based, responsible, transparent, clean, and efficient government, and related political mechanisms and organizations should play an active role in improving transparency, enhancing accountability, combating corruption, and improving performance. According to the authority granted by laws, work features, and the existing situation, government auditing may become the important force for improving national governance capacity.

TERMINOLOGY

The Third Plenum of the 18th Communist Party of China (CPC) Central Committee proposed that the overall goal of deepening the reform comprehensively is to improve and develop socialism with Chinese characteristics, and to promote modernization of the national governance system and capacity. This is the requirement for upholding and developing socialism with Chinese characteristics, and also for the socialist modernization. The national governance system refers to the institutional systems for governing the country under the leadership of the Party, including the systems, mechanisms, laws, and regulations in regard to economic, political, cultural, social, and ecological civilization, as well as Party building. National governance capacity refers to the capacity of managing social affairs through national systems, including reform, development and stability, domestic affairs, diplomacy, national defense, and governance of the Party, the state, and the military. The national governance system and governance capacity are organic and complementary. Without them, governance capacity cannot be enhanced; without enhanced governance capacity, efficiency of the national governance system cannot be achieved. ▪

(c) Government Auditing: Important Assurance of Governance Modernization

National governance modernization includes the modernization of the national governance system and governance capacity. A modern governance system and governance capacity should meet several basic requirements: forming and maintaining good governance order, effectively resisting various governance risks, and achieving high governance efficiency. Among them, good governance order is the basic precondition and realization approach, resisting risks is the basic requirement and assurance, and good governance efficiency is the goal. Based on statutory responsibilities and inherent characteristics, government auditing must effectively play this role, and a powerful security mechanism must be established.

First, government auditing is an important assurance for maintaining governance order. Forming and maintaining good economic and social order are necessary for governance and make up the basic premise and realization approach. As early as the Warring States period more than 2,000 years ago, Mozi proposed that "one unified standard should apply to a country; a national fundamental function is necessary to prevent chaos."[29] Hans Kelsen, representative of the normative school of law, points out that "The State is the community established in accordance with domestic laws and order, and the State as a legal person is the personification of this community or domestic laws and order constituting this community."[30] Government auditing's function of safeguarding national governance order is mainly reflected as follows: Firstly, by supervising and restricting the situation of administrative power exercise, government audit offices reveal, investigate, and punish major violations of financial laws and disciplines, improve the responsibility investigation and accountability mechanisms, and promote strengthening administration and management of administrative affairs according to law. Second, by supervising the situation of following market economy rules, government auditing can reveal in a timely way behavior violating market rules, and detect and check errors, so as to prevent economic risks and maintain market economy order. Third, in accordance with the laws, government audit offices, on behalf of the masses and taxpayers, supervise the duty performance of governments, departments, units, and state-owned assets management units, and reports to the people, which helps improve the level of national governance. In particular, government audit offices disclose audit information, and report audit results, audit-related problems, and rectifications to the public, to protect citizens' rights to know and participate, and to mobilize all parties to participate in state governance, so as to provide a strong foundation and assurance for the public "participatory governance."

Second, government auditing is an important assurance for controlling governance risks. Good risk prevention and control capacity are a basic requirement for national governance. Currently, China is undergoing integrated and coordinated development in economic, political, cultural, social, and ecological civilization construction. As national governance becomes more complex, the involved governance fields expand and governance contents become enriched, but governance risks also increase. One of the important goals of national governance is to minimize public risk, so as to ensure national security and sustainable economic and social development. By relying on unique status and organizational and technology advantages, government audit offices can identify and reveal important risks in a timely manner, and put forward measures and suggestions for strengthening risk control. Government audit offices also can analyze problems and offer proposals from a higher, macro-, and global perspective, so as to provide scientific decision-making opinions for assessing national strength and safeguarding national security.

Third, government auditing is an assurance for enhancing the efficiency of national governance. Governance efficiency is an important factor to measure the governance modernization degree, and the important goal of governance is to ensure national system advantages are transformed into governance efficiency. Government auditing is an assurance to enhance the efficiency of governance: Through audit supervision over government budget allocation and implementation and fund utilization and management, audit offices promote improved capability in using and managing financial funds, budget execution capability, and the financial fund usage of budget units. Furthermore, through supervision of the economy, efficiency, and effect of government work, audit offices function to improve the performance of administrative departments and further enhance the quality and efficiency of industries or sectors within their administrative jurisdiction. Finally, on the basis of detecting and disposing of various problems, government audit offices can deeply analyze from all perspectives and offer proposals for reforming systems, improving laws, systems, and institutions, strengthening management, and preventing risks, so as to enhance the macroeconomic performance of national governance.

To sum up, this cognition involves three aspects: firstly, government auditing is an important part of the power balance mechanism and the supervision control system, and also a basic institutional arrangement made in accordance with the Constitution and laws.[31] Secondly, by independently and fairly reviewing the truthfulness, compliance, and performance of various economic activities concerning national governance, government audit offices can understand the real situation, reveal hidden risks, reflect prominent problems, and analyze systemic and mechanism obstacles and defects, to solve the problems in a timely and effective way. That is to say, government auditing plays an "immune system" role of preventing, revealing, and resisting, and a cornerstone and assurance role for standardized, efficient operation of other national governance subsystems. Third, from a mechanism perspective, government auditing is comprehensive, specialized, and regular, and its supervision role is all-embracing. Government auditing is an important force in enhancing national governance capacity, and an important assurance for promoting the modernization of governance capacity.

The foregoing analysis shows that all aforesaid cognitions on the nature of auditing are based on audit practice in different periods, perspectives, and levels, playing an active theoretical guidance role for audit work. In general, they have the relationship of inheritance, development, and continuous deepening. Relatively speaking, cognition of the nature of auditing from the perspective of national governance is more comprehensive and in-depth than other aspects. It more clearly defines the fundamental property of auditing and audit practice, and pays more attention to audit functions, role, targets, and realization approaches. In recent years, China's audit offices, under the guidance of this theory, firmly uphold the scientific audit concept, comprehensively perform audit supervision duties, fully bring into play the vital role of government auditing in promoting improvement of national governance, constantly enhance the initiative, macro-, constructive, open, and scientific features, and constantly improve legalization and standardization based on science and information so as to make new progress in construction of audit teams, audit theories, and audit culture. These practices also show that the cognition on the nature of auditing from the governance perspective is in line with China's conditions in regard to socialist politics, economy, culture, and society, and is of great significance to improve the socialist audit system with Chinese characteristics and promote scientific development of the audit cause.

TERMINOLOGY

Socialism with Chinese characteristics consists of the road, theories, and systems. The road of socialism with Chinese characteristics is the realization path, theories of socialism with Chinese characteristics play the guidance role, and socialist systems with Chinese characteristics are the fundamental assurance. They are united in the great practice of socialism with Chinese characteristics. During the overall process, we should persist in taking economic construction as the central task, and promote economic, political, cultural, and ecological construction, and so on; adhere to the four fundamental principles[32] and the policy of reform and opening up; and emancipate and develop productive forces, gradually achieve the goal of common prosperity, and promote people's all around development. The theories of socialism with Chinese characteristics are the latest achievements of Marxism in China, including the Deng Xiaoping Theory and the important thought of the "Three Represents"[33] and the Scientific Outlook on Development. The socialist system with Chinese characteristics upholds the organic unity of the fundamental and basic political and economic systems and various institutional mechanisms, the organic unity of the national democracy and grassroots democracy systems, and the unity of the Party's leadership, people's status as the masters, and rule by law.[34] ▪

III. EVOLUTION OF GOVERNMENT AUDITING FOR NATIONAL GOVERNANCE

The evolutionary history of China's government auditing shows it is always closely related to national governance. In different historical periods, governance needs, objectives, and modes may differ, and government auditing may undertake different historical missions. The functions and roles of government auditing always adapt to the objective needs of national governance. But fundamentally speaking, government audit offices, through audit supervision, always function to promote power balance, monitor the governance process well, conduct real-time tracking of governance performance, reveal problems in a timely manner, and promote reform and improvement of governance systems and mechanisms so as to improve overall national governance.

(1) Evolution of Chinese Ancient and Modern Government Auditing

China has a long history of government auditing, and various dynasties witnessed the rise and fall of national governance (see Table 1.1). According to historical records, ancient Chinese used the words "investigating, listening, counting, checking, comparing," and so on to describe "audit" activities, indicating these presented different forms and played different functional roles through history. The Zhou Dynasty (1046–256 BCE) advocated the "rule by rites," and the governance goal of "defining the authority and ranks of the king, ministers and officials." To this end, the official rank of Zaifu was created with responsibility for supervising the implementation of decrees and rites; the holder of this office could report any problems to the Taizai (official rank) or even directly to the emperor.[35] In the Qin and Han dynasties that followed, rulers advocated "grand unification" and strengthening centralized governance, and established a set of highly authoritative supervisory systems, including the censor audit system. Auditing supervision function was added to the system of supervision by censors at the state, prefecture, or county level, and the mode of "comprehensive supervision and investigation, and united supervision and examination" was developed and used long after. The flourishing Tang Dynasty (618–907) is world-renowned for its political openness and economic prosperity. Under the Tang regime, the audit system was improved along with political system reform, and the system of "unity of special audit, concurrent audit and internal audit by different departments respectively" was established. With certain judicial authorities, the Pi-Pu was set up. This was completely independent of the Ministry of Revenue in feudal times, and was specialized in audit supervision; the audit supervision function of the Censorate was strengthened; and the system of internal auditing by the Ministry of Revenue, Financial Revenue and Expenditure Ministry, and Salt and Iron Management Ministry was established, which vigorously promoted national financial management. In the Southern Song Dynasty (1127–1279), the Review Department was renamed as the "Audit Department" or "Court of Auditors," which is the first institution of China specialized in auditing and using the term "audit" in its name.

TERMINOLOGY

The audit supervision activity was first described as "audit" formally in the Southern Song dynasty. *The Compilation of Song Regulations* recorded that "On May 11, the first Jianyan year during the reign of Emperor Gaozong, to avoid the tautonomy with the name of Emperor Gaozong (Zhao Gou ["赵构" in Chinese]), the Zhuangou ("勾" in Chinese, meaning review) Department was renamed as "Audit Department" because "勾" is a homonym of "构" in the name of Emperor Gaozong. Later, the Audit Department was changed to "Court of Auditors," specializing in financial supervision and supported by laws. It became the specialized audit organization worthy of the name.

In the Ming and Qing dynasties, with few exceptions, China's political environment was largely closed, and the royal court strengthened the system of autocratic monarchy while ignoring the construction of the system of checks and balances. In addition, supervision organs including the Court of Auditors lost some of their power, and even a eunuch dictatorship appeared, which resulted in serious corruption, treasury deficits, and increasing decline of national strength. During the Ming Dynasty, the Pi-Pu was canceled, marking the end of an audit system existing for over thousands of years. Later, Supervisory Censors from the Court of Censors and the Jishizhong (an official rank) from the Ministry of Official Personnel Affairs, the Ministry of Revenue, the Ministry of Rites, the Ministry of War, the Ministry of Punishments, and the Ministry of Works were collectively referred to as "kedaoguan" (supervisory officials), exercising certain audit powers. In this period, independent external professional audit organs were cancelled,[36] and an audit system featuring "unity of supervision and examination" was established, which catered to the needs of the imperial autocracy. It inevitably became an autocratic tool for rule by man, and accelerated the decline of the dynastic system. ▪

Autocracy and the policy of exclusion of the Qing Dynasty eventually led to its collapse and brought the Chinese nation to the brink of destruction. To save the Chinese nation and ensure its survival, people with vision launched the Westernization Movement, Constitutional Reform and Modernization, and the Constitutional Movement. In the preliminary constitutional process, the Qing Dynasty once planned to pattern itself on the political system of Germany and Japan, and established an independent Court of Auditors parallel with the Cabinet. The supreme ruler would directly take charge of the Court of Auditors.[37] However, due to the failure of the reform movements, the attempt to establish a modern audit system was eventually aborted. In 1928, under the Republic of China, the Nanjing Nationalist Government had set up the Court of Auditors that operated in parallel with government ministries, offices of supervision, judiciary, and examination, and other offices, and enacted an Audit Law. In 1931, the Court of Auditors became a subsidiary body of the Supervisory Ministry. The system of combining supervision and examination was introduced. Under the five-chamber political system, the audit offices of the Republic of China worked as an important organ of power supervision. It was independent of the government administrative systems, possessing a detached independent position of supervision, and played a positive role in consolidation of financial disciplines, investigating corruptions, increasing revenues and reducing expenditures, and assuring government operations. However, due to the corrupted political system, long-term chaos caused by war and the controlling power of a privileged stratum in the later period, social unrest, and financial chaos, financial tycoons

TABLE 1.1 Ancient Government Auditing and Governance Situation in Some Dynasties

Auditing systems and institutions	Dynasty	State governance and legislative status at that time	Notes
Merit system of the officials	Western Zhou Dynasty	Monarchs managed state affairs in accordance with *Rites of Zhou*, which is the starting point of the soft power of Chinese civilization.	Western Zhou dynasty set up a post "Zaifu" (an official taking charge of the qualification assessment of all the officials and reporting the results to the monarch) to perform audit responsibilities.
System of Administrative Reports	The State of Qi in Spring and Autumn Period	Duke Huan of Qi reunited the feudal princes nine times, and became the first of the "Five Hegemonies of the Spring and Autumn Period."	Guan Zhong, a legalist chancellor and reformer of the State of Qi, said that "If a country is dedicated to developing agriculture, industry and commerce, it will get rich; If a country can establish a legal system and common rules, scrutinize its policies, establishing routine, and cultivate competent officials, it will maintain prolonged stability."
System of Administrative Reports	Western Han Dynasty	Legalists of Qin Dynasty proposed the view of "rule of law." Following the system of the Qin Dynasty, the Han Dynasty achieved the combination of rites[38] and law and the Rule of Wen and Jing.	*Law of Administrative Reports System* made specifications on the "rule of law." The function of "rule of law" had been gradually weakened in the late Han Dynasty.
Pi-Pu (Department of Judicial Control)	Tang Dynasty	During the Tang Dynasty, the earliest code of China's *Law of Tang Dynasty* was formulated. It consisted of *Law of Yonghui*, *Law of Wude*, *Law of Zhenguan*, and other laws. Reign of Zhenguan and the flourishing age of the Kaiyuan Era were also formed during this period.	Pi-Pu fully performed its functions in the early Tang Dynasty. In the mid- and late Tang Dynasty, its relevant functional role had been gradually weakened, and even had been abolished in a certain period.

Court of Auditors	Song Dynasty	*The Penal Complex of Song* was promulgated. The commodity economy of the feudal society reached its peak during this period.	The Northern Song Dynasty set up the Review Department and Other Departments. Later it was renamed the Audit Department. This is the first time that the word "audit" appeared in history. In the Southern Song Dynasty, it was changed to "the Court of Auditors." Facing the invasions of Jin and Mongolia and other foreign countries, wars were frequent in the Southern Song Dynasty. The Court of Auditors was mainly responsible for auditing the army and fulfilling the general national audit functions.
Censorate, Jishizhong (an imperial attendant) of the Six Ministries in Feudal China	Ming Dynasty	*Law of Ming Dynasty* and *Da Gao* (a special criminal law in Ming Dynasty) were enacted in the early Ming Dynasty, which helped to achieve centralization of state power and contributed to the formation of the prosperity in the early Ming Dynasty during the Rule of Ren and Xuan (refers to the reigns of Emperor Hongxi and Emperor Xuande of the Ming dynasty, which was considered its golden age).	
Censorate, Jishizhong of the Six Ministries in Feudal China	Qing Dynasty	During the reign of Emperor Shunzhi, an Office for Making Laws was set up. Large-scale legislative activities emerged. *Collection of Laws of Qing Dynasty* was enacted by Emperor Yongzheng. *Ta Tsing Leu Lee: Being the Fundamental Laws, and a selection from the Supplementary Statutes, of the Penal Code of China* was compiled during the reign of Emperor Qianlong. The Kang-Qian Flourishing Age (also known as High Qing) appeared during this period.	During the reign of Emperor Yongzheng, Jishizhong of the Six Ministries in Feudal China was incorporated into the Censorate. The audit supervision was exercised by the Censorate, which strengthened the regulatory authority of the Censorate, and laid the foundation for good governance of the Kang-Qian Flourishing Age.

Source: Chief Editor Li Jinhua: *The History of Audit in China* (volume 1), China Modern Economics Publishing House, 2005.

who always manipulated the economic lifeline and military sectors who consumed huge financial funds and other privileged agencies repeatedly refused to accept audit supervision. It became harder and harder for auditing to play an effective role, and it remained in name only, which was an important factor in the growing decline and fall of the Nanjing Government.

In the long history of change of Chinese dynasties, vicissitudes were closely related to such national supervision systems as auditing. The dynasties and periods with high-level political civilization did well in the separation of state powers and checks and balances, whereas the decline of a prosperous dynasty certainly started from the weakness and even abolition of such systems. Therefore, a ruler should firstly manage accounting and auditing to govern the country well. The 800-year Zhou Dynasty represented the summit of the slave society, which was associated with its "Zhou Guan" system (emphasizing the separation of powers and checks and balances). The Tang Dynasty represented the summit of feudal society associated with the system of Three Councils and Six Boards. However, the comparatively short-term Ming and Qing Dynasties emphasized autocratic imperial power and personal totalitarianism. It is an eternal truth that "all powerful people are easily abusing their power," and absolute power will definitely lead to absolute corruption. If the ruler roused all his energies to make the country prosperous in the period of autocratic imperial power and personal totalitarianism, national governance might be normal in the short term only. However, autarchy and totalitarianism will finally lead to governance anomie, finance running out of control, and national strength declining.

(2) Government Audit System in the Period of Revolutionary War under the Leadership of the CPC

Before the founding of the PRC, the CPC adhered to the road of encircling the cities from the countryside, established and consolidated itself in the revolutionary base areas, continuously accumulated strength through armed struggle, and won revolutionary victory through arduous efforts. As the armed struggles needed a lot of funds, the Party adopted relevant measures to save every copper for revolution and war and asked cadres not to be tempted by power and money in order to ensure the support of the people. Strengthening audit supervision was one of the major measures. The Party formulated different auditing systems suitable for different periods according to their characteristics. During the period of Western Fujian Soviet power, the Party carried out audit work to meet the military needs of anti-encirclement struggle and promoting the founding of Soviet power. In March 1930, after the founding of the Soviet government in the main revolutionary area, the Party established the Financial

Review Board and also asked governments at different levels to set up their own boards to review the financial position. In September 1933, the Central Audit Committee, subordinate to the Central People's Committee of the Soviet area, was established for performing audit functions. The Committee carried out audits of the fiscal budgets and final accounts of the central government's offices and departments, counties directly under Ruijin, Guangdong Province, and Jiangxi Province, and in the financial revenues of central institutions and mass organizations, including the central printing house and the effects of the saving movements in the central Soviet areas. The result of each audit activity would be published on the official newspaper of the CPC central committee, *Red China.* In the most difficult period of the Chinese revolution, audit supervision played a key role in promoting the implementation of various financial budgets and government decisions, reducing various expenditures, and combating corruption. During the Anti-Japanese War, government audit supervision was mainly focused on such central tasks as meeting military needs in the base areas and promoting regime construction in border areas. In 1937, the government of the Shaanxi-Gansu-Ningxia border region set up the audit division to conduct audit supervision of budgets and final accounts, public property of the administrative bodies, income and expense data, treasury receipts and disbursements, valuation and disposal of public property and the public sector balance of payments of other relevant authorities, taxation, the requisitioning of grain, corruption, and fraud. Meanwhile, the Central Military Commission also set up an audit division under the Financial Committee to implement the system of preliminary review in regiments and secondary review in brigades and armies, and final review in divisions, strategic areas, and headquarters. The division played a key role in increasing incomes, reducing expenditures, supporting the revolutionary war, and dealing with corruption and waste. During the Liberation War, the audit work was carried out mainly to meet war needs. In order to ensure the preparatory work of governing the whole country proceeded smoothly, the audit work of the government of border region focused on providing financial resources for the war. At that time, all military authorities above regimental level set up audit committees to play active roles in ensuring the Party and army's spirit of hard work, laying a solid foundation for liberating the whole country, and founding the PRC.

(3) Establishment and Development of Government Audit Systems after the Founding of the PRC

The PRC's government audit system was gradually established and developed based on the inheritance of former national audit experience and reference to international practice. For some time after the founding of the PRC in 1949, China didn't set up independent audit offices but handled the supervision of fiscal and financial revenues and expenditures through the departments of finance and taxation in combination with industrial and business management. In 1978, the Third Plenum of the 11th CPC Central Committee made the strategic decision to shift the focus of work to the economic construction, requiring strengthened financial and economic management, establishment and improvement of the economic supervision system, and strong maintenance of the national financial and economic disciplines. Constitutional revisions in 1982 led to the establishment of the audit supervision system. The National Audit Office of China was formally founded in 1983, and local governments above county level generally set up their own audit offices within two years. Thereafter, audit offices at all levels actively created work conditions around the strategic objective, focus, steps, and policies associated with Chinese economic construction, carried out the key work of increasing revenue and reducing expenditure as well as seeking balance of the two, played their role in enforcing discipline in finance and economics, correcting accounting errors, strengthening management, and actively safeguarding smooth economic construction.

With the further deepening of reform and opening up, China gradually transformed itself from the traditional planned economy system into a socialist market economy, and accelerated progress in building a socialist country under the rule of law. Facing a more beneficial development environment, audit offices made great progress in gradual audit standardization. During this period, they launched industry auditing, special fund auditing, and special auditing investigations in a planned way, and gradually formed a regular audit system focused on national major deployments, including rectifying the overall economic order. Auditing expanded from enterprises to government departments, financial institutions, infrastructure investment, agricultural funds, and the utilization of foreign capital. The audit offices emphasized the truth and legitimacy of audit content, explored improved management and greater efficiency, and emphasized micro-auditing from a macroperspective. Audit supervision plays an important role in enforcing financial and economic discipline, promoting improvement and rectification, and safeguarding the smooth system reform. The Audit Law and the Implementation Rules were promulgated in 1994 and 1997 respectively. This was the point when the basic systems, including the principles of audit supervision, the responsibilities and authorities of audit offices, audit procedures, and legal responsibilities, were further defined and clarified, and the legalization, institutionalization, and standardization of audit work were initially realized so audit offices and individual auditors could deepen their understanding of audit work and associated laws.

The 16th Party Congress proposed to "strengthen the restrictions and supervision on the use of power." According to the requirement, audit offices adjusted their orientation, objectives, and priorities while continuing to adhere to basic audit policy: "to audit in accordance with laws, serve the overall situation, stay close to the center, stress the focus, and be pragmatic"[39] as they implemented the Audit Law revised in 2006. Through enhancing the level and quality of audit results, maintaining truthfulness as the basis, and exposing distorted or wrong accounting information as the focus, audit offices intensified the investigation and punishment of major violations of laws and regulations and economic crimes, strengthened the restriction and supervision of power, promoted audit results announcements and the handling of the performance audit, continued to deepen and improve the fiscal, financial, and business audits, actively explored the accountability audit, and built the "3 + 1" audit pattern. They also focused on strengthening the construction of talents, methods, and technologies, and enhanced the overall quality of audit teams, improving audit criteria and rapid adoption of modernized audit technical means. During this period, audit supervision played a positive role in maintaining economic order, deepening reform and development, strengthening restrictions on power, and promoting democracy, further improving the credibility, authority, and social influence of audit work.

Since the 17th Party Congress, audit offices have thoroughly studied and applied the *Scientific Outlook on Development*, firmly established a scientific concept of auditing, deepened understanding of the nature of auditing, and stayed close to the overall economic and social development. This required enhanced infrastructure construction of audit teams, and deeper study of law, information, culture, and theory in order to further promote audit work concerning fiscal affairs, finance, business, economic responsibility, resources and environment, and foreign capital. On the basis of ensuring truthfulness, compliance, and performance in regard to financial revenues and expenditures, more attention has been given to initiative, macroscopic, and constructive auditing and audit supervision of key areas, revealing and investigating major violations of laws and regulations, reflecting on problems in the system and mechanism, and conducting audit supervision at higher levels. Audit offices have sought to fully play the "immune system" function as a public finance guardian, actively promoted China's political, economic, cultural, social, and ecological civilization construction, and played a positive role in improving national governance, safeguarding state security, maintaining financial order, improving macroeconomic regulation and control, strengthening the creation of a clean government, managing state affairs according to law, deepening reform, and opening up economic and social development.

The 18th Party Congress established the historical status of the Scientific Outlook on Development, interpreted the rich connotation of socialism with Chinese characteristics and eight basic requirements to gain new victories, and proposed the objectives of building a moderately prosperous society in an all around way, comprehensively deepening reform, and opening up work on the major deployments. This included the Five-in-One overall arrangement—namely, socialist economic construction, political, cultural, social, and ecological civilization construction, and the major task of comprehensively improving the scientific level of Party building. Guided by this spirit, government audit offices treated rule of law and improved livelihood for the people through reform and development as the starting point and supreme goal, to fulfill their audit supervision responsibilities, promote overall implementation of the Five-in-One arrangement, facilitate the building of a moderately prosperous society in an all around way, and play a practical role in safeguarding the sound operation of the national economy and society and promoting national governance.

Through 30 years of development, the audit supervision system of socialism with Chinese characteristics has been basically established and became a modern government audit system. This covers a number of key fields:

- **To build a relatively complete audit law system.** Multilayered but inherently coordinated norms of audit law now exist on the basis of the Constitution, with the Audit Law and the Rules for the Implementation of the Audit Law as the core, supported by audit standards.
- **To safeguard the independent exercise of audit supervisory power in accordance with the law.** Government audit supervision responsibilities have to be exercised consistently within the national governance mode. The Constitution specifies that the government audit legal status should be independent of the decision-making and performance system, and free from restraints by any vested interests and interference by any other administrative organization, social group, or individuals.
- **To form an audit system suitable for China's national conditions.** The State Council has set up the National Audit Office, which exercises independent audit supervisory power under the premier's guidance. Local people's governments above county level set up audit offices with independent supervisory power under the guidance of the head of government at

the corresponding level and responsible to that government as well as to the next higher level of audit office.

▪ **To authorize extensive and effective responsibility and authority.** To ensure government auditing plays an active role in national governance, laws and regulations stipulate extensive audit responsibilities, including the accountability audit, and as defined by the Constitution, government audit offices are granted effective authority through such means as administrative coercive measures, transference of major issues, and audit sanctions.

▪ **To form a coordinated and efficient audit operating mechanism.** Through 30 years of exploration and practice, a complete, coordinated, and efficient audit operating mechanism suited to national conditions has been established for such aspects as audit work programs and plans, field implementation of audit projects, audit result reports, audit rectification tracking, and audit relief, ensuring government audit offices can fully exercise their responsibilities.

Over 30 years' development has laid a solid foundation for the improvement of government audit theories. Meanwhile, its functions have effectively promoted reform and opening up, as well as the construction of democracy and rule of law. Specific details are as follows:

▪ **Providing timely, objective, and reliable information for scientific decision making in national governance, so as to promote the implementation of needed policies and measures.** Chinese audit offices pay much attention to analyzing and reflecting on the implementation of relevant state policies and measures, management of major projects, and associated problems. In this way, support is given to scientific state decision making, improving macrocontrol policy and strengthening management of public investment projects. In order to ensure the timeliness of the information provided, various follow-up auditing methods have been used. In the past few years, follow-up auditing has been conducted for major projects like the Beijing-Shanghai High-Speed Railway, the second line of the West-East natural gas transmission project, the Three Gorges Project, and postdisaster reconstruction after the Wenchuan earthquake, as well as important events, including the Beijing Olympic Games, Shanghai World Expo, and the Asian Games. Policy implementation problems have been exposed and corrected in a timely manner. For example, for four consecutive years, more than 20,000 auditors conducted follow-up auditing of the anti-earthquake and relief work and postdisaster recon-struction after the Wenchuan earthquake, involving over 22,500 invest-ment projects. This had a positive impact on the smooth progress of relief and reconstruction.

■ **Playing a restriction and supervisory role in the state power system and promoting normalized allocation and exercise of power.** In accordance with the Constitution, the Audit Law, and other relevant laws and regulations, audit offices should conduct auditing or special auditing investigation of all units, projects, and events involving management or use of public funds. Since 1999, pursuant to provisions of the CPC Central Committee General Office and the General Office of the State Council on strengthening the accountability audit, audit offices at all levels have been required to further promote the accountability audit. In December 2010, the CPC Central Committee General Office and the General Office of the State Council promulgated *The Provisional Regulations on Accountability Auditing of Party and Government Officials and Leaders in State-Owned Enterprises*, summarizing the development and effect of over a decade of accountability auditing. These regulations stipulate that audit offices should conduct an accountability audit of the primary leaders and cadres of local governments at all levels, judicial and procuratorial organs, functional departments of central and local governments at all levels, public institutions, mass organizations, and legal persons of state-owned or state-holding enterprises. In recent years, audit offices nationwide have conducted an accountability audit of over 500,000 leaders and cadres. Through audit supervision, examination, and evaluation, the power of governments and officials has been restricted within the scope of people's authorization; thus the match of power and responsibility has been promoted and auditing's role of standardization, restriction, and supervision is brought into full play.

■ **Focusing on weak economic and social links and risks, so as to safeguard national security.** It will always be the primary task of national governance to ensure a country's survival and security, and a common responsibility for almost all departments of national governance. Audit offices have taken on safeguarding national security as a major task, focusing on energy and strategic resources, fiscal and financial operation, state information, internal governance and supervision of financial institutions, and protection of resources and the environment. They analyze weak links and potential economic and social risks in a timely manner and provide reliable information for safeguarding national security. Especially in 2011 and 2013, in accordance with State Council requirements, more than 40,000 auditors were mobilized to comprehensively audit the debts of local governments at province, city, and county levels. Through figuring out the basic situation, reflecting performance, revealing problems, and making suggestions, audit offices played a positive role in eliminating improper statements at home and abroad about Chinese national security and economic and social development, improving the fiscal administration system, revising relevant laws, and so on.

▪ **Revealing violations of laws and regulations as well as behavior involving abuse of power, and maintaining economic and social order.** Chinese audit offices always take it as their obligatory responsibility to ensure the laws are strictly observed and enforced, and law violators must be brought to justice so as to strengthen the "immunity" of the national governance system. They focus on studying the characteristics and laws of corruption cases under the new situation, and give attention to key sectors, positions, and links prone to corruption, thus becoming an importance force in combating corruption. Audit offices also focus on analyzing loopholes in institutional construction and implementation and positively promoting system improvement. In addition, for timely treatment of major law and regulation violations, a joint conference system and coordinated consultation mechanism has been established involving public security, procuratorial organs, and inspection departments. Treatment results of transferred audit cases have been publicized, promoting the deterrent effects of auditing.

▪ **Reflecting problems at the system, mechanism, or institution level, and promoting innovation in national governance.** Chinese government auditing is characterized by strong independence, a wide range of coverage, familiarity with laws and regulations, and mastery of full and accurate information. On the one hand, government auditing focuses on reflecting the problems of audited units in budget enforcement, financial management, and internal control, including less-stringent management, failure in ensuring system implementation, and low quality of accounting information, so as to strengthen management, supervision, and restriction. On the other hand, from the micro- and overall perspective, government auditing focuses on reflecting problems such as institutional barriers, mechanism distortions, and system defects, so as to promote reform in the fiscal and financial system, state-owned businesses and investment system, and so forth. Over the past 30 years, audit offices have submitted more than 40,000 reports, and promoted the formulation and improvement of an equal number of rules and regulations. The National Audit Office has made suggestions including refining government budget management, promoting disclosure, and strengthening local government's debt management. All the suggestions are conducive to improving national governance.

■ **Focusing on people's livelihood and resource and environment protection, endeavoring to safeguard people's fundamental interests, and promoting ecological civilization construction.** Protecting people's fundamental interests is the basic goal for audit offices. They focus on the management of livelihood projects or funds for the Three Rural Issues (i.e., agriculture, rural areas, and farmers), low-income citizens, education, medical treatment, housing, and social security; they also focus on fund use performance and implementation of policies and measures related to resource exploitation and development, as well as ecological environmental protection. For example, in 2012, more than 40,000 auditors nationwide conducted a full audit of the country's 18 social security funds. The audit work took seven years to complete and involved various departments including human resources, social security, civil administration, health, and finance at the province, city, or county level. Auditors have grasped the basic situation of the social security system, examined policy implementation and effect, revealed difficulties, and proffered advice for system improvement and standard management.

■ **Implementing the system of disclosing audit information and rectifying and tracking problems, and endeavoring to ensure people's right to know and participate in national governance.** With the development of democracy and legal construction, the audit offices have gradually improved the system of announcing audit findings and issuing audit information, and have insisted on investigating problems and promoting rectification and disclosure simultaneously. Thus, the supervisory role of auditing is brought into full play. Since implementing the system of announcing audit results in 2003, 24,000 audit results have been made public. Audit offices also disclose information on rectification and disposal of detected problems. For five consecutive years, the National Audit Office has disclosed the rectification and reform result of problems concerning central budget execution and financial revenue and expenditure, and each announcement comprehensively and objectively reflects the rectification and reform situation. At the same time, audit offices have invited news media to conduct follow-up reporting on major audit projects and reveal the whole audit process. Publicizing the audit plan, procedure, and results according to law not only serves as an important channel for promoting rectification of audit findings and fulfilling duties, strengthening the responsibilities and performance awareness of audited units, but also helps the public to understand the duty performance of governmental departments and participate in national governance.

TERMINOLOGY

At the beginning of 2003, the SARS epidemic aroused deep concern in China, and the government spent a vast amount of money to tackle the problem. How to manage and use these funds and their effects became key questions. The National Audit Office issued the No. 1 Announcement of Audit Findings in December 2003. Since then, the system to issue audit results to the public has become an important part of audit disclosure.

National governance goals change in different historical periods, and the requirements for government auditing are different, along with its responsibilities and missions. The function of auditing cannot be given full play in a more effective way until we understand, master, obey, and apply the laws throughout the whole process and continuously adjust the thinking of audit work. ▪

IV. CORE VIEW OF THE NATURE OF AUDITING FROM THE NATIONAL GOVERNANCE PERSPECTIVE

To understand and comprehend the nature of audit work from the national governance perspective meets the objective requirements for profound changes of the external audit environment. It stands for significant development and breakthrough in government audit theory. It is a significant innovation of socialist audit theories with Chinese characteristics, taking government audit practice in recent years into consideration. It is of strong guiding significance to socialist audit practice with Chinese characteristics and will also have far-reaching significance. The key points can be briefly described as follows:

▪ Government auditing is an important part of the national political system and is a kind of institutional arrangement to supervise and restrict power by power in accordance with law.
▪ Government auditing is an important aspect of national governance, and strengthening audit supervision is a significant approach and method to obtain improvement. The demand of national governance determines the emergence of government auditing; the goal of national governance

determines the direction of government auditing; and the mode of national governance determines the system of government auditing.

▪ Government auditing is one of the endogenous supervision and control systems of national governance; it serves the decision-making process, and supervises and restrains the execution system of national governance.

▪ Government auditing, as an "immune system" endogenous within the overall system of national governance, with functions of exposure, resistance, and prevention, is a cornerstone and important assurance for national governance.

To comprehend government auditing from the national governance perspective has profound implications for further clarifying the guiding ideology, fundamental objective, basic approach, and working guidelines. Under the direction of this theory, the National Audit Office of China advocates that government auditing must hold socialism with Chinese characters as its soul and guideline, and scientific audit concepts should be firmly established. The fundamental objective of auditing is to protect people's fundamental interests, which at the present stage can be specifically described as "to promote rule by law, reform and development, and to safeguard people's livelihood." The primary task for audit work is to safeguard national security and can be expressed as "to protect national economy security, to safeguard national interests, to promote democracy and rule of law, and to promote comprehensive and coordinated sustainable development." Government auditing must follow the guideline of "conducting audit according to law, serving the overall situation, focusing on the central task, highlighting the key points, and being realistic and pragmatic."

To comprehend government auditing from the national governance perspective reflects a new profound understanding and conclusion of the nature of audit work against a new historical background. This theoretical view has aroused broad consensus in China's audit theory and practice, and is widely recognized by audit circles of various countries. In 2013, the 21st International Organization of Supreme Audit Institutions Conference was held in Beijing, issuing the Beijing Declaration, stressing that it is the common objective for supreme audit institutions to promote good national governance. The Declaration provides an important basis and basic principles of setting the future development direction, tasks, and goals for audit offices of various countries. The International Audit Organization Strategic Plan (2011–2016) also clearly requires that supreme audit offices of all countries should exert more efforts to combat corruption and strengthen accountability, transparency, and good governance. It can be foreseen that with the development of audit practice and better performance, theories of auditing for national governance will also be continuously enriched.

BIBLIOGRAPHY

American Accounting Association. *Statements of Basic Auditing Concepts*. American Accounting Association, 1973.

Dunleavy, Patrick, and Brendan O'Leary. *State Theory—Politics on Freedom and Democracy*. Translated by Ouyang Jinggen, Yin Donghua. Hangzhou: Zhejiang People's Publishing House, 2007.

Erhang, Lou, Chief Editor. *Introduction to Auditing*. Shanghai: Shanghai People's Publishing House, 1987.

Flint, David. *Philosophy and Principles of Auditing—An Introduction*. London: Macmillan Education, 1988.

Fukuyama, Francis. *State-Building—National Governance and World Order of 21st Century*. Translated by Huang Shengqiang, Xu Mingyuan. Beijing: China Social Sciences Publishing House, 2007.

Li, Jinhua, Chief Editor. *Study on Audit Theories*. Beijing: China Audit Publishing House, 2001.

Mauts, R. K., and H. A. Sharaf. *The Philosophy of Auditing*. Sarasota, Florida: American Accounting Association, 1961.

Wen, Shuo. *History of World Audit*. Beijing: China Audit Publishing House, 1990.

Xiao, Yingda. *Comparative Auditing*. Beijing: China Financial and Economic Publishing House, 1991.

Yan, Jin'e. *Definition of Auditing*. Auditing Reserch, Issue 2, 1989.

Schandl, C. W. *Theory of Auditing*. Translated by Tang Yunwei, Wu Yunfei. Beijing: China Financial and Economic Publishing House, 1992.

NOTES

1. *Selected Works of Lenin*, Volume 2, People's Publishing House, 1995.
2. Lou Erxing (ed.), *Introduction to Auditing*, Shanghai People's Publishing House, 1987; Yan Jin'e, Definitions of Auditing, *Auditing Research*, Issue 2, 1989.

3. David Flint, *Philosophy and Principles of Auditing—An Introduction*, Macmillan Education, 1988.

4. Cai Chun, *Audit Theory Structure Research*, Southwestern University of Finance and Economics Press, 1993 edition.

5. Montesquieu, *Spirit of Law* (Volume I), Beijing: Commercial Press, 1961.

6. Li Jinhua (ed.), *Review of 25 Years of Audit Work in China and Prospect*, People's Publishing House, 2008, pp. 3–5.

7. *Collected Works of Marx and Engels*, Volume 9, Beijing: People's Publishing House, 2009, p. 436.

8. Wang Shizong, *Governance Theory and Its Adaptation in China*, Hangzhou: Zhejiang University Press, 2009, Introduction.

9. UNDP, *Reconceptualising Governance*, 1997, p. 9.

10. *Complete Works of Marx and Engels*, Volume 1, People's Publishing House, 1956, p. 338.

11. *Selected Works of Marx and Engels*, Volume 4, People's Publishing House, 1972, p. 166.

12. *Selected Works of Marx and Engels*, Volume 1, People's Publishing House, 1972, pp. 78–79.

13. *Complete Works of Marx and Engels*, Volume 3, People's Publishing House, 1956, p. 377.

14. *Complete Works of Marx and Engels*, Volume 25, People's Publishing House, 1956, p. 132.

15. *Complete Works of Marx and Engels*, Volume 1, People's Publishing House, 1956, p. P302.

16. Jerry D. Sullivan, Vincent M. O'Reilly, Barry N. Winograd, James S. Gerson, and Henry R. Jaenicke, *Montgomery's Auditing* (I), translated by the translation group of Montgomery's Auditing, Beijing: China Commerce and Trade Press, 1989, pp. 6–7.

17. Wen Shuo, *The World History of Auditing*, China Auditing Publishing House, 1990, p. 20.

18. Fremont E. Kast, James E. Rosenzweig, *Organization and Management: A System and Contingency Approach*, China Social Sciences Press, 2000, p. 127.

19. A country's public systems can be divided into basic systems and specific systems. Basic systems like building foundations pursue durability; basic systems like the building framework highlight stability; and specific systems like the functional decoration of rooms emphasize suitability and effectiveness, and can be adapted and changed according to changes in demand. Obviously, these three systems differ in effectiveness: basic systems pursue permanence; basic systems highlight long-term stability; and specific systems underline adaptability. Yan Jirong: *Modern National Governance and Institutional Building*, *Chinese Public Administration*, Issue 5, 2014, pp. 58–63.

20. Glenn Tinder, *Political Thinking: Some Permanent Questions*, translated by Wang Ningkun, Beijing: World Book, 2010.

21. Wang Fu (Han Dynasty), *A Treatise on the Latent Man. Shu She.*
22. Liu Jiayi, National Governance and Government Audit, *Social Sciences in China*, Issue 6, 2012.
23. Ibid., p. 64.
24. Ibid., p. 65.
25. Hu Angang, The Nature of Governance Modernization Is Institutional Modernization. *People's Tribune*. November 2013, p. 20; Wang Shaoguang, National Governance and Basic National Capacity. *Journal of Huazhong* University of Science and Technology, Social Science Edition, 2014, Issue 3 (Issue 424 in total).
26. Xi Jinping, Align Our Thinking with the Guidelines of the Third Plenary Session of the 18th CPC Central Committee, published in the *People's Daily*, January 1, 2014.
27. Naomi Caiden, Patterns of Budgeting. *Public Administration Review*, 1978, Vol. 38 (November/December), 539–543.
28. Speech delivered by CPC Secretary General Xi Jinping at the Symposium for Heads of Some Provinces and Cities, in Wuhan, Hubei, July 23, 2013.
29. Feng Youlan, translated by Zhao Fusan, *A Short History of Chinese Philosophy*, pp. 65–66, Beijing: Joint Publishing H.K., 2009.
30. Hans Kelsen, *General Theory of Law and State*, Beijing: Commercial Press, 2013, pp. 269–270.
31. Generally speaking, participatory governance is a process in which policy-interested individuals, organizations, and governments jointly participate in public decision making, resource allocation, and cooperative governance.
32. "The Four Fundamental Principles," as one of the two focal points of the CPC's basic line for the primary stage of socialism, refer to the adherence to the socialist road, the people's democratic dictatorship, the leadership of the Communist Party of China, and Marxism, Leninism, and Mao Zedong Thought. The Four Fundamental Principles reflect the fundamental interests and will of the CPC and people of all ethnic groups. They are the fundamental principles for socialist modernization, reform, and opening up, the basis of rejuvenating the country, and the political cornerstone for the survival and development of the Party and the state.
33. "Three Represents" means that the CPC always represents China's advanced productive forces, advanced culture, and the fundamental interests of the overwhelming majority of the Chinese people. It is the foundation of Party building, the cornerstone of governing, and also the source of force.
34. *Series of Important Speeches of General Secretary Xi Jinping*, 2014, People's Publishing House.
35. Li Jinhua (ed.), *The History of Audit in China* (volume 1), China Modern Economics Publishing House, 2004.
36. The Qing Dynasty once set up the auditing office—namely, the Huikaofu (an audit organization dealing with Money and Cereal affairs)—during the reign

of Emperor Yongzheng. After Emperor Yongzheng took the throne, he promoted fiscal consolidation, set up the Huikaofu to conduct large-scale auditing nationwide, rectified the official system, and punished corruption. All his reforms were effective. Unfortunately, after three years, the Huikaofu was dissolved. The main reason was the system of power balance strongly contradicted with the feudal autocracy.

37. In September 1906, Emperor Guangxu said in Decision on Yikuang and Others' Auditing of Administrative Offices of the Central Government that "To accept different advices, the Advisory Parliament should set up some new offices. Court of Auditors should be responsible for the auditing of the funds. Other offices should be set up under the control of Court of Auditors." Quoted in *The World History of Auditing* by Wen Shuo, 2nd edition, 1996, p. 134.

38. Zeng Xianyi and Ma Xiaohong, Traditional Chinese Legal Structure and Basic Concept Dialectic. Edited by Gao Hongjun, Alma Jianyin, and Lu Nan, *Jurisprudence Reading Literature*, Tsinghua University Press, 2010, pp. 55.

39. See the State Audit Policy in Section III of Chapter 4.

CHAPTER TWO

Audit Function

F UNCTION REFERS TO THE SPECIFIC properties of an object that can meet certain demands while maintaining a relatively stable and independent mechanism. Audit function refers to the capability and effect of auditing revealed in an economic and social operation. Such capability and effect are delivered through audit activities. Based on audit activities, one can judge and measure the capability and effect of auditing, which can be improved through enhanced audit efforts.

I. GENERAL COGNITION OF THE GOVERNMENT AUDIT FUNCTION

According to the functionalist theory in sociology, any social phenomenon has its own important functions. Auditing, as an important part of the national political system, must have its functions to meet national governance and social needs. Audit function reflects audit essence (nature of the audit) with its own intrinsic characteristics. Like other social systems, audit essence is closely linked with the function of economic and social operation. Audit function not only can directly reflect the audit essence, but also can explain the development and changes of auditing. Following the order of objective demand of social economy–structural function–structural form, we can find the most basic relationship between auditing and social economy.

The function, duty, and role of auditing are closely related. Audit function is achieved through audit supervision, certification, and evaluation. Audit function and duty often do not have any strict distinction, but the audit function and the audit role do have some obvious differences. Audit function is the ability the audit has to create a certain impact. Audit role refers to the actual impact produced. Audit function is a prerequisite for performing the audit role. The latter is the external manifestation of audit function, as well as the objective effect generated while auditing is conducted.

To some extent, the nature of auditing can be explained by the audit function. According to the functionalist theory, the audit function depends on the nature of the audit structure itself. If the nature of auditing itself changes, its function of maintaining overall economic and social development will naturally change accordingly. Auditing exists as part of the social life structure because it has a specific function.

Scholars have yet to reach a unified cognition of audit function due to differing ideas about the nature of auditing. For example, some scholars emphasize that the basic function of auditing is economic supervision (i.e., achieving the purpose of maintaining economic order, improving economic management, and strengthening macrocontrol by conducting such supervision). The scholars advocating the "economic cybernetics" theory believe that the audit function is to conduct control, meaning that audit institutions not only can identify problems but also can directly correct them. In practice, different views on audit function lead to different ways of using audit results. When audit results are used to address and punish violations of laws and regulations, improve relevant systems, deter or correct wrongful behaviors, people often believe supervision is the main audit function. When audit institutions conduct objective comprehensive evaluation of the auditee's duty performance according to certain criteria, issue or publish audit results to discharge accountability and win public trust, there is a belief the function of auditing is mainly to conduct evaluation or certification. For example, such accountability audit projects as the Beijing Olympics Games, Shanghai World Expo, and local government debt are all considered evaluation and certification audit projects.

There are generally two factors affecting the functioning of auditing: (1) the objective demand by national governance and (2) the subjective initiative of auditing itself. Demand by national governance provides the basis for the existence of audit function and represents the ability to satisfy the objective needs of national governance. The embodiment of audit function depends on the specific audit work (audit behavior). To what extent the audit work itself can perform its function depends on the audit adaptability to the surrounding environment and creativity of audit work. The need for national governance and economic society for audit is objective, and can be accurately understood and managed. Through continuous improvement of audit work itself, the subjective initiative of auditing to meet the objective needs of national governance can be achieved, and the function of audit can be fully played.

 ## II. "IMMUNE SYSTEM" FUNCTION OF GOVERNMENT AUDITING

The immune system is the important defense force in the human body against viruses and bacteria. Survival and maintenance of proper health in a lifetime depend on this strong defense system. If the immune system is not working properly, the result can be devastating. Therefore, many physicians describe the immune system as "an element of body and soul," "defender of life," "lifeguard," bodily "fighting force," and so forth.

A country is like a living organism. Through theoretical analysis of national organization, structure, function, and behavior characteristics, as well as integrated application of theory and method of system science, organizational behavior, political science, sociology, economics, medical science, and other disciplines, the complex organizational system—namely, the country with its life characteristics—can be resolved into the metabolic, immune, nervous, and behavioral systems. The immune system is a complex subsystem defending against natural, economic, social, and other risks, and is also the barrier[1] behind which the country can be run in an orderly, coordinated, and safe way. To maintain a good national economic and social order, each part of the country needs to perform its functions and duties in a harmonious and unified way.

In the living organism of a state, the government audit system is equivalent to the immune system. The two have a high degree of similarity, manifested in the following four aspects: The government audit as an important part of the national political system, like the human immune system, has an endogenous nature; the value of the government audit is to protect the country's economic and social operations, which is similar to the value of the body's immune system safeguarding human health; government auditing is indispensably responsible for defending national economic and social operations, just like the human body's immune system; and government auditing is professional. Audit institutions effectively play their role through coordination with other departments, very much like the mechanisms of the immune system.

According to medical immunology, the immune system has three basic functions:[2] immune defense, mainly referring to the body's immune protection against foreign antigen (e.g., microorganisms and toxins) attack; immune homeostasis, which is a physiological function wherein the immune system can promptly identify and remove the body's damaged or aging cells, without attacking any normal cells, in order to maintain a stable internal environment; and because of immune surveillance, while various factors in vivo and in vitro cause normal individual tissue cells to constantly mutate, the immune system can identify copying errors or mutant cells and clear them out in a timely manner.

According to a comprehensive study and analysis of government audit history and reality, the government audit as the "immune system" of a healthy national economic and social operation has three functions: prevention, exposure, and resistance.

It should be pointed out that the audit "immune system" function is nothing new, but rather reflects people's growing understanding from the macro-, continuity, and development perspectives in the process of economic and social development. Audit institutions of various countries adopt a similar approach to their work; however, due to differences in historical development, cultural traditions, and political systems, the focal point of the "immune system" function has a different emphasis in terms of its role and fields. For example, the U.S. GAO[3] focuses on public policy formulation and implementation and offering suggestions for improvement; the National Audit Office of China directly investigates and punishes violations of the laws and regulations, while, through uncovering and analyzing outstanding contradictions and major problems in the policy implementation process, offering targeted audit recommendations on reforming and improving macroeconomic policies.

The immune system function of government auditing can be studied in the following two aspects.

1. **Government auditing, above all, is "the immune system" ensuring the healthy operation of the national economy and society.**
   As an important part of national politics, government auditing belongs to the supervisory control system of national governance. Unlike other supervision functions derived from the specific management functions, government audit supervision is independent, full-time, and professional behavior conducted by specialized agencies and professionals, and is thus

an endogenous "immune system" of the national governance system, with prevention, exposure, and resistance functions safeguarding national economic and social health. As the endogenous "immune system" of the national political system, government auditing emerges, develops, and improves with the emergence and development of the country. The reason why the government audit function is compared to the bodily "immune system" is that the two functions share great similarities.

When studying the immune system function the government audit system has in ensuring healthy operation of the national social economy, health is an important concept. Initially, "health" was a physiological concept. In 1948, the World Health Organization (WHO) issued its World Health Organization Charter, stating, "Health is a state of good psychological and social adaptation, rather than just the absence of disease and weakness." In 1989, the WHO refined the concept, saying health included physical health, mental health, good social adaptation, and moral health. With growing understanding, people began to use the concept of health to describe the status of natural, economic, and social operations. The concept of health permeates many disciplines, from medicine to ecology, geography, sociology, economics, and so forth. The research field expanded correspondingly, especially regarding organizational systems. The concept of health is used to describe the good operating condition[4] of a complex system. "Health" of the national economic and social systems means their good operation. Due to different national political and economic systems, history, and culture, the pursuit of "health" in regard to national economic and social systems may differ. The view raised here of the government audit "immune system" function is based on the pursuit of ensuring the "health" of China's current economic and social system.

The government audit "immune system" recognizes an audit function elevated from the perspective of maintaining economic and social health and safety and based on the internal links of national governance and economic and social operation with audit development, thus achieving integrated innovation on a multidisciplinary ideological and theoretical basis. The government audit "immune system" has the following characteristics: (1) As the "immune system" of the national political system, it primarily maintains the accountability relationship between the country's political systems and ensures such a system is implemented. In this regard, government auditing is distinct from internal auditing and independent auditing. Internal auditing mainly involves promoting the performance of the internal accountability relationship within enterprises and administrative institutions; independent auditing primarily facilitates implementation of the accountability relationship between enterprises and their stakeholders. (2) Government auditing emerged with the emergence of a state and developed with the development of a state. (3) Government auditing was created by the political system and changes with the latter's development. Government auditing under the feudal autocratic regime focused on the subjects' accountability to the ruler, and maintained the rule of the feudal monarchy and the country's governance. Modern government auditing under the democratic political system focuses on the government's accountability to the public, aiming to promote good governance. The world's political system has many variations. Government audit systems also have their own unique characteristics. For example, compared with the federal audit system, the central audit office that the unitary state sets up to strengthen central control is responsible for not only the central behavioral level but also local-level governments.

Audit "immune system" theory is the dialectical cognition of audit function from the perspective of movement, contact, and development, inheriting and developing the economic supervision theory, accountability theory, and the principles of democracy and rule of law. For example, compared with the economic supervision theory, the "immune system" theory is an advance, as it clearly stresses that the audit should play the role of prevention, exposure, and resistance, implying the control is practiced at an earlier stage. Compared with the accountability theory, "immune system" theory expands the role and scope of the government audit to the operation and development of the economy and society, as well as national security and other fields, and enlarges the audit horizons to the higher level of national governance, thus involving a wider field of vision.

2. **The government audit involves preventability.** As a kind of system arrangement, government auditing has an endogenous deterrent role, which must be strengthened to inhibit a variety of "diseases" affecting the healthy operation of the economy and society. Government auditing, performing its supervisory responsibilities in accordance with the law, has the advantages of independence, objectivity, impartiality, and innovation, covering all aspects of economy and society, so it can detect problems in a timely manner by being able to detect problematic tendencies.

Government auditing must give full play to its exposing function. Checking for errors and correcting disadvantageous aspects are the basic requirement for audit supervision. Audit institutions must investigate and deal with violations of laws and regulations, economic crimes, loss and wastage, extravagance, damage to resources and environmental pollution that harm the interests of the people, endanger national security, destroy democracy and the rule of law, and so on. They must identify institutional barriers, deficiencies, distortions in the mechanism, and regulatory loopholes to safeguard economic and social health and safe operation.

Government auditing must give full play to its resistance function. Auditing should not only expose problems but also deeply analyze, reveal, and reflect their root causes from the micro- and macroperspectives, from the individual to the general, from the local to the global, from individual signs to overall trends, in order to promote institutional reforms, improve the rule of law, enhance the system, standardize mechanisms, strengthen management, prevent risks, improve the quality and performance of economic and social operations, and enhance their "immunity" so as to promote comprehensive, coordinated, and sustainable economic and social development. Therefore, we must comply with the development trends of the times, adapt to the needs of economic and social development, grasp the basic characteristics of auditing, follow the internal law of auditing, base all work on openness, initiative, service, and understanding of the overall situation, insist on criticism, supervision, microscopic investigation and disclosure, adaptability, and independence, unswervingly reveal and deal with major violations of laws and regulations and economic crimes, thoroughly reveal systemic problems, and resolutely propose regulations for standardized management and improving the system and regulations to effectively assume the historical "immunity" responsibility of the government audit.

III. CONNOTATION OF AUDIT "IMMUNE SYSTEM" FUNCTION

As mentioned earlier, government auditing is an important part of national governance, acting as an "immune system," with the functions of prevention, exposure, and resistance. Deep understanding of the connotation of the government audit "immune system" function is the premise and guarantee of good audit work.

(1) Prevention Function

The basic meaning of prevention in Chinese is "in advance preparedness."[5] The prevention function of government auditing means that, through its deterrence role and the advantages of independence, objectivity, impartiality, innovativeness, and the coverage of all aspects of the economy and society, government auditing can prevent risks in economic and social healthy operations and can strengthen the governance system's "immunity." The term "deterrent" stems from the fact that government auditing based on the Constitution and laws can serve as a regular monitoring system. Both the audit institutions and auditees are aware of the possible consequences of audit activities that become "common knowledge." Auditees know that the audit institution will check their economic and social activities. The audit institution also knows that the auditees may have problems in economic and social activities and seek to hide them. Game Theory points out that, on the basis of common knowledge, in order to maximize their profits (or utility), the strategies adopted by each player must be the best reaction to the expected strategies of other players. No one will be interested in deliberately violating this game equilibrium (also known as the Nash equilibrium), and rashly deviate from this "consistent" prediction leading to losses.[6] Thus, audit supervision is a deterrent for the auditee, and can play a role in prevention and early warning in case of violations. Meanwhile, by following up in a timely way and paying close attention to the safe operation of the whole economy and society, government audit institutions can detect trends and tendencies so as to perceive risks in advance, and play an active role in preventing illegal ideas turning into illegal activities and localized problems from becoming global ones.

Over the years, China's audit institutions have focused on disclosing and analyzing weaknesses and potential risks in the economic and social operation to safeguard national economic security. Through public finance auditing, they pointed out that with the scale of government debt growing, and that the potential financial risk is building up. In financial system auditing, they detected that the capacity of the financial risk supervision is insufficient and recommended that more attention be paid to systemic risks. Through the audit of state-owned enterprises and overseas government institutions, they found that loss of state assets has become serious and that the awareness of protecting state-owned rights and interests in international cooperation needs to be further enhanced. Through the audit of resources and environment, they highlighted that protection of land and mineral resources needs to be further strengthened, and that rapid economic and social development is increasing the pressure on the environment. Through the audit of key livelihood projects and funds, such as subsidies to grain growing farmers, government investment in affordable housing, and rural drinking water security, they identified the social security system needs further improvement, and reported that violations of public interests occurred now and then. For some major investment projects and key special funds they conducted auditing on a real-time basis, covering the entire process of projects. Thus they were able to disclose problems and potential risks in a timely way and ensured that these projects were conducted smoothly.

CASE 2.1: **WHOLE-PROCESS, REAL-TIME AUDITING OF THE CONSTRUCTION OF VENUES FOR THE BEIJING OLYMPIC GAMES**

From September 2005 to March 2009, the National Audit Office of the People's Republic of China (CNAO) organized a real-time audit of the financial revenues and expenditures of the Beijing Organizing Committee for the 29th Olympic Games, as well as of venue construction. To achieve the main objective of "serving and safeguarding the Olympic Games" and ensuring the central government policy of "holding the Olympic Games in an honest and thrifty way" be fully implemented, the audit was organized based on progress of projects and the following agreed audit priorities, stages, and levels. Under the principle of prevention first, the audit covered areas of construction period, quality, safety, investment control, and fund use. Auditors gave timely recommendations for corrections of problems, followed up to ensure the problems were rectified by the auditees, and urged project management departments and construction units to perform their duties and strengthen management so as to complete quality venue construction on time. Over a four-year period, the CNAO cumulatively conducted spot checks of more than 30,000 quality control documents involving the acceptance of completed work, materials receipt checks, and on-site supervision. The audit uncovered more than 350 tendering and bidding problems of various kinds, issued more than 240 individual audit reports, and offered nearly 800 recommendations.[7]

CASE 2.2: **WHOLE-PROCESS, REAL-TIME AUDITING OF FUNDS AND SUPPLIES FOR RELIEF AFTER THE WENCHUAN EARTHQUAKE**

From May 14th to late November 2008, the CNAO organized audit institutions of all levels nationwide to conduct a whole-process, real-time audit of funds and supplies for relief work regarding the Wenchuan Earthquake, covering a total of 18 central departments and units, 1,289 provincial departments and agencies of 31 provinces (autonomous regions and municipalities), the Xinjiang Production and Construction

(continued)

(continued)

Corps, 5,384 prefecture-level departments and units, and 24,618 county-level departments and units. The auditors extended their audit scope and travelled to 3,845 towns and 9,526 villages in the Sichuan, Gansu, Shaanxi, Chongqing, and Yunnan provinces (municipalities), and investigated 76,709 affected households. A total of four audit reports were issued in the process of auditing.

Audit institutions at all levels, according to the requirements of timely correction and adoption of standardized practice with regard to uncovered problems, offered recommendations and supervised and urged rectification activities. They offered more than 3,640 recommendations on strictly implementing national disaster relief policies, strengthening the receipt, distribution, and use of relief funds and supplies, and preventing loss and waste. All levels of governments, departments, and units attached great importance to the audit, with 2,940 recommendations adopted and 570 new rules and system operations made, ensuring the scientific, rational, and effective use of relief funds and supplies. For example, to solve the problem of overstocking relief materials in six seriously affected cities and prefectures, the Sichuan Provincial Earthquake Relief Headquarters formulated a document, *Opinions on Disposal of Remaining Relief Drugs and Medical Devices*. Following audit recommendations, Hanyuan County corrected the unreasonable policy practiced in some towns of requiring earthquake-affected residents to demolish the houses that were considered unsafe before they could be provided temporary relief funds and materials.[8]

(2) The Exposure Function

The exposure function of government auditing refers to the effect and capacity through certain ways and means for the government audit institutions to reveal the real situation of audited objects and issues and disclose existing problems. "Auditing is a systematic process of objectively collecting and evaluating evidence of economic activities and matters to determine the extent of consistency with established standards, and passing the results to the stakeholders."[9] Through supervising and inspecting the implementation of governance policies and measures, government audit institutions can objectively reflect the real situation and reveal problems, and promote better governance. By law, the primary responsibility of auditing is to supervise national governance activities. Auditing must uncover errors, remedy disadvantages, and correct deviated rules, order, and decision. Therefore, the important function of auditing is to reveal and punish violations of laws and rules, economic crimes, loss and waste, extravagance, irrational use of resources, environmental pollution, and acts damaging the interests of the people, endangering national security, and sabotaging democracy and the rule of law. Meanwhile, by revealing the systemic barriers, institutional deficiencies, distortions in mechanisms, and regulatory loopholes, the audit institutions can eliminate all kinds of improper interference in economic and social operations, and promote good implementation of national governance policies and measures for the achievement of healthy operation of the economy and society.

From the perspective of political science, auditing in the first place is an institutional arrangement at the national governance level. "In the beginning, government only cared about accounting for revenues and expenditures and collecting taxes. To this end, the government adopted control means including audit, to reduce errors and malpractices caused by the incompetence or fraudulent behavior of officials."[10] Ancient auditing focused on subjects' responsibility to the ruler, such as the tax audit in the Zhou dynasty, monarch's "grants" during the Western Han Dynasty, strengthening of auditing in the Song Dynasty, review of regulatory and accounting reports during the Yuan Dynasty, and the accounting examination in the Qing Dynasty; modern auditing focuses on government management performance and the government's responsibility to the public to promote democratic rule of law. Both ancient and modern auditing, by performing the exposure function of auditing, provide audit results to a particular object in order to achieve the audit objectives and play the audit role. The exposure function is one of the basic functions of auditing. Along with the continuous development of the government audit, its importance has become increasingly prominent. Of course, affected by the degree of economic and social development as well as changes in the external audit environment, the way, focus, and degree of performing the exposure function will differ in regard to time, area, or aspect.

Over the past 30 years or so, Chinese audit institutions gave full play to the exposure function of auditing and achieved good results. First of all, through revealing and dealing with all kinds of problems, they directly contributed to the increase in state financial revenue and decrease of expenditures, handed over evidence of economic crime to the judiciary and the discipline inspection and supervision departments, recovered substantial economic losses for the country, and also promoted further development of anticorruption work. Second, by revealing all kinds of deep-seated problems in the implementation process of government budgets, audit institutions promoted the reform of the financial management, transfer payments, and departmental budgeting systems, centralized treasury payments, and "separation between revenue and expenditure," and ensured stricter management of land and social security funds. Third, through auditing and audit investigation into special funds for "Three Rural Issues," education, health, social security, poverty relief, and environmental protection, they supervised the implementation of Party and state policies and measures to vigorously achieve national macrocontrol policy goals, and effectively protected the interests of the people. Fourth, through supervising and inspecting the truthfulness of accounting information and the conditions of state-owned assets, they dealt with fraud, illegal operations, asset management chaos, and other acts, to deepen reform and promote scientific development. Fifth, through revelation and supervision over the exercise of power, they audited for holding the leading officials to account, provided an important basis for monitoring and assessing government officials' performance, encouraged government departments and staff to exercise power in accordance with the law and perform their duties effectively, and also contributed to the establishment of accountability mechanisms.

TERMINOLOGY

"Three Rural Issues" involve rural areas, agriculture, and farmers. The purpose of researching "Three Rural Issues" is to increase farmers' income, agricultural growth, and rural stability. As a large agricultural country, China's three rural issues are related to quality of the nation, economic development, social stability, national prosperity, and revival. ▪

CASE 2.3: **SPECIAL FUND AUDITING**

From May to September 2012, the National Audit Office audited the special funds allocated by the central government and ten provinces (autonomous regions), including Shanxi, Inner Mongolia, and Liaoning in years 2010 and 2011, for the purpose of energy conservation and emission reduction, as well as 1,139 related projects. Audit results show that 44 projects (accounting for 3.86 percent of those audited) of 42 units (enterprises) did not achieve the expected effect with a total amount of 1.587 billion yuan of the special funds, accounting for 6.8 percent of the total funds audited. Meanwhile, 35 sectors and project implementation units used special funds totaling 270 million yuan in violation of the rules, accounting for 1.16 percent of total funds audited. Some special funds for energy conservation and emission reduction were not allocated according to budget requirements, and construction of some projects failed to meet the schedule for completion. Eight criminal cases were discovered, and transferred to relevant departments for further action.[11]

From November 2012 to March 2013, the National Audit Office audited the funds allocated by the central government and transferred to 18 provinces (municipalities), including Tianjin, Hebei, and Liaoning, from 2011 to 2012, for comprehensive utilization of renewable energy and resources, and energy conservation and environmental protection respectively. A total of 5,044 projects were audited, involving funds of 62.109 billion yuan, respectively accounting for 60.57 percent and 75.85 percent of the total. The audit discovered that 348 project units had misappropriated and made a fraudulent application and claim for a total of 1.617 billion yuan, accounting for 2.6 percent of funds involved; 102 project units fabricated false declaration materials, and defrauded the state out of 556 million yuan; and 29 project units misappropriated 226 million yuan for the purpose of production, operation, and business spending. Due to loose review by competent departments, and lack of due diligence by third-party review agencies, 217 project units obtained 835 million yuan in violation of rules by "exaggerating the actual scale and budget," and repeated declaration. Relevant local departments and project units returned 205 million yuan to the former funding channels, and the state was able to recover another 214 million yuan involved in fraud. The NAO transferred 29 cases involving 41 people to the judicial authorities.[12]

(3) The Resistance Function

The basic meaning of resistance is "withstanding,"[13] "defense,"[14] and so on. The resistance function of auditing means that, by improving and standardizing the system, government audit institutions can resist and inhibit various "diseases" in the economic and social operation and guard against all kinds of risks, thereby contributing to improved national governance performance. Relevant information on economic and social operations is the basis of formulating macroeconomic policies and evaluating the effect of macroeconomic policy. With its independent status, government audits function to conditionally and completely collect and provide relevant information, including that of microeconomic agencies and the industry and fields, to provide real, objective, comprehensive, and reliable data for corresponding decision-making and management departments. In the course of obtaining information, an audit institution not only identifies the situation and reveals problems, but also analyzes, reveals, and reflects the causes of these problems from both the micro- and macroperspectives, from the individual to the general, from the local to the global, from the individual signs to the overall trends, and from appearance to essence, in order to mobilize positive factors, prevent negative factors from invading the whole economic and social system, promote institutional reforms, improve the rule of law and the system, standardize mechanisms, strengthen management, and prevent risks, thereby improving the quality and performance of economic and social operations, and promoting comprehensive, coordinated, and sustainable economic and social development.

For years, Chinese audit institutions adhered to starting from the audit of fiscal and financial revenue and expenditure, focusing on ensuring accountability and improving systems, comprehensively integrating the truthfulness and legitimacy auditing of the financial revenues and expenditures with performance auditing, combining problem detection with system improvement, paying more attention to decision-making behavior of government departments and state-owned enterprises, the economic, social, and ecological benefits of major investment projects and key financial funds, and the institutional shortcomings and management loopholes of violations, and putting forward views of treating both symptoms and root causes. Over a period of 30 years, government audit institutions at all levels submitted more than 2.3 million audit reports of various types, and provided a solid and reliable information and decision-making basis for Party committees and governments at all levels and relevant departments to improve their management and systems.

CASE 2.4: **AUDITING OF IMPLEMENTATION OF CENTRAL MACROCONTROL POLICIES**

To address the 2008 international financial crisis, the Central Government proposed macroeconomic policies for maintaining economic growth, restructuring, reforming, and focusing on people's livelihood, and comprehensively implemented a package plan to promote steady and rapid economic development. From 2008 to 2009, under the organization of the CPC Central Committee and the State Council, audit institutions nationwide gave top priority to promoting steady and rapid economic development, and strengthened audit supervision of the implementation of various policies and measures. In the second half of 2008, NAO rapidly organized an audit and survey on the impact of the crisis on Chinese businesses, especially SMEs, commercial banks, financial derivative product business, overseas investment risk, and energy security. The purpose of the audit was to provide the government with decision reference. In 2009, all audit institutions focused on checking implementation of central policies and measures, organized auditing or real-time audits of 10 important fund projects and five major investment projects, and promoted the launch and implementation of various investment projects. According to the audit findings, NAO proposed to further speed up the implementation of central macrocontrol policies. Regarding local support funds, it was suggested that local governments at all levels should take further measures, make clear areas for support and responsibilities for the added investment funds, and accelerate fund allocation. NAO suggested the National Development and Reform Commission, Ministry of Finance, and other departments strengthen their tracking of the added investment projects, urge local governments and related sectors of all levels to strictly implement macrocontrol policies for energy conservation and emission reduction, conduct project selection and early preparation well, prevent low-level redundant construction and blind expansion, and constantly improve the economic and social benefits of investment.

After the exposure of related problems, relevant departments and local government organizations at all levels organized system rectification and ensured the implementation of central macrocontrol policies. For example, the National Development and Reform Commission issued an Emergency Notice on Further Solving the Related Issues concerning Local Supporting Investment for Added Central Investment Projects. Various places took measures to accelerate fund allocation and early preparation and promote the organization of physical work as soon as possible. The Ministry of Water Resources issued an Emergency Notice on Correcting Audit and Survey Problems about Reinforcement of Unsafe Dilapidated Reservoirs, and Emergency Notice on Strengthening Quality and Security Management of Projects of Reinforcing Unsafe Dilapidated Reservoirs under Construction, requiring all places to carry out rectification work within a specified period.[15]

IV. RELATIONSHIP AMONG THE THREE MAJOR FUNCTIONS OF THE AUDIT IMMUNE SYSTEM

Prevention, exposure, and resistance are the three ways in which government auditing performs its "immune system" function. They are interconnected and constitute an organic whole in the practice of audit work. Specifically, there are three types of relationships involved:

1. **The parallel relationship.** Exposure, resistance, and prevention are three methods through which the audit performs its "immune system" function, and jointly safeguards the healthy operation of the economy and society. Exposure and resistance are the means to correct existing problems, while prevention is in advance preparation to prevent them from occurring. The three are complementary and indispensable, and have equal importance. Just as firefighting is no substitute for fire prevention, and treatment is no substitute for disease prevention, without revelation there can be no resistance and prevention; without resistance, exposure and prevention will come to nothing; and without prevention, exposure and resistance will cause exhaustion in the audit process. It is not correct to separate the three or stress one more than the other.

2. **The complementary relationship.** Exposure, resistance, and prevention are closely linked and mutually serve as the condition and the purpose, and together meet the requirements of guaranteeing healthy operation of the national economy and society. Among them, exposure is the foundation. Without exposure, there will be no effective capability to resist and prevent; resistance is the key. Without resistance, the exposed problem cannot be effectively corrected and loopholes effectively closed. Exposure without resistance only makes the situation worse, for it cannot form a deterrent so that prevention is impossible; prevention, therefore, is the ultimate goal. A healthy society should not be full of problems. Healthy operation of the economy and society ensures fewer or even no problems, and this requires prevention in advance. The depth and breadth of prevention to some extent determine the health of the economic and social operations. Effective prevention itself contains strict requirements for exposure and resistance. The results of strict exposure and resistance are beneficial to effective prevention. Meanwhile, resistance and prevention cannot be independently completed by audit institutions, and often need coordination and cooperation with other relevant departments and units.

3. **The relationship between symptoms and root causes.** Performing exposure and resistance functions means merely alleviating the symptoms. Performing the preventive function is to address the root causes. Strengthening exposure and resistance not only can effectively curb behavior harmful to economic and social health, but also can have a deterrent effect by establishing good social morality. Strengthening prevention not only is beneficial to the healthy operation of the economy and society, consolidating the outcome of exposure and resistance, but also helps to reduce their operating costs as well as various economic and social

operational losses. Only through strict exposure and resistance as well as effectively curbing the behavior affecting economic and social health can the essential preconditions be created for prevention. Only by doing a good job of prevention and continuing from the source to eradicate problems can one fundamentally prevent and solve the problem affecting the economic and social healthy operation.

In the actual audit work, we must ensure exposure practices, focus on resistance, and aim at prevention. Protecting the healthy operation of the economy and society means we must strictly disclose the behavior hindering healthy operation and deeply analyze the causes; limitations in the powers of audit institutions, as well as the complexity of overcoming hindrances to economic and social operational health, determine that the correction and resistance aspects need to rely on forces outside the audit institutions. Resistance often becomes the focus in performing the immune system function.

- **Highlighting the intervention at an early stage feature of prevention.** Compliance auditing emphasizes exposure and resistance, focusing on postsupervision. Time lags and indirectness weaken the audit deterrent. Performance auditing requires bringing into play the prevention function, so it must highlight concurrent auditing and pre-auditing to better enhance the timeliness of the work. Highlighting intervention at an early stage by concurrent auditing and pre-auditing is reflected in terms of both organization and implementation of an audit and the role of auditing. Major projects or policies should be subject to real-time auditing to ensure the problem doesn't continue to fester uncured.
- **Highlighting the accuracy feature of exposure function.** The audit "immune system" function requires both sensitivity and judgment. In complicated circumstances, it is necessary to distinguish the priorities and accurately uncover problems with fundamental impact and significant long-term hazards. The actual situation will differ with the place, time, and nature of the project. In this regard, audit institutions and audit staff must analyze specific problems and make an accurate judgment. At present, China is in a triple superposition stage of "growth speed change, structural adjustment pains, and prestimulus digestion," and various deep contradictions and problems have appeared. Audit institutions should consider the new requirements for reform and development, correctly grasp the new situation and new problems concerning reform and development, truly disclose, analyze, and reflect emerging problems, objectively and prudently

conduct audit processing, and offer suggestions, to better promote smooth and healthy economic development. They should insist on auditing according to law, and severely investigate and punish serious violations of laws and regulations, abuse of power, and corruption; at the same time, they should insist on seeking truth from facts, instead of investigating and treating old problems according to the current rules and systems, or measuring current innovation matters according to outdated ideas. Any innovative initiative that breaks through the original systems or regulations, but is conducive to scientific development, deepened reform, and implementation of central policies and measures, should be supported, standardized, and improved, to eliminate institutional obstacles to economic development. The faults of reform and development cannot be corrected simply according to existing standards and regulations, but should be carefully studied and analyzed, be viewed historically, dialectically, and objectively, and treated prudently.

■ **Highlighting the thoroughness of resistance.** First, the cause shall be analyzed thoroughly. While correcting violations in regard to the auditee's financial revenues and expenditures, audit institutions should deeply analyze management methods, the decision-making mechanism, system construction, and so on in order to solve the problem at the source. Thus it can treat both symptoms and root causes, prevent recurrence of disciplinary violations, and effectively bring the role of resistance into play. Secondly, audit recommendations must be thorough. Whether the recommendations are comprehensive, thorough, objective, complete, macro, targeted, and operable is an important aspect of determining the resistance role of auditing. For the auditees, good audit recommendations should help correct a problem, improve internal controls and systems, standardize management, promote scientific decision making, and protect the safety and effective use of state-owned funds. For governments at all levels, auditing should focus on economic and social development objectives and a macroeconomic regulation and control policy orientation, and help to establish and improve institutional mechanisms, laws, and regulations. Thirdly, the rectification has to be thorough. The direct purpose of auditing is to rectify and resolve existing problems, so as to convert the audit results into execution and productivity as well as a driving force for administration according to law. Therefore, it is necessary to establish and improve the audit rectification system, improve the accountability mechanisms, and further strengthen follow-up examination of audit results; establish communication and coordination mechanisms with government departments and relevant organizations, strengthen collaboration, and effectively promote rectification work; and actively and steadily push forward the audit announcement system, gradually standardize the announcement forms, contents, and procedures to effectively influence public opinion, social supervision, and better promotion of rectification work.

V. SPECIFIC EMBODIMENT OF THE GOVERNMENT AUDIT FUNCTION

Achieving good national governance is an objective need for national development. Whatever the state system and political system, government auditing is an important part of the basic political system. Through performing the "immune system" functions of prevention, revelation, and resistance, it can promote continuous improvement of the national governance system, and the sustainable and healthy development of the economy and society embodied in the following seven aspects.

1. **Government Auditing Is an Important Measure to Supervise and Restrict the Exercise of Power.** Power allocation and constraints are the basic elements of modern national political system design, and also an important principle in establishing a national political system. To achieve effective control, management, and services of public affairs, a country should impose ways of restriction to prevent abuse of power. When power is not effectively controlled and restricted, a country won't have the value standard, moral system, and legal basis that are required. As a national power specified in the form of the constitution or laws, through the implementation of statutory supervision, revelation, and evaluation functions, government auditing restrains the power of government agencies and officials within the range authorized by the people, and publicly discloses the extent and level of fiduciary duties to be fulfilled by government agencies and officials for supervision by the people, creating a system whereby powers match responsibilities. Audit offices of all countries play a positive role in promoting effective government accountability. For example, when releasing the government auditing standards in June 2003, the U.S. General Accounting Office (GAO) stated that the concept of responsibility for the use of public resources was the key to the national management program, and the most basic element of a healthy democracy. In 2004, its

main function was defined as investigating the accountability of the federal government, and it was renamed as the "Government Accountability Office," to emphasize government audit functions in improving national governance. Britain, in 1866, specified that all government payments had to be reviewed by the auditor general on behalf of Parliament and independent of the government. The monarch appoints the auditor general, who can be dismissed only after getting the unanimous consent of both Houses of Parliament. To improve the efficiency of accountability, disposal, and punishment, France stipulates that the president of the Audit Court concurrently serves as president of the Court of Finance, Budget, and Discipline, to fundamentally ensure the effectiveness of audit accountability and rectification. Chinese audit offices have conducted more beneficial explorations and trials in realizing effective accountability and promoting the balance of rights and liabilities. For example, the economic responsibility auditing system[16] has become the important way for ensuring that the leading cadres abide by laws and discipline and conduct due diligence, as well as a means of strengthening supervision and restriction of the exercise of power, and also an important reference for assessing, appointing, dismissing, investigating the responsibilities of, supervising, and managing cadres.

2. **Government Auditing Is an Important Way to Promote Democracy and the Rule of Law.** Democracy and the rule of law are the optimized selection of national governance in a political system, and are an important sign of political civilization construction. The rule of law is the social management mechanism, social activity pattern, and social order status taking democracy as the basic premise, strict compliance with the law as the core, and power constraints as the key. Democracy can be traced back to ancient Greece, and literally means "the people's rule." In modern constitutional theory, democracy means that the most basic rights in political affairs belong to the people. In the history of the development of democracy, embodiment of the democratic ideals in national governance cannot be separated from rule of law. This is a long-standing concept. The Western rule of law stems from Solon Reform, already basically theorized in the era of Aristotle (384–322 BC). Its core is the national governance way featuring "rule of law." Some scholars have pointed out that the rule of law ensures democracy is institutionalized and legalized, creates actionable, stable operational and developmental space for democracy. Democracy injects new content and motivation to the rule of law, so that the latter serves for the protection of human rights, freedom, and happiness.

Therefore, the ultimate goals of democracy and the rule of law are the same, becoming the optimized choice of national governance in the political system, gradually harmonized through long-term practice.

The largest impact of rule of law on the modern government audit lies in providing the legal basis for audit offices and audit work, safeguarding the independence of government auditing, and providing specific audit standards. The establishment setting, functions, objectives, tasks, and procedures of modern government audit bodies are often stipulated by laws. In particular, the institutional setting is often stipulated constitutionally. For example, the Constitution of Japan stipulates that national revenues and expenditures and final settlement have to be reviewed by the Board of Audit each year, and the Cabinet then submits a final settlement and review report to parliament in the following year. The Italian constitution stipulates that the Court of Audit has to conduct antecedent supervision over the legality of various government decrees, and conduct ex post supervision over the legality of the implementation of state budgets.[17] Article 91 and Article 109 of the Constitution of the People's Republic of China also stipulate the establishment of the central and local audit offices. All countries pay attention to bringing into play the important role of government auditing in promoting the rule of law and the administration by law. For example, the U.S. GAO evaluates whether the formulation of any regulations complies with statutory procedures in advance. In recent years, the EU Court of Auditors focused on auditing implementation regulations concerning foods, and found many problems, including organic agricultural products' failure to meet EU standards, and weak security supervision of organic agricultural products.[18] In recent years, China's audit offices firmly investigated and dealt with the problems of failure to abide by the law, loose law enforcement, and failure to punish law-breakers, made suggestions on formulating and amending laws and regulations, promoted the formulation of the Law on the State-Owned Assets of Enterprises and the Regulation on the Implementation of the Tendering and Bidding Law, participated in the coordination of more than 700 laws and regulations, and vigorously promoted the construction of democracy and the rule of law.

In modern society, governments are entrusted by the people to govern the country. Modern government auditing meets the requirements of democratic politics, continues to expand the field of auditing with the deepening of government responsibility, deepens the supervision content, gradually extends audit content from the real legality of fiscal and financial revenue and expenditure to the overall economy, efficiency, and effect of government activities and to the security, sustainability, and equity of the national governance, in order to meet people's supervisory requirements in regard to government performing their functions, exercising their powers, and assuming responsibility, reveal any acts that seriously damage the dignity of law and order, and ensure due punishment. Meanwhile, through audit results announcements and information disclosures, the transparency of governance is enhanced. China's audit offices make public all audit findings except state secrets and business secrets, organize the media to track and report major audit projects, disclose the audit process and progress in a timely fashion, and provide important channels for the public to understand government departments' performance of duty and oversee their fiscal revenue and expenditure activities.

3. **Government Auditing Is an Important Guarantee for Policy Implementation.** With the rapid development of a new public management movement in the world, various countries have conducted many useful explorations and trials in improving public governance, and audit offices have played their due role. In particular, many government audit offices conducted follow-up and performance audits of policy implementation, and helped government departments to improve management, economy, efficiency, and effectiveness of using and managing public resources.

Practice has proved that auditing can improve national governance capability mainly according to the following three aspects: Firstly, auditing can enhance budgetary constraints, and improve budget execution and management. The budget execution audit is the eternal and basic function of government auditing, which is extensively reflected in laws of different countries. In recent years, they have paid much attention to the role of auditing in improving budget execution capability. For example, the U.S. GAO, in view of the major internal control loopholes and false asset reporting of the federal government in the process of making consolidated financial statements, refused to express audit opinions for 17 consecutive years. Since 1995, the audit offices of China have submitted audit reports on annual budget execution to local governments each year, and presented audit reports to national people's congresses to strengthen normative budget execution and promote the rational allocation, normalization, and efficient use of financial resources. Second, auditing is conducive to increasing revenues, reducing expenditures, and improving economic governance capability. For example, since 2008, Chinese audit offices have strengthened auditing of the true and legitimate benefits of financial revenue and expenditure, directly contributing more than 100 billion yuan from revenue increases, expenditure reductions, and recovery (excluding more than 1 trillion yuan involved in major cases investigated since 2008). According to the National Audit Office, the auditing expenditure of each yuan can generate the audit results of more than 100 yuan, and each auditor can annually audit the funds of more than 40 million yuan.[19] The real time audit of the implementation of governance policies and measures facilitates policy implementation and improvement of the governance level. For example, the EU Court of Auditors paid close attention to the effectiveness of economic recovery and remedial measures after the European debt crisis, audited the implementation of related policies, and released audit reports on losses incurred by the Spanish banking industry. In recent years, audit offices of China have audited the implementation of the Central Eight Provisions and the "Three Provisions" of the State Council, conducted special auditing of the management and use of three public expenses and conference expenses, conducted special surveys on the governments' reform promotion, and operating and expenditures of county-level agencies, to ensure smooth reform.

TERMINOLOGY

The Central Eight Provisions refer to the eight provisions of the Political Bureau of the CPC Central Committee on improving the work style and maintaining close ties with the masses, which were adopted and released at the meeting of the Political Bureau of the CPC Central Committee on December 4, 2012. The provisions involve improving investigation and research, streamlining meetings, briefing documents and reports, normalizing visit activities, improving security work, improving news reports, making strict publications, and practicing thrift. The "Eight Provisions" reflect the fundamental requirements for managing and running the Party strictly.

The "Three Provisions" of the State Council were proposed by Premier Li Keqiang when meeting with Chinese and foreign reporters after the First Session of the 12th National People's Congress on March 17, 2013. Concrete contents are as follows: during the term of office, construction will not be allowed of any new government building; there will be no increase in financial support personnel; and public spending on receptions, going abroad, and purchasing vehicles cannot increase. The "Three Provisions" reflect the concrete requirements for building frugal governments under the new situation. ▪

4. **Government Auditing Is a Powerful Tool to Strengthen the Anti-corruption Struggle.** Corruption involves the use of public power to promote personal interests; it means alienation of public power and is a serious threat to national governance. Promoting the anticorruption campaign is the role of government auditing as the "immune system" of national governance, and is determined by the endogenous nature of government auditing. It is independent of auditors' will, and is not the special task of the government audit offices during a certain period, but an important duty that all government audit offices cannot avoid. There are many reasons, but primarily these are: most of the corruption and fraudulent activities ultimately relate to money. The audit work always focuses on the nation's wealth, and can easily find the direct misappropriation or indirect encroachment of national wealth; secondly, government auditing is independent, and has no conflict of interest with the audited unit and object, and can objectively reveal problems; and thirdly, government auditing is a regular monitoring system, covering all financial funds and government agencies, and can uncover clues to major cases in a timely and effective manner.

For a long time, National Audit Offices have been paying attention to major illegal problems uncovered during auditing and have become an important force in anticorruption work. They always regard investigating major violations of laws and regulations and promoting anticorruption work as an important duty, effectively highlighting the management, distribution, and use of financial funds as well as audit supervision over budget and final account in engineering construction, bidding and procurement, land transfer and displacement, exploitation and transfer of state-owned resources and mineral resources, loan issuance of financial institutions, bill discounting and insurance claims, foreign investment of state-owned enterprises, asset disposal and enforcement of the "Three Importance and One Greatness" system, and so on, establishing coordination mechanisms with the police, prosecutors, and supervisory and other relevant departments, and strengthening communication and coordination with these departments to deal with serious violations in a timely manner.

Supreme audit institutions around the world attach great importance to playing the role of auditor in fighting corruption. For example, the U.S. GAO launched a special audit of then Vice President Dick Cheney's alleged fraud, and revealed the truth of the collusion between government officials and businesses in the United States; the European Court of Auditors and the UK Audit Commission conducted a thorough investigation into members' acts of fiddling expenses and claiming subsidies illegally, and so on. The French media paid great attention to presidential spending compliance problems disclosed by the French Court of Audit. The South Korean Board of Audit and Inspection deeply probed fraud by senior officials.

5. **Government Auditing Is an Important Guarantee for Safeguarding National Security.** Safeguarding national security has always been the primary task of the national governance and the common responsibility of almost all sectors in the national governance system. As an important part of the national governance, government auditing, in fulfilling its supervisory responsibilities, has always paid close attention to national security, making a unique contribution. First, government auditing can provide timely, objective, and reliable information for national governance, so as to provide scientific decision-making reference for the assessment of national strength and safeguarding national security. The audit of local government debt in 2011 and the comprehensive audit of national government debt in 2013 launched by the CNAO are good examples. Second, government auditing focuses on revealing and reflecting weaknesses and risks in economic and social operations related to national security. Third, government audit supervision, given its independent status, can truthfully reveal problems, offer audit suggestions and opinions, promote rectification, continue to regulate and restrict the operation of powers, and maintain and improve the economic and social order in order to safeguard the national security.

Audit institutions all over the world have made many efforts in safeguarding national security. In 2010, the CNAO released the new auditing standards, and further clarified that safeguarding national security is the objective of the government audit. Article VI of the new standards clearly pointed out that "The main objective of the audit institution is, through overseeing the truthfulness, legitimacy and effect of audited unit's financial revenue and expenditure as well as economic activity, to safeguard national economic security, promote democracy and the rule of law as well as clean government, and protect the healthy development of the national economy and society." The interpretation of the new standards for the government audit objectives is from the Audit Law, and is more explicit. In recent years, national-level audit institutions have always seen safeguarding national security as a major task of audit work, focusing on fiscal and financial operations, energy and strategic resources, national information, local government debt, internal governance and supervision of financial institutions, security of state-owned assets and operational risks of SMEs, resources and environmental protection, and so forth, analyzing and exposing weaknesses and potential risks in the economic and social operation in a timely manner, and providing reliable information for safeguarding national economic security. In 1990, the U.S. GAO began to release its list of high-risk fields of government work. Especially in recent years, it focused on auditing the projects needing emergency concerns and transformation. For example, after the 9/11 terrorist attacks, the United States strengthened auditing the projects concerning land security, international affairs, and national defense. In the following 10 years, of more than 1,000 audit reports released, there were more than 500 national defense reports. After a disastrous hurricane in 2005, the GAO included national flood insurance programs in the high-risk list in March of the following year.

6. **Government Auditing Is an Important Force to Promote the Deepening of Reform.** Reform is the self-improvement and development of national governance to keep pace with the times. By reforming and changing the aspects and links in the productive relationship no longer considered capable of adapting to productivity demands, it can gradually improve the mechanisms of economic and social scientific development, and achieve more efficient allocation and use of resources. The purpose of auditing is not only to reveal problems, but also, even more important, to correct errors, improve the system, and deepen reform. By improving the system in all aspects and managing affairs, personnel, and wealth within the system, audit institutions can fundamentally ensure the safe use of state funds and effectively guard against many criminal acts seeking private gain through abuse of power, in order to achieve good national governance. Government auditing is characterized by strong independence, wide contact areas, familiarity with policies and regulations, and ability to grasp detailed situations. It can analyze problems from a macro and global viewpoint, and propose solutions from institutional and mechanism-related aspects, so as to continue to promote reform in various fields. This is not only the responsibility legally placed on government auditing, but also an important way for it to play a role in national governance.

Audit institutions around the world always seek to play up the constructive role of auditing in promoting reform. Going back in history we find that, in 1714, the Prussian Highest Accounting Office evolved from an organization providing simple document and account auditing to providing political advice; in 1761, the Accounting Office, the predecessor of the Austrian Court of Audit, was founded. In addition to uncovering accounting errors and pointing out deficiencies, a major task was prevention control—namely, expressing opinions on pending economic matters before the imperial court made a decision. In 1967, the U.S. Congress issued the first request to the GAO to assess the effect of a project; in 1969, the congressional government management committee held extensive discussions on the potential ability of the GAO to become a source of congressional information, and concluded that "if the GAO concentrates on project impact evaluation, review on economic activity and providing new suggestions, their work will be more meaningful and useful."

In China, government auditing has played an active role in promoting the continuous development and improvement of the socialist system with Chinese characteristics. Centering on the establishment and improvement of the market economy system and starting from fiscal and financial revenue and expenditure auditing, Chinese audit institutions at all levels focus on responsibility performance and accountability, integrate the conventional audit and performance audit, strengthen supervision and inspection over the implementation of existing laws and regulations, carefully identify the problems and loopholes in policies, systems, and management, and propose solutions to problems at the system and mechanism level, effectively protecting the smooth progress of reforms, and playing a positive role in establishing institutions and mechanisms conducive to scientific development.

7. **Government Auditing Is an Effective Means to Safeguard People's Livelihood.** Whether livelihood problems can be properly addressed not only is a vital expression of national governance but also determines the political direction to a considerable extent, and is related to its basic soundness and credibility. Since ancient times, China has mentioned "people's livelihood" and "national plan" in the same breath.

In China, the policy of safeguarding the interests of the people is established as the fundamental goal of government auditing, to promote harmony and sustainable development of the economy and society, which plays a constructive role in promoting the protection and improvement of people's livelihood, building a resource-saving and environment-friendly society, and so on. Chinese audit institutions always attach importance to the supervision and inspection of implementation of policies and measures related to people's livelihood and resource environment protection, problems involving people's vital interests and fund management related to the "three rural problems" and support of urban low-income people, as well as education, health, housing, and social security programs. They aim to reveal and reflect the poor implementation of policy and objectives, correct any problem threatening serious impact and damage to people's interests, and play an important role in ensuring and improving people's livelihood and promoting the harmony and sustainable development of the economy and society. In recent years in the United States, the GAO proposed four strategic audit objectives, including countermeasures to the challenges faced by the welfare of the American people and overall financial security, and the challenges and threats of globalization, promoting the transformation of federal government functions, meeting twenty-first century challenges, and maximizing the value of GAO work. Three of GAO's eight major audit concerns are directly related to people's livelihood: the U.S. economy in times of change; population aging and diversification; and quality of life. Canada's Office of the Auditor General takes serving the public interest as its primary value; the South Korean Board of Audit and Inspection stresses the establishment of a just and equitable society through auditing and monitoring. Thus, livelihood problems are of universal concern.

 BIBLIOGRAPHY

Audit Research Institute. *Exploration and Thought on Audit Immune System Function*. Beijing: China Economic Times Press, 2009.

Brown, Alfred Reginald Radcliffe. The Functional Concept of the Social Sciences. Liu Dacheng, Trans. *Ethnic Renditions*, 1985 (5).

Gong, Feili. *Medical Immunology* (2nd edition). Beijing: Science Press, 2007.

Kurt Zanker. *The Body's Immune System—the Body and Soul Elements*. Translated by Jiang Lan. Changsha: Hunan Science and Technology Press, 2001.

Su, Guoxun. Neo-functionalism: New Integration in the Contemporary Sociological Theory. *Foreign Social Sciences*, 1990 (8).

Xigelite, Schmidt. *Key to "Immune System" Health*. Translated by Mao Jie. Taibei: Taiwanese Lin Yu Cultural Enterprise, 2002.

Yang, Duogui, and Zhou Zhitian. *National Health Report*. Beijing: Science Press, 2008.

Yang, Shanhua. *Contemporary Western Sociological Theory*. Beijing: Peking University Press, 1999.

Yu, Guangjun. Evolution and Development of Functionalist Theory. *Journal of Shangqiu Vocational and Technical College*, 2010 (3).

NOTES

1. Yang Duogui, Zhou Zhitian, *National Health Report*, Beijing: Science Press, 2008, p. 34.
2. Gong Feili, *Medical Immunology*, Beijing: Science Press, 2007, p. 3.
3. In 1921, the United States introduced the national audit system and set up the U.S. Federal Audit Office, which is a constitutional institution independent of the U.S. administration but performs the duties of supervision of government. In 2004, the U.S. Federal Audit Office changed its name to the U.S. Federal Government Accountability Office to emphasize that the duties of the state audit are to strengthen the government's responsibility and improve the governance of the country. At present, China still refers to it as the U.S. Federal Audit Office or U.S. Audit Office.
4. Yang Duogui and Zhou Zhitian, *National Health Report*, Beijing: Science Press, 2008, pp. 29–30.
5. *The Modern Chinese Dictionary*, Yanbian: Yanbian People's Publishing House, 2002.
6. Shi Xiquan, *Game Theory*, Shanghai: Shanghai University of Finance and Economics Press, 2000, pp. 31–34.
7. 8th China's Audit Results Announcement in 2009: Follow-up audit result of the Beijing Olympics' financial revenue and expenditure and the Olympic venue construction projects.
8. China National Audit Office on Wenchuan Earthquake Relief Funds and Materials Audit Bulletin (No. 4).
9. Committee on Basic Auditing Concepts, *A Statement of Basic Auditing Concepts*, Sarasota, FL: American Accounting Association, 1973, p. 2.
10. Jerry D. Sullivan, Richard A. Gnospelius, Philip L. DeFliese, and Henry R. Jaenicke, *Montgomery's Auditing* (10th edition). Beijing, China: Citic Press,1985.
11. 16th China Audit Results Announcement in 2013: Audit Result of 1,139 Energy-Saving and Energy Emission Reduction Projects.
12. 25th China Audit Results Announcement in 2013: Audit Result of 5,044 Energy-Saving, Recycling and Comprehensive Use Projects.
13. *Modern Chinese Dictionary*, Beijing: Commercial Press, 1995.
14. *Modern Chinese Dictionary*, Yanbian: Yanbian People's Publishing House, 2002.
15. 3rd China Audit Results Announcement in 2009: Audit Situation of National Audit Office on Implementation of Central Government Policy on Stable and Faster Development of the National Economy.
16. In 1999 the CPC Central Committee and the General Affairs Office of the State Council issued the Provisional Regulations concerning the Below-the-County-Level Party and Government Leading Cadres' Economic Responsibility Audit and the Provisional Regulations concerning Leading Personnel of the State-Owned Enterprises and State Holding Enterprises with Respect to Economic

Responsibility Audit during Their Terms, both for trial implementation. In 2006, the PRC Audit Law increased provisions of the economic responsibility audit, making it possible for this system to gradually embark on a legal track. In October 2010, the General Affairs Office of the CPC Central Committee and the General Affairs Office of the State Council issued the Regulations concerning Economic Responsibility Audit for Leading Cadres of the Party and Government and Leaders of State-Owned Enterprises, making all kinds of leading cadres at all levels fully open to economic audit. In July 2014, seven member units of the Central Economic Responsibility Audit Joint Meeting issued the Rules for the Implementation of Regulations concerning Economic Responsibility Audit for Leading Cadres of the Party and Government and Leaders of State-Owned Enterprises, further promoting the standardization of the economic responsibility audit system.

17. Li Jinhua, *Audit Theory Research* (2nd edition), Beijing, China: Modern Economic Publishing House, 2005, p. 204.
18. Scientific Research Institute of the China National Audit Office, *Introduction to Foreign Audit Supervision System*, Beijing: Modern Economic Publishing House, 2013, p. 12.
19. China National Audit Office Report. Source: China National Audit Office website.

CHAPTER THREE

Research on the Government Audit Objective

THE OBJECTIVE IS THE RESULT OR TARGET of an activity, expected by an organization or individual. Objective determines orientation. Research on the audit objective has an important role in specifying audit work direction, guiding audit practice, and completing the audit task. This topic defines the basic concept of government audit objectives, analyzes their characteristics and the factors affecting them, expounds the connotation of the fundamental and realistic goals of government auditing, and systematically proposes primary tasks and priorities.

 ## I. CONCEPT OF GOVERNMENT AUDIT OBJECTIVES

(1) Connotation of Government Audit Objectives

Auditing as a purposeful activity also has its own specific objectives. Audit objectives are the expected results of audit automation as well as the purpose to be achieved by audit behavior. As an important part of auditing's theoretical system, audit objectives form the guide to Audit Law and an important factor determining the main audit value orientation and work ideas, and play the role of leading the direction and standardization of audit work. The degree of realization of audit objectives determines the effectiveness of auditing.

Audit offices are expected to meet government audit objectives. They can be divided into fundamental, realistic, and immediate objectives. The first is to safeguard the fundamental interests of the people. The realistic objective is to promote the rule of law, safeguard people's livelihoods, and promote reform and development. The direct objective is to monitor and evaluate the reality, legality, and effectiveness of the financial revenues and expenditures of audited units. The three are interrelated and interdependent. The fundamental objective is the highest-level goal and the ultimate purpose of audit work as well as the premise and foundation of determining the realistic and immediate objectives in a certain period. The realistic objective is both the embodiment of the fundamental objective and the direction and guidance of the immediate objective within a certain period. The realization of government audit objectives is also dependent on the completion of the main audit tasks in various periods.

(2) Features of Government Audit Objectives

As a special public activity, government auditing pursues objectives quite different from that of internal auditing, social auditing, and other types of auditing, which have the following three aspects:

1. **Publicity.** The nature of government auditing determines the objective. As an important part of the national political system, government auditing emerged and developed to meet the demand of national governance. It works as the "immune system" with the functions of exposure, resistance, and prevention within the national governance system, and it is the cornerstone and a guarantee of national governance. This determines that government audit objectives must be determined from the perspective of safeguarding public interests and focusing on public power performance, formulation of public policy, provision of public service, and establishment of the public, in order to reflect the public will and safeguard the public interest.

2. **Hierarchy.** The government audit objective has many levels. Overall, it includes fundamental and realistic objectives. The priority and focus of auditing are the concrete manifestation of realizing these objectives. The hierarchy of audit objectives is determined by the nature of the state, the situation and tasks at a particular stage, the essence and characteristics of audit matters. In practice, audit offices should set priorities when

implementing specific audit projects. The realistic objectives can be achieved by a series of audit projects, so that the fundamental objective can be ultimately achieved through the completion of realistic objectives at various stages. Meanwhile, the achievement of the future objectives should be based on realization of the previous objective.

3. **Dynamics.** The socioeconomic environment varies in different periods, and so does the audit demand. In order to better adapt to such changes, the audit objectives, especially the realistic objectives, should be adjusted accordingly, which represent the dynamics of government audit objectives. This requires audit offices to always focus on socioeconomic development trends, and adjust the audit task and work priorities accordingly.

(3) Main Factors Affecting Audit Objectives

In general, three factors affect audit objectives: the objective needs of the audit environment and the ability and level of auditing.

1. **Development and changes of national governance.** A country's historical heritage, cultural traditions, and level of economic and social development determine the objective of national governance, which accordingly determines the direction of the government audit. At different stages, the phased objectives and the key of national governance differ, and so do the realistic objectives and immediate objectives of the government audit. The 18th CPC National Congress determined objectives of building a moderately prosperous society in an all around way and the overall layout of "Five-in-One," covering the political, economic, cultural, social, and ecological civilization. The Third Plenary Session of the 18th CPC Central Committee established the overall goal of comprehensively deepening reform (i.e., improving and developing the socialist system with Chinese characteristics, and promoting modernization of the national governance system and ability). The Fourth Plenary Session of the 18th CPC Central Committee proposed the overall objective of building a socialist legal system with Chinese characteristics to create a socialist country under the rule of law. This is a guarantee for achieving the "China Dream," including the great rejuvenation of the nation, and also specifies the direction and goals of national governance in a new era. Meanwhile, the basic national conditions, that China will remain in the primary stage of socialism for a long time, do not change. The social principal contradiction between people's growing material and cultural needs and backward social production remains.

China's international status as the world's largest developing country is unchanged, which is the maximum reality facing Chinese national governance. Accordingly, it determines that the government audit must focus on the main contradictions and problems in socioeconomic development and play an active role in advancing the rule of law, safeguarding people's livelihoods, promoting reform and development, and modernizing national governance.

TERMINOLOGY

The "China Dream" is an important guiding ideology and governance concept proposed by General Secretary Xi Jinping since the 18th CPC National Congress. The core objectives can be summarized as "two centenary goals"—namely, by 2021 (the hundredth anniversary of the CPC's founding), GDP will double compared to that of 2010, urban and rural residents' income per capita will double compared to that of 2010, and a moderately prosperous society in all respects will be achieved. By 2049 (hundredth anniversary of the PRC's founding), China will become a prosperous, democratic, culturally advanced, and harmonious modern socialist country. ■

2. **Legal environment.** Modern society is ruled by law. Any organizational or individual behavior must conform to the law, including government auditing. As the audit is conducted in a specific legal environment, the establishment of its goals is inevitably affected by the environment. In a nutshell, the better the legal environment, the higher the degree of legalization. Therefore, the audit objectives can better meet the needs of national governance, and the audit role can be brought into better play. The impact of the legal environment on the audit objective is mainly reflected as follows: On the one hand, the audit objectives must comply with laws and regulations. While giving the government audit certain oversight powers, the law also stipulates the limitations of its system, scope, authority, and so forth, and the law is the fundamental basis for determining the audit objectives. Audit offices must exercise their powers strictly in accordance with their statutory authority and procedures to ensure the work is legal, objective, and fair. On the other hand, audit offices must carry out their work, and conduct audit evaluations, audit conclusions, audit processes, and audit sanctions, according to the facts and the law, which provide the

fundamental basis and standards. The Constitution and the Audit Law have made provision in this regard.

3. **Audit ability and level.** Audit ability and level have significant impacts on the development and change of audit objectives. These reflect the audit demand for national governance and socioeconomic development. If auditing lacks the ability and level to meet this demand, the audit objectives cannot be achieved. Therefore, to determine the audit objectives, we should fully consider social needs and audit ability and seek a balance.

II. FUNDAMENTAL OBJECTIVE OF GOVERNMENT AUDITING

The fundamental objective of government auditing is the highest objective, reflecting the ideal situation and the final result. Always adhering to CPC leadership is the basic political principle. The Party's purpose is to sincerely serve the people, and government auditing under CPC's leadership works to achieve this purpose. This requires that audit offices should always uphold and obey the political, ideological, and organizational leadership of the Party, by conducting independent audit supervision according to the law, fully fulfilling the audit responsibilities conferred by the Constitution, and consciously implementing the Party's principles and policies so as to safeguard the fundamental interests of the people.

On the one hand, under the Constitution, the people are the master of the country, and the ultimate effect of national governance should be reflected in safeguarding their fundamental interests. People's congresses are the organs through which the people exercise power, chosen by democratic elections, responsible to the people, and subject to their supervision. All administrative, judicial, and procuratorial organs of the state are created by the people's congresses by which they are supervised. The National Audit Office is a government department, responsible to the people's congress, and should consciously take safeguarding the core interests of the people as its fundamental objective. On the other hand, the power of an audit office is given by the law reflecting the people's will, and the results of audit work ultimately will be judged by the people. Audit offices, on behalf of the people and the taxpayers, supervise the performance of government departments in fulfilling their responsibilities, as well as units involved in state-owned asset management and usage, subject to the people's supervision and evaluation.

The fundamental interests of the masses include economic, political, and cultural aspects. Economic interests refer to meeting people's material needs. Material interests involve the quantity, opportunities, and conditions of material wealth acquired by the people, the efforts paid by the people to the material gained ratio, and the degree of the match between the improvement in the quality of material life and overall social productivity growth. Meeting people's political needs includes the democratic rights stipulated by law—namely, democratic election, democratic decision making, democratic management, and democratic supervision, as well as opportunities, conditions, and the extent to which people can exercise these rights, and above all the status of the people as the master of the country. Cultural interests are the demand from people's spiritual life, including the right of being educated and the right of enjoying cultural achievements.

The multiplicity of people's fundamental interests derives from the diversity of human needs. Economic interests are related to material needs, mainly involving challenges to human existence, and are the most basic demands of human beings. Political interests are related to people's social needs, which deal with human concerns over their social status and rights. Cultural interests are related to people's cultural needs and solving problems in their spiritual lives. Human demands for diversity cannot be isolated as it is interactive. Thus, the economic, political, and cultural interests of the people are closely related. Economic interests are of decisive significance, ranking the premise of achieving political and cultural interests.[1]

The fundamental interests of the people are dynamic, historical, and three-dimensional. The specific content and emphasis of multiple interest demands constantly change in different periods of socioeconomic, political, and cultural development. When the development level of social productive forces is low and material wealth is relatively poor, people are more concerned about their material needs. When the economic interests of the people are satisfied to a great degree, they will have higher levels of interest demands in such areas as politics and culture. At present, China is in the primary stage of socialism. For most people, the most pressing demand is to improve their living standards. This means that, among the current multiple interests of the people, material interests still remain the core of the people.

Implementing, maintaining, and developing the fundamental interests of the people is a systematic project involving various socioeconomic fields. In this process, government audit offices should always put safeguarding the fundamental interests of the people as the chief objective, comprehensively perform audit duties, and play an active role in socialist economic construction, political construction, cultural construction, social development, and ecological civilization with Chinese characteristics.

III. REALISTIC OBJECTIVE OF GOVERNMENT AUDITING

The realistic objective of government auditing, against the background of socioeconomic development at a certain stage, is the phased objective to realize the fundamental objective. At present, China's economic and social development is at a strategic stage, facing historical opportunities with a number of risks and challenges. The Third Plenary Session of the 18th CPC Central Committee established the overall goal of comprehensively deepening reform—namely, promoting the modernization of the national governance system and ability. The Fourth Plenary Session proposed the overall objective of building a socialist legal system with Chinese characteristics and a socialist country under the rule of law. Focusing on the two overall objectives, government auditing needs to make promoting the rule of law, safeguarding the people's livelihood, and promoting reform and development as the current realistic objective. This also meets the demand of social and economic development, indicates the important role of government auditing in national governance, and enhances systematic modernization.

(1) Promoting the Rule of Law

The rule of law is a long-standing concept. In western history, it emerged from the Solon Reform, and was framed as a theory by the time of Aristotle. He believed rule of law should contain a twofold meaning: the enacted law should be universally obeyed, and the law obeyed by everyone should be the well-developed law.[2] Rule of law is a social management mechanism and a social activity pattern with a certain social order. It takes democracy as the premise, strict compliance with the law as the core, and power constraints as the key. It requires confirming the legal authority in national governance and social management, and takes implementation of the law as the most basic form of social adjustment. Rule of law pursues fairness, justice, equality, and freedom, and provides protection for the harmony of humankind and nature and the harmony of humankind and society. It provides systemic resources for social development. It is an important indicator of social development and progress. And it is the premise in protecting the national stability and maintaining people's fundamental interests.

The Fourth Plenary Session of the 18th CPC Central Committee opened a new chapter in this regard when it adopted the "Decision on major issues about promoting the rule of law," and proposed the overall goal of building a social-ist legal system with Chinese characteristics and a socialist country under the rule of law. Specifically, under CPC leadership, we uphold the socialist system with Chinese characteristics, implement socialist legal theory with Chinese characteristics, form a complete legal system, an efficient legal implementation system, a strict legal supervisory system, a strong legal guarantee system, and a complete inner-party legal system. In order to enhance the building of a legal country, a legal government, and a legal society, it is emphasized that national governance should follow rational legislation, strict law enforcement, fair jus-tice, and legal behavior, and finally realize the modernization of the national governance system and capacity. The Fourth Plenary Session of the 18th CPC Central Committee clearly stipulated that the major task of comprehensively promoting the rule of law was to improve the Constitution-centered socialist legal system with Chinese characteristics and strengthen implementation; fur-ther promote administration according to law, and accelerate the building of government ruled by law; ensure judicial justice, and improve the credibility of justice; enhance people's cognition of the rule of law, and promote the construc-tion of society governed by law; strengthen the workforce related to law; and strengthen and improve the CPC's leadership for comprehensively promoting the rule of law. Law is an important tool for state governance. Rule of law is a fundamental way of managing state affairs, and an important basis for modern-ization of the national governance system. Therefore, promoting the rule of law will inevitably become an important realistic goal of government audit work.

The Fourth Plenary Session of the 18th CPC Central Committee took a big step in strengthening audit work and stressed the need to improve the system and to protect the right to exercise audit oversight independently. Auditing supervision is listed in the national supervisory system, including inner-party supervision, NPC supervision, democratic supervision, administrative supervi-sion, judicial supervision, social supervision, and public opinion supervision, which fully demonstrates that government auditing is a systematic instrument to promote democracy and the rule of law. Government auditing helps to estab-lish a complete legal system, an efficient legal implementation system, a strict legal supervision system, and a strong legal security system, and provides an important guarantee for the rule of law in national governance.

(2) Maintaining People's Livelihood

The people are the foundation and the root of economic and social develop-ment. Solving problems related to people's livelihoods lies in the concept of safeguarding people's fundamental interests, and it is a condition for building a harmonious socialist society and realizing scientific development. The Report to the 18th CPC National Congress stated that

> The CPC must purposefully take putting people first as the core requirement for thoroughly applying the Scientific Outlook on Development. We must always make realizing, safeguarding and developing the fundamental interests of the majority of the people as the starting point and the goal of all the work of the CPC and the country. To achieve new victories for socialism with Chinese characteristics under new historical conditions, we must maintain the people's principal position in the country, safeguard social fairness and justice, strive for common prosperity, and promote social harmony. To achieve the goal of building a moderately prosperous society in all respects, deepening reform and opening up in an all-around way, we must comprehensively improve the people's living standards, and urge to deepen reform in key sectors with greater political courage and vision. In order to strengthen social development and achieve social harmony and stability, we must give high priority to ensuring and improving the people's well-being, and strive to give them a better life. In order to improve rational construction of the CPC in all aspects, we must put people first, exercise governance for the people, and always maintain close ties with them.

Thus, all aspects of Chinese national governance adhere to the core idea of the people first, highlighting the goal of continuously improving living standards.

Livelihood improvement is a long-time and complex systematic project. The key is to solve the most pressing and practical problems of the greatest concern. We should keep making progress in ensuring that all people enjoy their rights of education, employment, health care, aged care, and housing. After a period of development, China's social productivity has grown rapidly, overall national strength has been significantly enhanced, and people's living standards have been improved. Especially in recent years, more emphasis has been given to the bottom line and promoting fairness, with system construction as the starting point. A more comprehensive social security network of compulsory education, basic health care, basic pension, and housing has been gradually established. Livelihood undertakings flourish. The urban and rural social security system has been basically established. Urban and rural free compulsory education has been comprehensively implemented. The national healthcare system has been initially formed. Great changes happened in people's living standards. However, China is still in the primary stage of socialism. The income gap is still too wide, urban and rural development remains uneven, the social security system is incomplete, and other issues remain to be solved, which have become important factors affecting the long-term stable development of the economy and society. People are looking forward to solving them. Strengthening social construction and improving people's livelihoods currently are the major practical goal of government auditing.

(3) Promoting Reform

In China, reform means self-improvement and development of the socialist system and profound social change. The fundamental purpose of the reform is to form a new system compatible with the basic national conditions at the primary stage of socialism in every respect. The new system is full of vigor and vitality, beneficial to promoting the development of productivity and building socialism with Chinese characteristics. Since 1978, China's tremendous achievements in economic and social development have fully proved that reform and opening up are the only road to achieve national prosperity and people's happiness. The powerful energy has inspired the Chinese people; socialist China and the CPC embark on a steady path of prosperity and happiness, which has made a historic contribution to the world's economic development and progress of human civilization. In terms of the depth, breadth, and historical status of reform, China's reform was indeed a revolutionary change.

At present, China is in a triple positional stage: shifting the growth phase, enduring the structural adjustment, and digesting the stimulus policy. Reform and development face many problems and difficulties. Interest obstacles and institutional barriers must be broken in order to coordinate reform in various fields. Facing the new situation of reform, the CPC held the Third Plenary Session of the 18th Central Committee, specified the overall objective of improving and developing the socialist system with Chinese characteristics and promoting the modernization of national governance system and ability, and formed an action program and specific measures to deepen reform in various fields as an important milestone in socialist construction.

To ensure continuous reform, promote domestic political and economic sustainable development, and cope with the challenge of globalization, many countries pay attention to the constructive role of auditing, giving the government audit offices both the right to reveal and the right to report. They are required to put forward audit-based recommendations on reform and improvement. The ultimate goal of this constructive role is to promote continuous reform. The National Audit Office of China, as a comprehensive supervisory department, should make promoting reform a realistic goal, consciously become integrated into overall economic and social development, give full play to the advantages of strong independence, wide audit areas, familiarity with policies and regulations, and abilities to grasp the detailed situation from a macro- and global viewpoint, and be able to review the audit situation and analyze and reflect on audit problems. Accordingly, the National Audit Office of China should make recommendations on the following subjects: enhancing system reform, improving the rule of law and supporting system, standardizing mechanisms, strengthening management, preventing risks, and effectively promoting the implementation of measures of comprehensively deepening reform.

(4) Promoting Development

Development is a global theme. From the perspective of China's specific national conditions, development is a process of socialist modernization, and is the basis and prerequisite for solving various problems at the current stage. Only through development can we solve the contradictions between the people's growing material and cultural needs and backward social production, achieving the purpose of safeguarding the fundamental interests of the people.

In over 30 years of reform and opening up, China has always made development a key theme of socialism with Chinese characteristics and the top priority in governing and rejuvenating the country. Economic construction has been at the center of the work of the CPC and the state with remarkable achievements. At present, China's economic aggregate ranks the second in the world, but its per capita GDP is still behind developed countries. Irrational economic structure and the mode of extensive economic growth have not fundamentally changed. Economic and social development between urban and rural areas, among different regions, is not coordinated. Increasing pressure on population, resources, the environment, and other issues are still outstanding. To solve these complex contradictions and problems on the road ahead, the sole pursuit of accumulation is not enough; we must also rely on rational development in order to achieve a breakthrough in "quality." General Secretary Xi Jinping has pointed out that, amid comprehensive deepening reform, we must adhere to the major strategic judgment that development is still the key solution. In adhering to rational development, we must follow the general theme of steady improvement and the important strategy of innovation and development. We should put the safeguarding of the fundamental interests of the people first and make the overall development of the people the objective both currently and in the long term. And also we should let the people share the fruits of development, meanwhile persisting in making economic construction the core. We should continue to deepen reform and opening up, accelerate the transformation of the economic development mode, and promote coordinated development of urban and rural areas.

At present, China's development opportunities and challenges are unprecedented. We must have a profound understanding of the new features appearing in China's economic and social development, scientifically analyze the new opportunities and challenges of economic globalization, and profoundly overcome contradictions emerging in industrialization, urbanization, economic internationalization, and in-depth development. Development concepts must be integrated into the entire process of audit work. We must consciously contribute to the overall economic and social development, and strengthen audit supervision over the implementation of policy, exercise of power, economic operations, and environmental protection, and so forth. We should pay close attention to the outstanding contradictions and potential risks restricting healthy economic and social operation, actively make recommendations for rational development, and promote green, safe, and efficient development.

IV. PRIMARY TASK OF GOVERNMENT AUDITING AT THE PRESENT STAGE

The achievement of government audit objectives is dependent on the completion of the main audit tasks. According to China's current situation, the key task is to safeguard national security, especially economic security. National security refers to the country's current and future interests, as well as the national development situation. National security means that there is no existing threat or potential threat to national interests. National security is the basic premise of national survival and development, which requires urgent modernization of the national governance system for overall stability, forming an important guarantee in building a moderately prosperous society in an all around way and realizing China's great rejuvenation.

Development and changes in the national security situation determine that government auditing must give priority to safeguarding national security. General Secretary Xi Jinping pointed out that, at present, China's national security has more space and time for improvement, considering that internal and external factors are more complex than at any time in history. We must adhere to the overall concept of national security, with security of the people as the purpose, political security as the foundation, economic security as the base, the military, cultural, and social security as the protective shield, and promotion of international security as the backing, heading on the road of national security with

Chinese characteristics. To implement the overall concept of national security, we must pay attention to both external and internal security: seek internal development, change, and stability to build a peaceful China, and seek international peace, cooperation, and win-win situations to build a harmonious world. Great importance should be attached to both territorial security and nonterritorial security. People should be emphasized as the foundation of national security. We should devote ourselves to building a national security system integrating political security, territory security, military security, economic security, cultural security, social security, IT security, information security, ecological security, resource security, and nuclear safety, paying attention to both development issues and security issues. Development is the foundation of security, and security is a condition for development. Therefore, we should pay attention to both China's safety and common security of the international society, build a common destiny, and encourage various parties to embrace the objectives of mutual benefit and common security. Government auditing, in safeguarding national security, particularly economic security, must be able to adapt to changes in the situation.

To safeguard national security, government audit offices must first safeguard national economic security. This means that the fundamental economic interests of a country, as an independent sovereign economy, are not hurt in any way. This can be achieved by ensuring a sovereign economic independence, a solid economic base, steady growth of a rational economic structure, and sustainable development. This includes fiscal security, financial security, state-owned asset security, and so forth. A safe national economy guarantees economic independence, self-defense, and competitiveness in international economic life, and an ability to avoid great losses and defuse regional and global economic crises.[3] Economic security is an important aspect of national security, and is a foundation for economic development and strong national defense. Without economic security, national security and national interests have no guarantee, and the progress of the socialist society will lose its foundation and protection.

Currently, the National Audit Office should primarily safeguard national security in six ways.

(1) Maintaining Fiscal Security

National fiscal security means that the financial status of a nation is maintained at a stable, balanced, and steady rate of growth, ensuring that the government can cope with any crisis with powerful financial strength. National fiscal security guarantees the normal operation of the national economy and society. To maintain fiscal security, audit offices are required to check budget management, draft final accounts and budget execution results of the government at the corresponding level, as well as the financial management of the government at a lower level, investigate major issues of illegality, maintain financial and economic order, promote improvement of budgetary execution effects, promote effective use of financial funds, reveal potential risks in financial operations, propose comments and suggestions to strengthen financial management and deepen financial reform, maintain financial security, and protect the healthy development of the economy and society.

(2) Maintaining Financial Security

Financial security means that, under the conditions of globalization, a country's financial development has the ability to defend against various domestic and international threats and invasion, to ensure that financial sovereignty is not infringed, and to ensure the financial system maintains normal operation and development. Any economic activities directly related to money circulation and credit belong to financial security. For maintaining financial security, audit offices are required to conduct audit projects and special audit investigations of various types of financial institutions and regulatory authorities, as well as the implementation of monetary policy and its effects, focus on revealing major irregularities in the management of financial institutions, disclose prominent risks affecting the healthy development of the financial system, analyze risk-related reasons in terms of policy and mechanisms, put forward proposals to safeguard financial security, prevent financial risks, and promote stable financial development.

(3) Maintaining the Security of State-Owned Assets

State-owned assets are various assets legally owned by the state on behalf of the people, and specifically refer to various types of property or property rights achieved by virtue of national power or recognized according to law in various forms of investment, income, grants, and donations, including operating and non-operating state-owned assets and those in the form of natural resources. Security of state-owned assets involves many aspects, including total quantity, structure, and efficiency. Safeguarding their security means to improve asset utilization efficiency, protect the rights and interests involved in the assets, seek to achieve an increase in value and prevent losses, and ensure that state-owned assets fully play a positive role in the national economy and social development. To provide such safeguards, audit offices are required to conduct audit projects and audit investigations of the authenticity, lawfulness, and efficiency of the audited entity's financial revenues and expenditures as well as the management and use of state-owned assets, in order to promote the accountability of state-owned assets.

(4) Maintaining the Security of the People's Livelihood

The security of the people's livelihood means that citizens' rights to live and develop are guaranteed. At the present stage, it mainly involves the right to education, employment, fair income distribution, housing, medical care, and social security. The security of people's livelihood is closely related to their fundamental interests and is the most important factor in social stability. Safeguarding livelihood security is a basic tool for promoting economic development and social progress. Therefore, audit offices are required to conduct audit projects and audit investigations of funds, projects, and policy implementation related to people's livelihood, protect the compliance and effects of livelihood fund usage and management, and promote effective implementation of livelihood policies and improvement in the relevant institutions, mechanisms, and systems, constantly improving the quality of people's lives and protecting people's interests.

CASE 3.1: **AUDITING OF SOCIAL SECURITY FUNDS**

From September 2009 to February 2010, the government audit office audited the collection, management, and use of the funds for subsistence allowances to urban residents, as well as the implementation of relevant policies in the period 2008–2009, in 18 provinces and regions, such as Liaoning, Heilongjiang, and Sichuan. Focusing on auditing these areas, 48 cities and 130 districts and counties were involved in the audit. The National Audit Office pointed out problems in fund management, urged the Ministry of Civil Affairs to conduct special law enforcement supervision of social assistance policies and the management and the use of special funds on a national scale, and urged various regions to establish and improve relevant systems and methods.

In 2012, based on the instructions of the State Council, the National Audit Office organized 40,000 strong auditors nationwide and set up over 3,000 audit groups to carry out a comprehensive audit of national social security funds. As of the end of October 2012, violations of disciplines and regulations have been rectified, reaching 31.57 billion yuan. Altogether problems amounting to 202.771 billion yuan were corrected by means of recovering funds, clearance and standardization, implementing financial aid and recovering social security premiums, and modifying and improving relevant policies. Based on audit recommendations, various areas have established and improved 1,173 pieces of social security regulation. Individual accounts of basic pension insurance for 6,218,300 insured have been set. A total of 1,290,700 citizens meeting requirements have been absorbed in the system, while 2,113,300 were removed according to relevant regulations.

(5) Maintaining Security of Resources and Environment

Conserving resources and protecting the environment is China's basic national policy, and an important foundation and condition for its economic and social sustainable development. It means that national resources and the environment are in rational use and under effective management. Development and use of national resources should not undermine the overall stability of the system, so that the threefold relationship among economic development, resource supply guarantee, and the natural ecological environment remains harmonious. Currently, the contradictions between supply of China's important resources, such as oil, metal ores, wood, water, and arable land, and social and economic development needs have become increasingly prominent. Resource utilization efficiency is still not that high. Foreign dependence in regard to resources is increasing year by year. Environmental pollution is serious. The trend of ecological environment deterioration has not been effectively curbed. To cope with requirements of maintaining the security of resources and environment, audit offices need to monitor the implementation of policies and regulations regarding national resources and the environment and the management and use of funds. Audit offices need to focus on exposing problems of disorderly development, inefficient use, and ecological destruction, as well as poor implementation of energy conservation and emission reduction policy. They should put forward recommendations on improving systems, laws, and regulations, promote the conservation of resources, protect the environment, and achieve sustainable economic and social development.

(6) Maintaining Information Security

As an important part of national security, information security refers to the overall security of information, information networks, and information systems under the trend of integrated computerized social information. With the rapid advance of information technology, national information security has become an important part of national security, involving the country's political, economic, technological, cultural, military, and social development. Maintenance of national information security is the objective requirement for protecting China's healthy economic and social development. Accordingly, audit offices are required to conduct information system audit projects and audit investigations of policy implementation, reveal security risks and hazards, promote the establishment of a sound national information security system, improve information security prevention, control, and protection ability, and protect the simultaneous development of information security and information construction.

V. FOCUS OF GOVERNMENT AUDIT WORK AT THE PRESENT STAGE

Based on the foregoing objectives and major tasks, combined with the government audit environment at present and development in the future, audit offices should actively adapt to the new situation and new tasks of national governance development, focus on "anticorruption, the reform, the rule of law, and the development" to conduct comprehensive audits of public funds, state-owned assets, state-owned resources, and the accountability of leading officials, continue to detect major violations of laws and regulations, significant losses and waste, significant potential risks, and poor performance of duty, promote the deepening reform and the rule of law, and improve performance. Therefore the two engines of "anticorruption" and "reform" can drive the "development" of the steamer heading smoothly on the track of "the rule of law." Its focus is as follows:

1. **Strengthen the real-time audit of the implementation of central major policies and measures, and ensure smooth policy implementation**. It is necessary to closely combine national policies and measures with regional economic development characteristics and the working scope of relevant departments. Audits should focus on departments' ability to develop specific implementation measures, task decomposition, work progress, and system improvement in accordance with working scope and task division. According to different development conditions of various areas, audit offices should make specific implementation procedures, detailed execution plans, clear accountability bodies, and guaranteed mechanisms, to ensure targeted auditing contents, schedules, maps, implementation progress, and actual results are achieved when conducting auditing on various localities and relevant departments. Audit offices should concentrate on major issues affecting economic development, such as key links, key projects, and important contents of policies and measures, reveal and reflect the major problems, positively propose suggestions for improvement, and promote the upgrading of rational and effective macrocontrol.

2. **Reveal and reflect potential risks in economic and social operations, and safeguard national economic security.** We must always make safeguarding national economic security the primary task of audit work, pay close attention to weaknesses and potential risks in budgetary issues, financial matters, and problems related to people's livelihoods,

state-owned assets, energy, resources, and the environment, and focus on social instability that probably rose from economic problems, especially local government debt, regional financial instability, and so forth. We must identify trends and problems, actively put forward suggestions, plug loopholes in a timely way, properly dispose of and avoid losses, and ensure the security of economic and social development.

3. **Seriously expose and deal with major violations of laws and rules and promote construction of a clean government.** Major violations of laws and rules found in the audit should be investigated thoroughly. The focus should be on the allocation of financial funds, major investment decisions and project approvals, significant procurements and biddings, loan issuance and securities trading, state-owned assets and equities transfer, and land and mineral resources trading. Furthermore, auditing should concentrate on anticorruption, highlighting issues related to the abuse of power for personal gain, bribery, opacity trading, and other issues. We have to pay attention to the root of corruption, carefully study and analyze the characteristics and patterns of corruption cases, and fully promote the establishment of anticorruption mechanisms.

4. **Strengthen auditing of the implementation of laws and regulations, and promote the building of democracy and the rule of law.** We have to make strong efforts to check the implementation of laws and regulations, and reveal failures and breaches in law enforcement in which someone has suppressed the law with power or broken the law for personal gain. We must effectively promote administration according to law, and build democracy and the rule of law. It is required to reveal problems that were skipped by laws and regulations, or those not stipulated legally that might hinder rational development. It is required to positively improve the legal framework, promote a sound and comprehensive system of laws and regulations, and finally provide an institutional guarantee for the rule of law. It is necessary to deepen the transparency in CPC and administrative affairs, improve the audit results publicity system, promote the establishment of a sound fiscal balance and information disclosure system, gradually improve democratic supervision, and provide information and channels for public participation in national governance.

5. **Strengthen the supervision and control of power, and promote a sound and comprehensive accountability mechanism.** Auditing should focus on the exercise of power and the execution of duty and promote sound fiscal management and operation of power. We must deepen economic accountability auditing of leading officials, explore auditing of

off-term officials regarding natural resources and assets, and focus on supervision and inspection of officials' compliance with laws and disciplines so as to achieve strengthened accountability.

6. **Enhance the performance audit, and improve quality and efficiency.** Auditing should highlight the effectiveness of the national governance system and fully implement the performance audit. During audit processes, several aspects have great importance, such as integrated efficiency, performance, and accountability. Comprehensive analysis should be conducted on economic, social, and environmental benefits. Problems found by auditing related to severe extravagance and waste, significant resource damage, environmental pollution, and low efficiency should be highlighted, for the purpose of maintaining efficient and sustainable development. It is necessary to strengthen budget implementation and other audits of financial revenues and expenditures, focus on the use of incremental funding, revitalize the stock of capital, and guard public funds.

7. **Strengthen the audit of public welfare projects, and maintain people's fundamental interests.** The interests of the people must always be the fundamental objective of auditing, so we have to focus on the outstanding problems damaging the people's interests in the fields of corporate restructuring, land acquisition, and environmental protection. We should also pay great attention to the development of public education, public health, public culture, and public mechanisms including social employment, social distribution, social security, and social order. We should promote fair and rational distribution of public resources, public assets, and public services, and promote social equity and justice.

8. **Focus on revealing problems at the institutional level, analyze the causes, and make recommendations to promote the deepening reform.** From the perspective of national governance, we must reflect the deep-rooted contradictions constraining structural adjustment and shifts in the development mode, in order to reveal institutional obstacles, mechanism distortions, institutional shortcomings, and management loopholes that block rational development and deepening reform in key areas and key links. We have to correctly grasp the new situation of reform and development, identify outdated provisions that restrict development and hinder reform in a timely manner, and promote relevant improvements. We must pay close attention to the coordination of the reform measures, and conduct a systematic, integrated, and coordinated reform.

BIBLIOGRAPHY

China Audit Society. *Audit Project Research and Report (2008–2009)*. Beijing: China Modern Economics Publishing House, 2010.

The Decision of the CPC Central Committee on Some Major Issues concerning Comprehensively Deepening the Reform. Beijing: People's Publishing House, 2013.

The Decision of the CPC Central Committee on Some Major Issues concerning Comprehensively Promoting the Rule of Law. Beijing: People's Publishing House, 2014.

Interpretation to the 12th Five-Year Plan—Q&A for the Study of CPC Members. Beijing: People's Daily Press, 2010.

Li, Jinhua, Chief Editor. *Audit Theory Studies*. Beijing: China Modern Economics Publishing House, 2005.

Propaganda Department of the CPC Central Committee. *Scientific Concept of Development Learning Reading*. Beijing: Learning Press, 2008.

Theory Office, Propaganda Department of the CPC Central Committee. *Six "Why"—Answer to Several Major Issues*. Beijing: Learning Press, 2009.

NOTES

1. Pan Junling, Summary of Fundamental Interests of the People, *Hubei: Theory Monthly*, 2007 (10); Huang Weili, Interpretation of Fundamental Interests of the People, Shanghai: *Journal of Shanghai Jiaotong University* (Philosophy and Social Sciences), 2004 (1).
2. Aristotle, *Politics*, translated by Wu Shoupeng, Beijing: Commercial Press, 1965, p. 199.
3. Lei Jiaxiao, Basic Questions about the Research on National Economic Security, Beijing: *Management Review*, 2006 (7).

CHAPTER FOUR

Research on the Features of Government Auditing

"FEATURES" REFER TO THE SIGNS and symptoms characteristic of humans or things. Audit features, as the external expressions and signs of the essence of auditing, serve as important ways to differentiate government audit supervision from other economic and social supervision systems. As for the definition of government audit features, from the perspective of government audit nature, we can identify the inherent natural properties and general features of universality that it possesses and those where it differs from other things; from the perspective of government audit essence, we can trace the development stages and target location of national governance in various countries, to interpret the features of operating government auditing at various times, which reflect its distinctive social properties.

I. GENERAL FEATURES OF GOVERNMENT AUDITING

We have mentioned already that government auditing, as an institutional arrangement supervising and checking the exercise of power, is an important component of national governance. It has striking characteristics—namely, legality, independence, professionalization, and comprehensiveness. These allow government auditing to significantly boost national governance capability and further play a role as the cornerstone and important assurance for modernization of the national governance system and its capabilities. In the course of long practice, these features have even more concrete manifestations and imposed specific demands on auditing.

(1) Legality

Legality acts as the fundamental feature of government auditing, the functional basis as well as the essential guarantee for its authority and enforcement in its work. It is a crucial component and an important embodiment of the spirit of rule of law, as well as a critical carrier of law-based governance. The legality of government auditing mainly takes the following forms:

1. **Legality of auditing authority.** The Constitution of the People's Republic of China has endowed audit offices with the right of independent supervision and inspection with strong authority, and this institutional arrangement profoundly influences the national governance system and its activities. Apart from the explicit constitutional stipulation, the *Audit Law*, the *Rules for the Implementation of the Audit Law*, the *Economic Responsibilities and Audit Requirement of Leading Officials of the Party and Government and Leading Personnel of State-Owned Enterprises*, and other laws and regulations further define the basic responsibilities of audit offices in five categories (i.e., audit supervision over the truthfulness, compliance and performance of legal items, special audit investigation in terms of specific matters, submitting reports on audit results, submitting audit work reports as entrusted by corresponding governments, and guiding and supervising internal auditing as well as verifying related audit reports issued by public audit institutions) and eight basic authorities (i.e., the right to request the submission of materials, right to examine, right to investigate and obtain evidence, right to adopt administrative compulsory measures, right to seek assistance, right to transfer and recommend, the right to process and punish, and the right to notify or publish auditing results).

2. **Legality of audit evaluation standards.** The fundamental principle is to audit in accordance with the law. Laws and regulations serve as the criteria for auditing and evaluating right and wrong, decisions on precedent in issuing audit opinions and making audit decisions, which safeguard the objectivity and fairness of government auditing. All these determine the need for auditing based on facts and in accordance with

laws, and guaranteeing the legality of audit items and procedures as well as the qualitative treatment of problems to assure audit quality, speeding up the legality and standardization of audit work, optimizing the system of government audit laws, regulations, normative systems, and professional audit guidelines, and refining the work flow to guarantee all work follows procedures and is based on appropriate evidence and inspection as required by law.

3. **Enforcement of audit work**. Government auditors are protected by the law when performing their duties, and no organization or individual can refuse cooperation or hinder the work, otherwise the audit offices are entitled to take necessary measures. Audit offices shall issue opinions directed at specific situations after auditing the targeted units, and make audit decisions within the legal boundaries regarding the fiscal and financial revenue and expenditure of the auditees violating state regulations, as well as issuing penalties. The auditees must carry out any instruction or imposed penalty in due time, otherwise the audit offices are entitled to order immediate fulfillment, or appeal to the court for compulsory execution, and hold the auditees to account.

(2) Independence

Independence is the soul of auditing and the most basic feature of government auditing. This means audit offices can objectively and fairly investigate and report without interference. Practices and experiences home and abroad indicate that, to safeguard audit independence, we must attach adequate guarantees to organizations, personnel, work, and funds. In order to assure that audit offices can exercise their right of audit supervision independently, they must be full-time organizations set up independently; that means they have no affiliation relationship in any form with auditees. In order to ensure auditors can investigate in a practical manner and evaluate and report objectively and fairly, auditors shall not be in any form of financial relationship with auditees nor participate in the operations and management activities of auditees in any way. Auditors are protected by national laws when performing their audit functions in accordance with the law. Audit offices and individual auditors are required to exercise the right of audit supervision in accordance with the law, including carrying out evidence collection, making audit judgments, expressing audit opinions, and submitting audit reports based on the stipulated audit objectives, contents, and procedures and strictly in line with the requirements of audit standards and criteria. Audit offices and individual auditors must maintain spiritual independence in terms of their vocation, and not be subject to interference by any other administrative organs, social groups, or individuals. Audit offices shall have their own source of funds or certain economic revenue so as to guarantee they have enough funds to carry out audit activities independently and autonomously and are not tied to auditees.

The *Mexico Declaration on the Independence of Supreme Audit Institutions* issued by the International Organization of Supreme Audit Institutions (INTOSAI) has reiterated the significance of auditing being independent as well as the eight principles[1] to which they should adhere. To guarantee the independence of government auditing, most countries have defined the functions and authorities of government auditing in their constitutions. The Chinese Constitution issued in 1982, the *Audit Law*, the *Rules for the Implementation of the Audit Law*, and other laws and regulations issued after 1982 have established and safeguarded the independence of government auditing. The specific embodiment is as follows:

1. **Independence in terms of organization**. Government audit offices shall be set up independently, and not be subject to any other departments or business organizations. The National Audit Office is under the leadership of the Chinese Premier, and the local audit offices at different levels are under the leadership of the heads of the corresponding local government; meanwhile, audit offices are independent from the auditees and have no administrative affiliation or organizational relationship.

2. **Independence in terms of personnel**. The auditor general of the National Audit Office is nominated by the premier and appointed by the Standing Committee of the National People's Congress. Those in charge of the local audit offices at various levels are nominated by corresponding local governments and appointed by corresponding Standing Committees of the local people's congress. Additionally, the appointment, removal, and transfer of officials in charge of audit offices at a lower level must involve consultation with the audit offices at a higher level.

3. **Independence in terms of work**. Audit offices and individual auditors must not participate in daily economic planning and management work. Auditors work in line with the functions endowed by law, including compiling audit plans independently, collecting evidence and examining this independently, issuing an evaluation, making audit conclusions independently, and coming up with audit opinions; no administrative organ, social group, or individual may interfere. Such supervision has legal effect.

4. **Independence in terms of economy**. The audit funds for government audit work should be reliable sources and under no constraints. The funding is listed in financial budget guarantees at various levels with assurances of independence and objectivity in regard to law enforcement. According to the audit regulations formulated in the *Audit Law* and by the National Audit Office, audit offices have the right not only to examine in terms of the financial revenue and expenditure considered to violate state stipulations as well as the illegal and nondisciplinary activities of the auditees, but also to carry out administrative processing and apply for judicial processing, which is a further indication of the strong independence of audit offices.

Moreover, during the past 30 years since Chinese audit offices were set up, the construction of the professional ethics, development of audit normalization and standardization, and the reform and continued exploration of Chinese audit systems have further enhanced the independence of government auditing.

(3) Professionalization

Government auditing, highly professional and policy-based, is a full-time and professional supervisory behavior with high requirements in professional knowledge and practical skills. The professionalization of government auditing requires practitioners with wide professional knowledge and business skills, able to maintain an independent status and comply with professional ethics. Government auditors need to master broad, basic theoretical knowledge about auditing, be familiar with the application of audit approaches and technologies as well as the requirements of audit standards and regulations, be familiar with public finance, accounting theories, and techniques, have a good comprehension of related national principles, policies, laws, and regulations, and be equipped with certain management and legal knowledge. They must have rich audit work experience and relatively high analytical and judgmental capabilities, be able to use computers, and be equipped with certain foreign language proficiency, high oral and literal expression, and communication capability. Auditors must have favorable professional moral quality, adhere to the related principles, be honest in performing their official duties and devoted to duty, carry out audit work objectively and fairly, and strictly adhere to work regulations like confidentiality.

The enhancement of audit professionalization is vital given the growing specialization of audit work to ensure audit quality. The Fourth Plenary

Session of the 18th CPC Central Committee proposed "to promote the construction of audit professionalization." This reflects the need to optimize the human resources management system for auditors, set up competency and qualification management and a vocational guarantee system for auditors, optimize the training system, and improve the quality of auditors in a planned way. Specifically, we need to improve the professionalism of staff in audit offices, establish and optimize the competency and qualification management system of auditors, carry out unified recruitment, ordered communication, and selection grade by grade, and enhance professional skills and comprehensive management capabilities. We need to establish a management system complying with the characteristics of audit work. In addition, we must optimize the vocational education and training system. In line with age grades, job requirements, and work realities, we need to enhance the training and education system, combining medium and long-term training with short-term training, theoretical study with practices, improve theoretical bases, professional qualities, and operational levels, and effectively intensify competency and qualification capabilities.

(4) Comprehensiveness

Comprehensiveness is a crucial guarantee for the deterrent effects of government auditing, and is mainly manifested in the application and management of public funds, public goods, and public resources. As long as it is related to public interests, it should be under the supervision of government auditing. In the course of audit practice, the features of comprehensiveness are mainly reflected in the full coverage of audit supervision. This means full coverage of supervised targets. Any departments, organizations, or individuals related to the management, allocation, and application of public funds, state-owned assets, and state-owned resources must come under audit supervision and cooperate with audit work in accordance with the law. Comprehensive audit work should be carried out in terms of truthfulness, compliance, the performance of the management and application of public funds, state-owned assets, and state-owned resources and related economic activities, the performance of economic responsibilities of leading Party and government officials as well as leading personnel of state-owned enterprises, and the safety, reliability, and efficiency of information systems related to fiscal revenue and expenditure, financial revenue and expenditure, and the related economic and business activities in various departments and units. Secondly, audit work should closely follow budget compilation, execution, adjustment, final settlement, and other processes, faithfully focus on capital allocation, management, application, people's livelihood funds, and projects such as "agriculture, rural areas and farmers," social security, education, medical care, poverty alleviation, disaster relief, and affordable housing. We need to intensify audit work over pollution control and environmental protection of natural resources like land, mineral resources, and water, as well as key watersheds and related industries, and optimize the supervision of all natural resources. Next, while adhering to postauditing and real-time supervision, we need to actively move to the stage of pre-auditing and gradually realize whole-process audit supervision.

In order to do so, we should coordinate and integrate resources and formulate the audit planning. The National Audit Office, based on the current auditors, has proposed carrying out annual auditing in terms of budget implementation and drafting final accounts of governments, key departments, and units; at least one economic responsibility audit within the term of office of leading officials in key positions; and at least one audit within five years for other auditees. On the other hand, we need to reform audit approaches, improve efficiency, try to realize the diversification of supervisory approaches, explore the transfer from ex post, static, micro-, and critical supervision to a preclusive, dynamic, macro-, and constructive modern supervision concept, and advocate comprehensive, multilevel, and three-dimensional supervision.

II. OPERATING FEATURES OF GOVERNMENT AUDITING

When investigating the operating features of government auditing in a country, we need to base any analysis on the country's economic and social situations, national governance progress, and the development stage of government auditing. In modern China, the operating features of government auditing of socialism with Chinese characteristics, centered on the promotion of the modernization of the national governance system and its capabilities, are as follows:

- ▪ Based on constructive essence and a critical approach
- ▪ Based on serving and adhering to supervision
- ▪ Based on the overall situation, and adhering to detecting and solving problems from a microperspective
- ▪ Based on initiative and adhering to adaptation
- ▪ Based on openness and adhering to independence

(1) Based on Constructive Essence and a Critical Approach

A critical approach means that audit offices do not easily accept any conclusions without examination and tests, do not simply accept unproven facts, and maintain professional vigilance in order to systematically check and analyze auditees or audited items. In terms of modern government auditing, audit offices should observe and analyze items from a viewpoint of supervising the process and results of economic and social operations, being alert to various risks and possible infringement of economic security.

The constructive essence of government auditing means that audit offices not only uncover and investigate existing or potential problems, but also actively put forward solutions and measures to help auditees and related departments improve laws, regulations, and implementation rules to play a constructive and preventative role in improving management levels and preventing such problems. In terms of modern government auditing, the constructive essence of auditing determines its vitality, the extent of safeguarding national economic security and national interests, and the scope of promoting sustainable socioeconomic development and promoting democratic legal construction and rule by law.

The audit office's fundamental responsibility is reflected through uncovering problems, revealing risks, and dealing with them, as well as performing the overall critical functions of auditing. Moreover, the audit office is responsible for putting forward constructive suggestions to show the social value of government auditing.

The critical aspect of government auditing is the forerunner and foundation of its constructiveness, which, in turn, is a kind of abstraction and sublimation of criticality. Government auditing should identify problems and fulfill its critical function, as well as providing some opinions and suggestions on the constructive function to promote and improve the work in all aspects and development stage. Being based on criticality and maintaining constructiveness represent the unity of opposites between government auditing's two inseparable aspects.

According to the requirements of criticality and constructiveness, an audit office must innovate its audit approaches. This should extend from the legal and compliance audits to performance auditing primarily, thus enhancing the potential of audit supervision; moving from postauditing (as an old saying goes, "better late than never") to follow-up auditing, and improving audit supervision's preventive and warning functions; from the postaccountability audit to greater reliance on the accountability audit itself, combining the two, and promoting supervision and restriction in audit supervision; and from postaudit investigation to audit investigation in the course of the work, so as to give full play to the consulting and assistance function of audit supervision.

(2) Based on Serving and Adhering to Supervision

As an important part of the national political system, modern government auditing is the product of democracy and the rule of law; it is also a means to promote democracy and the rule of law. It requires that the government audit serve the construction of national governance and national political power by fulfilling its supervisory responsibilities.

Basing work on serving refers to complying with the needs of reform and opening-up policy and socialist economic construction, focusing on the central tasks of the Party and the country, and consciously safeguarding national economic security. This will be effective in promoting rule of law, reform, and development, and maintaining people's livelihoods, thus achieving the goals of reform.

Adhering to supervision means that an audit office should independently examine, supervise, and urge truthfulness, compliance, and performance of financial revenues and expenditures and other economic activities of auditees in accordance with the law. In China, supervision is an important responsibility of government audit institutions. According to the *Regulation for the Implementation of the Audit Law of the PRC*, audit offices' responsibilities are as follows: In accordance with the law, conduct auditing supervision over the budget enforcement condition of the people's government's departments of finance at the corresponding level, the budget revenue condition of the tax collection departments at the corresponding level, the budget performance and final settlement of departments and units that handle budgetary payments and appropriations to the people's government's departments of finance at the corresponding level, the budget performance and final settlement of the subordinate people's governments and other financial revenue and expenditure conditions; and conduct auditing supervision over units and projects that receive financial funds in terms of truthfulness, compliance, and performance in the use of financial funds approved by the people's government at the corresponding level.

In government auditing, service and supervision represent a dialectical unity, featuring close interrelations and discrepancies. Supervision is the basic means of government auditing, while serving is the fundamental objective. "Supervision" means detection and exposure, evaluation and publication, and rectification and reform, and thus helps auditees and other relevant departments and units to work in a normative, orderly, and efficient way. There can be no quality service without supervision and no meaningful supervision without serving. The two should be combined with neither one neglected. The relationship between supervision and serving should be handled properly to the extent that both can be coordinated and promote each other. Moreover, "redundant interference," "dereliction of duty," and "inappropriate leading" should be avoided during supervising and serving.

On the basis of providing services and persisting in supervision, government audit offices must safeguard social and economic order and protect the people's interests by revealing problems and detecting violations of laws and regulations, and create a favorable environment for the rapid and sound development of society and the economy through helping improve the social, legal, and economic systems. To improve service and supervision, audit units should do the following.

On the one hand, they should improve audit functions and efficiency to serve the overall situation of socioeconomic development under a philosophy of "focusing on the central task and serving the overall interests." The philosophy, a significant strategy of auditing, means focusing on the central task and conducting auditing on the basis of the overall situation of the work of the Communist Party of China and the country to serve the overall situation of opening-up and social and economic development. Audit practice in the past few years has shown that the only way to win public support and recognition is to set the audit on a higher level where it can deeply reveal existing risks and proffer advice to rectify flaws, enhance management, and promote reform.

On the other hand, they should strengthen self-consciousness of auditing to serve the overall situation of socioeconomic development under the philosophy of the "Six High Self-Consciousness." As auditing is the cornerstone and important assurance of national governance, audits should encompass the overall situation and integrate auditing with social and economic development; promote rule by law and the construction of democracy and rule of law through auditing; detect major violations of laws and regulations and pragmatically improve governance efficiency and fiscal performance through auditing; deepen reform and help transform governments' functions through auditing; promote combating corruption and upholding integrity through auditing; and promote rectification, reform, and normative management and propel the establishment of the accountability mechanism and the improvement and implementation of the responsibility investigation system through auditing—all these with high self-consciousness.

(3) Based on the Overall Situation, and Adhering to Detecting and Solving Problems from a Microperspective

Government auditing is an important part of national governance and performs certain national functions. Therefore, audit offices should plan and deploy on the basis of the overall situation, and analyze and judge audit items from a national, global, and macroscopic perspective. Audit units and auditors should have awareness of the overall situation and system and hold a macroperspective in order to plan long-term socioeconomic development; follow and serve the central tasks of the Party and government and the overall layout of opening-up and economic development with socialist characteristics; and solve problems from a macroscopic perspective.

Government audit institutions shall adhere to microscopic investigation and exposure. Audit offices independently take advantage of their own professional knowledge and skills to carry out audit work in regard to specific departments, units, and matters; reveal and investigate specific actions in violation of laws and regulations as well as policies and guidelines of the Party and government. Thus, this kind of auditing, exposure, and investigation is localized and microscopic, which requires audit offices and individual auditors to seriously carry out their work in accordance with the law, carefully implement each audit project, and carefully investigate violations of laws and regulations.

According to the principle of materialistic dialectics on the whole-part relationship, government auditing's feature of being based on the macroscopic, overall situation as well as adhering to microscopic investigation and exposure shows good understanding. Materialistic dialectics hold that all things are an organic whole composed of individual parts. The whole and the part are inseparable: The part is whole-oriented and subordinated to the whole. The performance and change of the whole will influence the performance and change of the parts, while the parts also have significant impact on the performance of the whole. Therefore, according to the materialistic dialectics, we should set up overall viewpoints, making efforts on both the whole and the part and letting the whole give full play to its functions.

This feature is a basic requirement set by the Party and government for government auditing, as well as a public expectation. The two factors of this feature, based on the macroscopic and overall situation as well as adhering to microscopic investigation and exposure, are mutually connected and unified, being indispensable for fulfilling government auditing's functions. Government auditing serves the objectives of national governance, which requires audit offices to use systematic thinking to analyze problems in systems, institutions, and policies, so as to find out the real reasons and offer audit opinions and suggestions instead of judging a case as it stands.

This requires audit offices to: carry out audit work on each audited unit and project from a macroviewpoint and in an overall perspective, so as to enhance the investigation on individual cases; pay attention to exposing and analyzing microcosmic problems so as to enhance the depth of audit work; on the basis of these individual cases and microcosmic problems, offer improved solutions in regard to institutions, systems, and mechanisms. In brief, audit work should be implemented from both a micro- and macroview and we should use experiences of each point to lead the whole.

(4) Based on Initiative and Adhering to Adaptation

This is a requirement raised for audit work from different angles. Basing on initiative refers to audit offices actively treating objective needs and changing the audit environment. That is to say, audit offices and individual auditors should exert their subjective initiative to actively get involved in social economic operations, so as to promote reform and development through audit work. Adhering to adaptation means that, as audit work changes with the objective needs and environment, audit offices and individual auditors will adjust their objectives, contents, emphasis, and organization modes and techniques so as to better meet the demands of socioeconomic development and deal with the challenges caused by the changing audit environment.

The feature of basing on initiative and adhering to adaptation shows that government auditing is an important part of national governance. Adaptation without initiative and initiative without adaptation are both partial and meaningless. What initiative emphasizes is exerting a subjective initiative and carrying out audit work actively and creatively; what adaptation emphasizes is following objective laws and requirements as well as realizing subjective and objective unification.

Basing on initiative requires audit offices actively to blend into national socioeconomic development, adjust their work ideas and focus, improve work methods, reveal potential risks, rectify and investigate violations of laws and regulations, analyze the reasons for problems, and offer audit opinions and suggestions. That is to say, initiative requires audit offices to focus on institutional aspects in the long run, so as to further perceive risks, reveal problems, and offer suggestions about using various resources to resist infection. Adhering to adaptation requires audit offices to get a clear understanding of the new situation of audit work, new requirements of governments and departments, and new expectations of the people.

(5) Based on Openness and Adhering to Independence

As mentioned in Section I, adhering to independence refers to audit offices staying independent in organization, personnel, work, and funding. That means that audit offices should be independent, full-time organizations; individual auditors should not have any financial relationship with auditees and not participate in their operational and management activities; and individual auditors should exercise their right of audit supervision independently in accordance with the law to make audit judgments, offer audit opinions, and issue audit reports. Audit offices should have their own source of funds.

Basing on openness refers to integrating audit work into the Party and the state's overall work, and expanding contacts and communications with the parties concerned so as to further enhance the objectivity and authority of audit work. From the perspective of system theory, national governance is a large system while government auditing is its supervisory control system. In national governance, different organizations undertake responsibility for decision making, execution, and supervisory control, thus forming an interrelated, interactive, and interdependent system. Government audit offices should ascertain problems in a timely manner during policy execution through tracking and supervising the implementation situation. In this way, they can make all the necessary decisions and deployments that are coordinated with policy orientation, mutually advanced in implementation and mutually complementary in actual results, so as to exert the overall force and comprehensive effect of governance to the highest degree. Government auditing restricts authority by exerting authority in accordance with the law. It needs to keep a relatively independent and open relationship with other subsystems of national governance. On the one hand, government auditing should obtain vigorous support and coordination from relevant external parties to maximize the working effect; on the other hand, the audit systems need to learn from other fields and even from other countries to constantly improve their work. When making plans, audit offices shall take into account the demands of Party committees, People's Congresses, governments, and their departments at all levels as well as all walks of life; when carrying out on-site auditing and implementing punishment, they should draw on the assistance and coordination of audit objects and related departments; and audit offices should inform the relevant units and departments in a timely manner and make public audit products and information.

In terms of the essence of auditing, there is no auditing without independence. If audit work cannot rule out interference from various aspects, it will hardly play its function of revealing, resisting, and prevention. When openness, questions, suggestions, and information from auditing are limited then auditing's function of revealing, resisting, and preventing cannot be completely exerted. In practical work, while keeping independence, audit offices and individual auditors should closely work with relevant departments, competent authorities, research units, and the auditees. As long as individual auditors integrate with other related personnel and fully take advice, they can reveal problems more accurately, resist contradiction more thoroughly, and prevent risks more effectively. At present, there are still many problems in working based on openness and adhering to independence in such aspects as audit plan, audit implementation, and audit openness. For example, in adhering to independence, some audit offices do not fully perform their duty of audit supervision independently under the leadership of the administrative head of government at the same level; they do not completely make decisions on "what to be audited" and "how to audit" independently; they do not suppress interference totally in audit processing; and they do not report the audit results and audit recommendations truly and completely in accordance with the law. Some audit offices do not fully listen to the opinions of the relevant departments and of the public in making audit plans; they do not make full use of all kinds of audit resources and social resources; they do not fully listen to the opinions of the auditees in reaching audit conclusions and implementing audit punishment; and they do not work together with other supervisory bodies.

Therefore, while adhering to independence, audit offices should improve openness in the following ways. First, they should closely surround the center and consciously open the supply market of audit products. That is to say, in accordance with the law, audit offices should produce and make open what Party committees, governments, People's Congresses, and the common people require. The second way is to be broad-minded. In every step of developing audit work, audit offices at various levels cannot indulge in self-gratification and should have the courage to go beyond the existing work level and work mode, so as to unceasingly reform and innovate. The third way is to open the audit process and consciously accept supervision of society from various aspects, including the formulation of an audit plan, implementation of an audit project, and preparation of audit reports and audit information. Audit offices shall listen to the opinions of and take advice from various sectors so as to ensure the justice, fairness, high quality, and good effect of auditing and strengthen audit credibility. The fourth way is to use all kinds of resources to form an overall supervisory force, which includes: audit offices taking advantage of engineering technicians from outside to make up for lack of professionals within and improve an unreasonable personnel structure; in the audit process, making full use of internal audit data and results proven to be reliable and credible through examination; and, in the process of audit planning and decision making, making full use of the work by organizations such as the audit research institute, audit academic society, and some social organizations. The fifth way is to improve the audit results announcement system and promote administrative openness and transparency.

III. WORK POLICY OF GOVERNMENT AUDITING

In recent years, in conformity with the new requirements for socioeconomic development and relying on practical experiences, audit offices set up the work policy of "auditing according to law, serving the overall situation, surrounding the center, highlighting the focus, and staying realistic and pragmatic." Based on truthfulness and emphasizing removal of the counterfeit and various types of disorders, they strengthened the investigation of and the penalty for major violations of laws and regulations as well as economic crimes, better performing the duties of audit supervision pursuant to the law.

"Auditing according to the law" is the specific embodiment of China's strategy of ruling the country by law in the auditing field, the profound reflection of the spirit of democracy and the rule of law in the auditing field, and the spirit of the rule of law to which audit work must always adhere. The Constitution and laws make clear stipulations for the duty and authority of auditing. Audit offices and individual auditors must conduct supervision and standardize their work totally based on the Constitution and laws, and the legal authorization, responsibility, and limits of authority and procedures.

"Serving the overall situation and surrounding the center" are the strategic positions to which audit work must always adhere. Moreover, it is the right choice for audit work to constantly adapt to the development requirements of socialism with Chinese characteristics. "Serving the overall situation" means to serve for the overall situation of economic and social development and the fundamental interests of the broad masses. "Surrounding the center" is to surround the central tasks of the Party and governments. "Serving the overall situation and surrounding the center" require audit offices and individual auditors to uncover problems, and specifically carry out proposals to stop a leak, reinforce management, promote reform, and improve the system regarding the overall situation of socioeconomic development and the people's basic benefits at a higher level. Consequently, audit work can acquire the attention and trust of the Party and government as well as public support and recognition.

"Highlighting the focus" is a significant strategy to which audit work must always adhere. It is also an effective strategy and method to deal with audit risk. It requires audit offices and individual auditors to focus on the problems concerning overall socioeconomic development as well as key, hot, and difficult problems closely related to people's livelihoods, democratic rule of law, and combating corruption and upholding integrity. Audit offices and individual auditors should also grasp problems influencing the overall situation and the future. After pinpointing the "fire condition" and "fire source," they should weigh the priorities, concentrate on auditing, and give full play to the function of the "immune system."

"Staying realistic and pragmatic" is an ideological style and work style to which audit work must always adhere. "Staying realistic and pragmatic" requires audit offices and individual auditors to stick to seeking truth from facts, being objective and fair, being practical and doing solid work, and achieving fruitful results. They should also recognize and handle problems from a long-term perspective so as to promote sound institutions, systems, and mechanisms, ensure the comprehensive implementation of lines, policies, and guidelines of the Party and the state, and assure the smooth realization of various development objectives.

BIBLIOGRAPHY

Li, Jinhua, Chief Editor. *The Study of Audit Theory*. Beijing: China Audit Press, 2001.

Shi, Aizhong, and Hu Jirong. *Audit Research*. Beijing: Economic Science Press, 2002.

Yu, Mingtao, Chief Editor. *The Establishment of a Socialist China's Audit System*. Beijing: China Audit Press, 1999.

NOTE

1. INTOSAI, Mexico Declaration on SAI Independence. Source: www.intosai.org/en/documents.

CHAPTER FIVE

Audit Modes

A UDIT MODES REFER TO THE FORMS and methods by which audit institutions carry out audit activities. Research on audit modes is aimed at promoting rational and effective use of various audit resources, improving the modes of organization and management, and continuously enhancing audit quality, efficiency, and effect. Traditional audit modes are mainly postauditing, on-spot auditing, and manual auditing, usually isolated and unitary. Along with the steady innovation and development of audit work, modern auditing gradually becomes diversified and often with various audit modes organically integrated.

I. SPECIAL AUDIT INVESTIGATION

Special audit investigation, as an important audit mode, has been universally recognized and widely used by audit institutions at all levels in China. Audit institutions at all levels have had outstanding results and accumulated useful experiences by actively exploring and conducting special audit investigations. Practice proves that special audit investigations are both a category of independent audit business with Chinese characteristics and a special audit mode. At the same time, they are the main form of carrying out performance auditing.

(1) Concept of Special Audit Investigation

(a) Origin of Special Audit Investigation

As a unique category of audit undertakings and specific audit mode in China, special audit investigations came into being along with the establishment of the audit supervision system in China and have been continuously enriched and improved along with the progress of China's audit undertakings. As early as 1984, when China's socialist audit supervision system was established, audit institutions began audit investigation activities. It can be said that this was a special audit investigation in embryo. Coupled with the progress of audit work, audit investigation activities became more and more important in audit work. In this regard, the CNAO started special arrangements and required audit institutions at all levels to carry out audit investigations within certain scopes, setting forth recommendations as references for the government and relevant departments to make macropolicy decisions and improve work. The arrangement and requirements of the CNAO and the variegated audit investigation practice successively carried out by localities played an active role in formulating and improving the system of special audit investigation with Chinese characteristics.

Along with the ever deepening practice of special audit investigation by audit institutions, laws and regulations related to audit investigation were also successively formulated and improved. Article 27 of the Audit Law of the People's Republic of China, promulgated in 1994, clearly defines the legal status of special audit investigation for the first time, enabling it to become a statutory responsibility for China's audit institutions. In order to better meet the needs of development of special audit investigations, the CNAO thereafter specially formulated standards and norms for special audit investigation and clearly stated in the CNAO Audit Work Development Program 2006–2010[1] that equal stress must be put on auditing and special audit investigation and that the proportion of special audit investigation projects carried out every year should account for about half of all the projects.

(b) Concept of Special Audit Investigation

The Audit Law of the People's Republic of China, promulgated in 1994, lays down the provision for the functions and responsibilities of special audit investigation.

It was the outcome of summarizing China's own audit practice and experience as well as drawing experience from the performance audit investigations of the United States and other countries. The International Organization of Supreme Audit Institutions (INTOSAI), the International Federation of Accountants (IFAC), the United States, and some other countries do not have special audit investigations in their classification of audit categories. It is not a universally used working method. In other countries, while investigations are carried out through auditing, the connotations are not entirely the same as the special audit investigation carried out by Chinese audit institutions. According to the provisions of existing audit laws and systems in China, special audit investigation is a category of independent audit undertaking having equal importance with auditing. Meanwhile, it is also an effective method of supervision (i.e., to achieve specific audit objectives through the means of audit investigations). Special audit investigation has become a unique form of Chinese audit professional work and unique audit mode.

The Audit Law defines the legal status for audit institutions to carry out special audit investigations and endows them with specific connotations and requirements. This law defines at the legislative level the functions and responsibilities as well as limits of authority of audit institutions for carrying out special audit investigations:

> With regard to particular matters relating to the State's budgetary revenues and expenditures, audit institutions shall have the power to carry out special investigations through auditing among relevant localities, departments, and units and report the results thereof to the people's governments at the corresponding levels and to the audit institutions at the next higher levels.

This provision has clear limitations: There is no clear definition of procedures and methods for special audit investigations, and the scope of special audit investigations is limited to "particular matters relating to the State's budgetary revenues and expenditures." But the matters relating to financial revenues and expenditures are excluded from the scope, hence making it too narrow for investigation.

It is clearly stipulated in the Standards for Audit Institutions to Conduct Special Audit Investigation promulgated by the CNAO in 2001: The term special audit investigation mentioned herein refers to activities of special investigations carried out by audit institutions mainly through audit methods into relevant localities, departments, and units in terms of particular matters relating to state fiscal revenues and expenditures or assigned by people's governments at corresponding levels to audit institutions to handle. This provision of the CNAO defines the audit methods that can be used in special audit investigations, while the issue of audit procedures has been left unresolved. Meanwhile, the scope of special audit investigation has been expanded to "particular matters relating to State fiscal revenues and expenditures or assigned by people's governments at the corresponding levels."

In accordance with the practical needs of special audit investigations, the Regulations for the Implementations of the Audit Law of the People's Republic of China, revised in 2010, lend greater specificity to the functions and duties of audit institutions for special audit investigations in the Audit Law of the People's Republic of China:

> With regard to the special matters relating to the State revenues and expenditures, including budget management, management, and use of State-owned assets, and so on, audit institutions may, in accordance with the procedures and methods prescribed by the Audit Law—these Regulations as well as other relevant provisions of the State—carry out special audit investigations among the relevant local authorities, departments and units.

This provision resolves fairly well the legislative problem of limitations of special audit investigations and is conducive to promoting the healthy development of special audit investigations.

In short, the concept of special audit investigations can be defined as follows: In accordance with laws, regulations, and relevant provisions of the state, audit institutions carry out special audit investigations among relevant local authorities, departments, and units with regard to budget management or special matters relating to state revenues and expenditures, including the management and use of state-owned assets, by mainly relying on relevant audit procedures and methods.

(c) Organizational Form of Special Audit Investigation

Audit institutions generally adopt two kinds of organizational forms in actually carrying out special audit investigations.

Carrying out special audit investigations independently (i.e., to carry out audit investigations into a certain matter, certain system, certain trade, or certain issue among a number of audit investigation targets with specific purposes and within a specified scope and time limit). Their main features are: to determine the target and scope of audit investigations in accordance with special audit investigation purposes and the clues and doubtful points already in hand, and to adopt different procedures and methods for audit investigations in line with different targets and scopes. They have specific scopes of contents (i.e., involving issues in only one aspect with a specified time limit and scope; that is, it is required only to reach the objectives and accomplish the task relating to the matter for audit investigations within the prescribed time limit and scope). By using such a method, audit investigations will be able to determine the direction of investigations, focus on the objectives, and prioritize key points, thus facilitating the tracking of problems and discovery of deep-rooted problems. It may cater to the requirements of the leadership at various levels to get to know the actual situation and discover and rectify problems in a timely manner through the implementation of economic, administrative, and policy-based laws and regulations.

Carrying out audit investigations in integration with audit projects (i.e., to carry out combined special audit investigations into relevant specified matters related with audit projects, and on this basis to carry out comprehensive analysis and summaries, to report the situation and problems to the government and departments concerned, and put forward audit recommendations). In carrying out special audit investigations in integration with audit projects, audit institutions should, after conclusion of the audit, combine the relevant situations reflected in the audit report and the result of investigations to form a special audit investigation report. Carrying out audit investigations in integration with audit projects will not only solve the problem of repeated entries into an entity (i.e., to accomplish two or more tasks by one entry), but also enhance the quality, depth, and efficiency of audits and special audit investigations through the sharing of data and information.

(2) Features of Special Audit Investigation

Special audit investigation has such features as macro-objectives, a content orientation, scope extensiveness, methods of flexibility, and a timely report on what happens.

(a) Macro-Objective

Auditing and special audit investigations are both important modes for audit institutions to perform their audit and supervision functions, but they have different objectives and different focuses. Comparatively speaking, auditing is mainly aimed at various specific projects and units. Its major objective is to determine and appraise the truth, lawfulness, and effect of the financial revenues and expenditures of the auditee, with focus on discovery, rectification, and handling of existing problems, while special audit investigation is mainly aimed at carrying out systematic investigations, analysis, and research of specific matters bearing overall, universal, tendentious, and embryonic natures, reporting the situation to the government and departments concerned, exposing problems, analyzing the causes at the levels of institutions, mechanisms, and systems, making recommendations for strengthening management and improving regulations and systems, providing the basis for decision making by governments and relevant departments at all levels, and serving macro-regulation of the state. Therefore, with more macro-objectives, special audit investigations are more conducive to bringing into play the constructive role of audit supervision and can enable auditing to provide an even better service for macropolicy decisions at a higher level.

The macronature of special audit investigation objective requires intensified macroconsciousness in subject selection, project identification, investigations, evidence collection, analysis of problems, and conclusions to investigations. In subject selection, it is necessary, in line with the central tasks of the country, to select with meticulous care and carry out audit investigations into hot and difficult issues with significant impacts on economic and social development that the people are universally concerned about and the society focuses its attention on. In investigations and evidence collection, it is necessary to analyze from the macro-angle, see through the appearance to perceive the essence, and screen out focal points for investigations and evidence collection from typical problems relating to the overall situation of social and economic development, instead of attending to everything, big or small, at once without regard to priority. In the course of analyzing the situation and forming conclusions to the investigations, it is necessary to summarize and classify all kinds of collected materials, make systematic analysis from a macro-angle, discover typical experience and problems of universality bearing on the development of macroeconomy from the analysis, and find the causes of the problems and the solutions.

(b) Contents Orientation

Auditing, covering considerably comprehensive content, implements comprehensive auditing and appraisal of the fiscal and financial revenues and expenditures of the auditee as well as their relevant economic activities, and exposes and makes known all the problems of law and regulation violations in the auditee's fiscal and financial revenues and expenditures, while special audit investigations mainly focus on selected matters relating to state fiscal and financial revenues and expenditures, including the management of budgets and the use and management of state-owned assets. By "special" it is meant that the contents of investigations in special audit investigations are more concentrated (i.e., focusing on particular matters within a prescribed time limit and scope). In actual special audit investigation work, audit institutions may, in line with the focused attention of the leadership, focus on hot issues the society is widely concerned with and difficulties in the reform drive, and carry out extensive and in-depth investigations into one subject or matter in different localities, departments, and units. As compared with auditing, special audit investigation contents are more concentrated, more unitary, more concrete, more typical, and more oriented.

The clear orientation of special audit investigation contents requires scientific and rational selection of the investigation subject. First of all, it is necessary to get to know the different appeals from various sides, fully get information from all sides, accurately and correctly select the investigation subject, and prevent the practice of attending to each and every aspect of a matter and going after the grandiose. Then, it is necessary to identify the objective of the investigations, and prioritize the focal points, key links, and focal units. Still next, it is necessary to pool audit resources together, do everything with a definite purpose in mind, do an in-depth analysis, and dig deeply into problems so as to ensure the depth of investigations.

(c) Scope Extensiveness

Audit scope is targeted mainly at a particular unit or project. Apart from investigations and evidence collection in other units and individuals when necessary, it involves very few units and individuals beyond the auditee. Therefore, the target scope is relatively narrow and the collected situations and ascertained problems are rather unitary, while special audit investigations must have a certain amount of scope and coverage in order to ensure that the results are believable and convincing. The wide scope of special audit investigations is manifested mainly in two aspects: investigation target and source of materials. In the aspect of investigation target, all localities, departments, units, and individuals related to matters for investigation are within the special audit investigation scope. In the aspect of source of materials, it can be either financial or nonfinancial accounting data, or even other materials relating to matters for investigation collected through concerned visiting personnel.

The wide scope of special audit investigations requires rational identification of the investigation scope to ensure accuracy of investigation conclusion. The wider the scope, the closer the learned situation will be to reality, the more accurate the investigation result, and the more convincing the investigation conclusion. Otherwise, there might be errors between the investigation conclusion and the reality, leading to audit risks. However, the audit investigation scope is affected by such factors as the human and financial resources of audit institutions, which are unable to carry out comprehensive investigations into units and individuals related to matters for investigation, but can carry out investigations only into a selected part of a total entity by using the audit sampling theory in accordance with the reality. Therefore, it is necessary to uphold two principles in determining the audit investigation scope: When identifying the audit investigation scope, if the investigation costs permit, the scope should be as large as possible, so that the investigation results will reflect a whole picture of reality to ensure the accuracy of investigation conclusion. When selecting the target for specific investigations, it should prioritize the focal point by stressing the representativeness of the target for investigations. To this end, units related to matters for investigation can be divided into several categories. From each category, a number of representative units can be selected for substantive investigation, so as to find the internal links and problems of a common nature, and form a highly accurate and strongly convincing conclusion to the audit investigation.

(d) Methods Flexibility

Organically integrating the methods of auditing and investigations, special audit investigations can, through auditing, keep abreast with the overall surface situation on the one hand and get to know and have a command of more specific live situations on the other. It can be either a unitary special audit investigation or audit investigations in integration with project auditing. It can be carried out either through the examination and verification of the accounting and statistics materials of the auditee, or through such methods as holding discussions, visiting relevant units and individuals, and distributing questionnaires among relevant units and individuals.

The flexibility and diversity of special audit investigation call for the most appropriate method according to the specific situation so as to ensure high quality and low costs of investigations. Generally speaking, it is necessary to determine the method on the basis of the status and impacts of the audited matter according to the whole picture, as well as the degree of difficulty of investigations. With regard to matters bearing on the overall situation of economic development, it is necessary to carry out comprehensive, systematic, and detailed investigations. With regard to other matters, sampling investigations may be carried out. With regard to representative auditees, it is necessary to carry out on-spot investigations. With regard to other auditees, investigations through questionnaires can be carried out.

(e) Timely Report on What Happens

The purpose of special audit investigations is mainly to provide the government and relevant departments with the basis for macromanagement and policy-decision making. The time effect of making audit investigation conclusions and recommendations is particularly important. It means that conclusions and recommendations must be made before the government and relevant departments make policy decisions. Otherwise the opportunity will be lost, and thus special audit investigation would lose its due value. To enhance the time effect of special audit investigations will be conducive for the policy-decision making stratum not only to be aware of and keep abreast of the situation, adopt measures for rectification and malady prevention, and stem the spread of relevant problems, but also to adopt and improve laws and systems in a timely manner, thus forestalling all possible troubles and resolving problems at the source.

To enable audit investigation results to be used by the government and relevant departments to the maximum extent, it is necessary to ensure the time effect of audit investigations in the following two aspects: First, subject selection of audit investigations should echo the calling of the times and be foresighted. It is necessary, in line with the status quo of social and economic development, to analyze and command the overall tendency of social and economic development and, in close line with the central tasks of the country, select universal and embryonic problems existing in the area of fiscal economy for special audit investigation. Second, it is necessary to enhance work efficiency. In such links as investigations and evidence collection, analysis and sorting out of materials, making audit investigation conclusions and producing reports on audit investigations, it is necessary to enhance work efficiency, and strive to submit reports on investigation results to economic policy-decision making departments with the fastest speed and within the shortest time.

(3) Procedures for Special Audit Investigations

Special audit investigation procedures are identical to audit procedures in general but somewhat different in specific procedures and requirements, mainly in the initiation and result of audit investigations.

(a) Initiation of Special Audit Investigations

Whether a special audit investigation will achieve its effect and whether its result will be valued by relevant leadership and policy makers depend, to a large extent, on whether the initiation of audit investigations is rational. Therefore, preparations for a special audit investigation plan constitute an important link.

The identification of audit investigation projects should abide by the Audit Law of the People's Republic of China and the Regulations on its implementation. It should be carried out for specific matters closely relating to state fiscal revenues and expenditures, including budget management and the management and use of state-owned assets. Meanwhile, these matters should be the focus: hot and difficult issues that the government and the general public are concerned about, or universal, tendentious, and embryonic problems already found in auditing. What's more, audit institutions indeed can play a macro- and constructive role in the investigations into these matters. The audit investigation result is influential to a certain extent.

The national audit standards, setting forth guidance for projects suitable for arranging special audit investigations, stipulate that, with regard to specific matters relating to state fiscal revenues and expenditures, including budget management or the management and use of state-owned assets, special audit investigations may be considered in the following circumstances: issues involving macro-, universal, policy-based, or institutional mechanism natures; cross-trade, cross-region, and cross-unit matters; matters involving large amounts of nonfinancial data; and other matters suitable for carrying out special audit investigations.

(b) Special Audit Investigation Result

After the finish of on-spot work of special audit investigations, the investigation team should lose no time in pooling together the materials from investigations and evidence collection, holding meetings to hear reports on audit investigations at a suitable time, exchanging information on investigations, discussing main problems found in the investigations, analyzing causes for the problems, studying recommendations and countermeasures for the solution of problems, and drafting and revising reports on audit investigations. Apart from the elements and contents conforming to the requirements in ordinary audit reports, special audit investigation reports should analyze macro-, universal, policy-based, or institutional and mechanism problems and set forth recommendations for improvement in line with the special audit investigation objectives and focal points. Where problems found in special audit investigations require rectification by the auditee, special audit investigation reports should also set forth requirements for rectification, specify the time limit for rectification, and require the auditee to submit a written report on the rectification to audit institutions. Before submitting a special audit investigation report, the audit investigation team should solicit the auditee's opinions, further verify the problems listed in the report, and, when necessary, revise or supplement the special audit investigation report.

The specific procedures and requirements for the reexamination, deliberation, approval, and service of a special audit investigation report should be handled in line with the corresponding procedures and requirements of the relevant audit report in accordance with regulations.

In special audit investigations, the audit investigation team should produce and submit to audit institutions an audit report in accordance with the prescribed procedures on acts of violations of state regulations on fiscal and financial revenues and expenditures or other law and regulation violations by departments and units subject to the supervision of audit institutions. Audit institutions should handle and mete out corresponding punishment according to law. When the handling and punishment are within the statutory power of the institution, it can directly handle and mete out the punishment. When the handling and punishment are beyond the statutory power of the institution, the case should be referred to relevant departments and units for handling.

(4) Attention in Special Audit Investigations

In order to give full play to the advantages of special audit investigations and avoid confusion between special audit investigations and audits, it is imperative to pay special attention to the following four points in the course of carrying out special audit investigations:

(a) Clear-Cut Special Audit Investigation Objectives. In carrying out special audit investigations, audit institutions must determine the objectives for audit investigations. The main purpose of special audit investigations is to get to know through investigations the specific policies serving as the basis for fiscal and financial revenues and expenditures of relevant localities, departments, and units, implementation of laws and regulations, or the operations and trade profiles of specific capital and projects, so as to do an analysis at the level of institutions, mechanisms, and systems, trace the causes in aspects of policy, system, and management, deep-rooted causes in particular, and produce audit investigation ideas and recommendations to provide information support for the government and relevant departments to boost macroeconomic management and improve policy decisions.

(b) Rational Decision on Special Audit Investigation Content. In carrying out special audit investigations, it is necessary to make a good selection of the investigation contents in accordance with the specified investigation objectives. Generally speaking, special audit investigations may be carried out on the following matters: implementation of state financial laws, regulations, and policies; trade economic activities; raising, distribution, and use of relevant capital; and other matters as assigned by people's governments at corresponding levels, organized or authorized by audit institutions at higher levels, or decided by audit institutions at their own level.

(c) Accurate Grasp of the Scope of Special Audit Investigation Targets. One, it is imperative to carry out audit investigations in accordance with the scope of jurisdictional limits prescribed in the Audit Law of the People's Republic of China. According to the provisions of the existing audit law and regulations, the jurisdictional limits of special audit investigations are completely identical to those of audits (i.e., jurisdictional limits divided according to the affiliating relationship of auditees' fiscal and financial affairs or the relationship of supervision and management of state-owned assets). The vastness of areas and big numbers of departments and units should not constitute the reason for carrying out special audit investigations beyond the jurisdictional limits. Furthermore, in principle, auditees involved in special audit investigations should be mainly units as the targets for audit and supervision by audit institutions according to law. In the course of practical investigations, audit institutions may also familiarize themselves with the real situation through investigations in other units and with individuals not belonging to targets of supervision by audit institutions but related to matters to be investigated. In addition, it is necessary to rationally grasp the scope of targets for audit investigations. Investigation costs permitting, the scope may be expanded as much as possible. Meanwhile, it is necessary to pay attention to focal points and stress the typicalness of targets so as to enhance the credibility of the conclusion of audit investigations.

(d) Provision of Necessary Audit Resources. As compared with project auditing, special audit investigations make higher demands on audit personnel in various ways. They should possess not only basic knowledge of audit inspection of accounts but also, more importantly, management knowledge and professional knowledge compatible with investigation content. Meanwhile, they should be good at making analysis and putting forward high-level and weighty audit opinions and recommendations, and have a certain degree of macroconsciousness, policy level, and writing capability. Therefore, in carrying out special audit investigations, audit institutions must take into consideration the provision of audit resources. It is necessary to have sufficient guarantee of time, manpower, and financial and other audit resources. Corresponding audit resources should be provided as far as possible according to the objectives and tasks of the specific special audit investigation so as to enhance efficiency and achieve the anticipated audit investigation outcome.

CASE 5.1: **SPECIAL AUDIT INVESTIGATION**

From June to September 2011, the CNAO carried out SAI of the building of rural medical and health service systems in 45 counties (cities and districts, hereinafter all referred to as 45 counties) under the administration of Beijing, Tianjin, Liaoning, and seven other provinces and municipalities, with spot-auditing focused on 76 hospitals at the county level, 131 hospitals at the township level, 677 clinics in rural villages, and 148 construction projects. The audit investigation results are as follows:

1. Remarkable achievements of the building of medical and health service systems in rural areas: substantial increase of input in infrastructure facilities, considerable improvement of functional housing and basic equipment supply in rural medical and health institutions at three levels; increase of medical institutions and medical personnel, further strengthening of the building of rural medical and health service systems covering the three levels of county, township, and village; steady progress of the basic pharmaceutical system and gradual improvement of relevant supporting and reform measures; and conspicuous increase of person/times receiving diagnosis and treatment in rural medical and health institutions, remarkable uplifting of the level of basic medical and health services the rural residents are entitled to. Along with the further improvement of access to and facilitation of basic medical and health services in rural areas, person/times receiving diagnosis and treatment have increased by a big margin.

2. Main problems found in audit investigation and their rectification: As the audit investigation results show, the overall situations of the use of capital and project management in 10 provinces and 45 counties were good and no major law or regulation violations were found. However, in some areas and medical and health institutions, there existed such problems as time-lag of the building of the contingents of health personnel and substandard management of construction and weak links in drug management. After the audit pointed out the problems, relevant localities and units have already corrected or are rectifying them.

(continued)

(continued)

In addition, audit investigations also found weak links in drug management in some areas. For instance, some basic-level medical and health institutions run by the government continued to purchase and use medicines and sell basic medicines at added prices after the implementation of the basic pharmaceutical system. Some hospitals at the county level sold medicines at added prices. The prices of medicines bidding for regularized procurement were too high, and so forth. Offices in charge of health and pricing in relevant provinces and counties have combed through the local medicines and prices and, through handling regulation violations and confiscating unreasonable incomes from added prices, have strengthened the implementation of the basic pharmaceutical system by stepping up supervision, dissemination, education, and other measures.[2]

II. REAL-TIME AUDITING

As one of the audit modes, real-time auditing (RTA) was primarily used in the area of auditing governmental investment at the beginning and gradually extended to other audit areas later on. The CNAO Program for the Development of Audit Work 2008–2012[3] and the CNAO Program for the Development of Audit Work during the 12th Five-year Plan[4] both clearly set forth the following: RTA shall be carried out in the entire process of major construction projects bearing on the people's livelihood, matters relating to particular resource development and environmental protection, major emergencies relating to public matters, and implementation of major state policies and measures. Since 2008, audit institutions at all levels have explored and carried out RTA in many areas, accumulated useful experience, and achieved remarkable effects that have won wide acclaim from all circles of society. Practice proves that RTA is not only an effective mode for carrying out performance auditing, but also an important channel for displaying the "immunity system" of audit functions.

(1) Concept and Features of RTA

(a) Concept of RTA

RTA is the mode to carry out auditing in keeping with the progress of the matter to be audited. Whether RTA is necessary mainly depends on the progress of the audited matter. Therefore, RTA refers to the involvement by audit institutions at a certain key link during the course of the progress of the audited matter and a kind of persistent dynamic supervision activity following the progress of the audited matter.

(b) Features of RTA

RTA has both the common characteristics of auditing and its own distinct features. It is an innovation in audit modes. As auditing, it should maintain independence from the beginning to the end, accurately command its identity, rationally delimit the responsibilities of the audit and the auditee, and refrain from engaging in the auditee's vocational, productive, and operational activities, so as to prevent audit risks. Main features of RTA are as follows:

- Preventive audit objective. RTA cares for not only the result of the audited matter but also, more importantly, the progress of the audited matter. It lays stress on the timely discovery of problems and the timely setting forth of rectification ideas. It lays more stress on prevention and gives a better play to the "immunity system" of audit functions. RTA objective lays particular emphasis on promoting the smooth progress of the audited matter to ensure that "No problems, less problems, or at least no major problems will occur."[5]
- Timely audit involvement. Different from the audit carried out after the end of the audited matter (time-lag), RTA involvement is early, with the checkpoint moved forward and stress laid on simultaneous progress with the development of the audited matter, so that RTA will run through the entire process of the development of the audited matter.
- Continuity of audit process. RTA involvement implements entire-process supervision over the development of the audited matter, embodies the continuity of audit process, enhances the frequency of audit supervision, and forms multiple audit supervisions over one and the same matter at different points of time. The audit cycle is generally rather long, featuring several times of on-spot audit or even on-spot residence in some cases.
- Extensive scope of audit contents. RTA is all-dimensional audit supervision. Apart from an audit of the truth and lawfulness of fiscal revenues and expenditures, it lays special emphasis on the management and performance of the audited matter. The audit scope and contents are more extensive and comprehensive.

(c) Specific modes of RTA

According to different features of the audited matter and the status quo of audit resources, audit institutions, in the process of carrying out RTA, may adopt different specific modes including periodic real time, selected-point real time, and on-spot real time. Periodic real time means that the audit team divides the entire auditing process into a number of phases in which it carries out auditing in regular intervals or at stages; selected-point real time means that the audit team divides the work on the audited matter into a number of links from which it selects some focal links for auditing. On-spot real time means that the audit team is stationed on the site of the audited matter and carries out simultaneous auditing along with the development of the audited matter. In planning to adopt the RTA mode in the implementation of audit projects, audit institutions should state clearly the specific RTA mode and requirements in their annual plans for audit projects.

(2) Identity and Superiority of RTA

(a) RTA identity

On the basis of RTA's clarified concept, features, and modes, it is necessary to do an in-depth analysis of and to grasp RTA's identity in order to have a more comprehensive and accurate understanding of RTA.

- RTA is one of the audit modes. It is generally believed that the audit work of Chinese audit institutions mainly consists of the categories of audits and special audit investigations. Audits can be divided into financial audits and performance audits. In addition, accountability auditing is a kind of audit with Chinese characteristics. It can be said that the three categories of audits are all independent audits, while a special audit investigation is both an independent audit and a unique audit mode. RTA is different. It is only a unique audit mode but not an independent category of audit. The distinctive feature of RTA is the time for audit involvement in the process of the development of the audited matter, and the audit implementation process moves forward simultaneously with the development of the audited matter. As a matter of fact, financial auditing, performance auditing, and special audit investigations on the one hand and RTA on the other are not mutually exclusive. In actual work, they can all adopt the RTA mode.
- RTA basic functions remain independently supervised. As mentioned earlier, with the checkpoint moved forward, early involvement, wide scope

of involvement, and in-depth involvement, RTA displays the distinctive feature and outstanding superiority of simultaneous progress of audit implementation and the development of the audited matter. In its implementation process, it is necessary to maintain audit independence, and prevent supervisors from deviating from their identity and playing the role of managerial personnel, thus leading to offside or bad positioning of audit functions. For instance, audits should not voice any opinions about matters relating to management, including whether a project should be initiated. They should not provide the auditee with any consultancy on the latter's specific businesses. They should not directly engage themselves in the auditee's managerial or productive and operational activities, such as helping the latter's code standards, calculation, and quality-certification and price fixing of materials, playing the roles of both supervisors and managerial personnel, and confusing audit responsibilities with managerial responsibilities.

▪ RTA is an effective channel to exercise the audit function "immunity system." It is imperative to exercise the audit function "immunity system" to integrate auditing work into the large pattern of economic and social development. Sometimes it is difficult for traditional auditing to discover problems in time, enabling many law violations to become established facts, resulting in irretrievable losses and the fact that the proposed ideas and recommendations can serve only as a kind of experience to learn from or an admonition. Owing to early involvement, wide scope and contents of involvement, in-depth involvement, and simultaneous progress with the development of the audited matter, RTA is able to discover problems and find the loopholes in management in time. RTA's objective is to nip the problem in the bud and resolve the problem in the process so that the auditee and audited matter will have no problems or fewer problems, or at least no major problems. Laying special emphasis on prevention, RTA can better perform the audit function "immunity system."

(b) Main superiorities of RTA

Traditional audit mode is mainly after the event static audit, with time-lagged involvement in a passive way. Traditional auditing can differentiate the responsibilities between the auditor and the auditee, contribute to capital-saving, and enhance effects. However, owing to the lack of real-time auditing in the process of the development of the audited matter, it is impossible or difficult for traditional auditing to discover problems in time, enabling many law violations to become established facts and resulting in irretrievable losses. Traditional auditing is only like "waiting until the dust settles to square accounts," and "mending the fold after a sheep is lost"—not conducive to the settlement of issues. This is the inherent limitation and deficiency of the traditional audit mode.

By stressing forward movement of checkpoints and entire-process supervision, RTA can nip the problem in the bud. By involvement in the progress of the audited matter, it can grasp information in time, discover weak links and existing problems in management, and set forth recommendations with clear aims. RTA involvement embraces comprehensive contents. This multidimensional audit supervision has expanded audit thinking, broadened audit areas, and deepened audit content. Thus it can give effective play to the role of the "immunity system" of audit functions. Therefore, RTA is a new mode in modern auditing and a development and improvement of the traditional audit mode. It has realized the transformation from static, passive auditing to entire-process, dynamic auditing.

RTA has also met challenges in practice, mainly as follows: In actual RTA, sometimes it is difficult to differentiate the audit responsibilities and the auditee's management responsibilities. Its implementation takes a fairly long time, creates a heavy workload, and has high audit costs. It requires higher demands on audit technology and methods, and some of the existing audit personnel find it difficult to be qualified. Employment of considerable numbers of personnel from intermediary agencies and relevant professional personnel from the society increases management difficulties and audit risks, including confidentiality and clean and honest conduct. It has set forth new requirements for audit outcome and assessment and appraisal of the performance of audit personnel.

(3) Procedures of RTA

As compared with project auditing, RTA procedures have the following five features:

1. **Audit project initiation.** Initiation of audit projects should usually take into consideration three factors apart from the tasks assigned by the superior level. First, whether it is necessary to adopt the RTA mode: In theory, all audit projects can adopt the RTA mode. However, owing to various reasons, RTA has not been applied to all audit projects. Initiation can start only with matters that need RTA and can have RTA carried out. Next, whether it can yield the anticipated benefit: Initiation can start only with

matters that can yield economic, social, macro-, and microbenefits. Finally, whether audit risks can be controlled: Initiation can start only with matters whose risks can be effectively controlled and audit quality assured.

With regard to cross-year projects that adopt RTA mode, the implementation should be listed as "follow-up audit" in the audit project plan of the corresponding year in the succeeding years after the year of initiation.

2. **Auditing program.** RTA projects jointly implemented by a number of audit teams under the unified organization of audit institutions or one category of an audit project implemented separately should have a program prepared for audit work on the said project or category of project, according to which relevant audit teams formulate RTA implementation programs. With regard to cross-year RTA projects or RTA projects to be implemented several times, audit institutions and relevant audit teams should formulate audit working programs and audit implementation programs in the first years of implementation, or at the time of first implementation, make unified and overall arrangements for the entire RTA process and, in each of the successive years or each time of auditing, formulate a separate annual plan or audit working program and audit implementation program.

Before preparing for audit programs, audit institutions should carefully carry out investigations into the overall situation of the auditee and the matter to be audited, analyze relevant materials obtained from the investigations, and rationally determine the audit objective, contents, and focal points. The overall situation of the auditee generally covers the affiliation of fiscal and financial affairs, the auditee's basic functions and scope of businesses, its major business activities, internal control situation, its professional features, and so forth. The overall situation of the audited matter, apart from relevant policy background and objectives, should focus on the sources, scale, and managerial and operational procedures of capital.

Each audit carried out annually in the successive years or after the second time should pay attention to its linkage with the audits already carried out, such as maintenance of relatively stable audit personnel and prevention of excessive staffing or excessively frequent changes of personnel; full use of the situation and materials already in hand from previous audits to prevent divorce of successive audits, still less groundlessly contradicting successive audit conformations; incorporation of rectification outcome of previous audits into the current RTA as important contents for supervision, implementation, checkup, and verification. The preparations for an RTA work program and audit implementation program, procedures for approval, focal points of content, and requirements for RTA work are not much different from those of a normal audit.

3. **Audit notification.** According to RTA features such as multiple times of implementation and long time span, audit institutions may, in the first year or at the first time of RTA implementation, work out and serve once and for all an audit notification in which the specific RTA mode and requirements are listed and the rough frequency and time limit of successive RTA are specified. There is no necessity for repetition in each of the successive years or each time after the second time. Audit notification may also be worked out and served in accordance with necessity.

4. **Audit results.** In the RTA implementation period, audit institutions may, through the form of "Circular on Audit Situation," in a timely fashion keep the auditee and its competent departments informed of the audit situation and problems found in the audit, set forth RTA opinions and recommendations with clear aims, and require rectification by drawing inferences from one instance about other cases. In order to simplify the operational procedures and enhance efficiency, a "Circular on Audit Situation" may be directly served to the auditee in the name of an audit team with authorization of audit institutions. In order to prevent audit risks and ensure audit quality, the contents of the circular should go through certain procedures, such as audit review, examination, and approval according to specific circumstances. After going through such procedures, the circular should be served in time as required by regulations to the auditee, which should carry out rectification accordingly. The auditee's rectification situation and results should be grasped.

   Apart from setting forth audit opinions and recommendations through the form of a "Circular on Audit Situation" in the course of audit implementation, audit institutions should, after the entire RTA process is over, produce a complete audit report to comprehensively and systematically reflect the basic situation of the entire RTA, main problems found in the audit, audit opinions and recommendations, and the rectification of the auditee. Main problems found in the audit cover mainly important problems already rectified and problems yet to be rectified. With regard to a cross-year RTA project, the audit team should submit every year to audit institutions an annual report of the current year. The annual report usually covers the basic situation of RTA in the current year, problems found in the audit, audit opinions and recommendations, and the rectification of the auditee. Annual audit reports and the complete audit report after audit completion should, in strict accordance with the regulations of the Audit

Law and Audit Standards, go through corresponding procedures, such as soliciting written opinions of the auditee, as well as review, examination, and approval by audit institutions.

5. **Audit files and announcements.** Audit institutions should require audit teams to designate special personnel to regularly place audit documents on file. With regard to cross-year RTA projects, the audit team may designate special personnel to take charge of the collection, sorting out, and preserving of RTA materials for filing. It may also place the materials in a file as a complete audit project after the RTA project is over.

Audit institutions should, in accordance with the principle of "making announcements while auditing; he who carries out the audit shall make the announcement," announce the RTA results in accordance with the principles and procedural requirements for announcements of audit institutions respectively in the process of RTA, after annual RTA and after completion of the entire RTA project. With regard to audit projects in which different levels of audit institutions participate at difference times under the unified organization of audit institutions, the RTA results should, in principle, be announced in a unified way by the audit institution in charge of the project.

(4) Categories of RTA

According to different contents of audited matter, RTA can be divided into three main categories: RTA of a project, RTA of capital, and RTA of a policy. The main contents of RTA of a project are investment projects and resources environment development projects, such as the audit of Olympic sport venues and the Three Gorges Project. The main contents of RTA of special capital are fiscal capital or various categories of special capital, such as the audit of the capital for the comprehensive development of agriculture, and audit of the capital for social security. The main contents of RTA of a policy are the implementation of relevant policies, such as the audit of the implementation and effect of the central measures for expansion of domestic demands to promote development.

In actual audit work, sometimes it is very difficult to differentiate project, capital, and policy. An RTA matter often simultaneously involves the three aspects of project, capital, and policy. For instance, RTA of special capital usually takes the raising, distribution, management, and use of capital as its main content. However, in order to deepen RTA of special capital, it is necessary to carry out auditing of projects involving special capital or of the implementation of the policy relating to the special capital. Therefore, audit personnel should rationally command the relationships among project, capital, and policy and determine the audit contents and focal points according to actual necessity. In carrying out RTA of a project, the audit should focus on the initiation, construction, and effect of the project. Meanwhile, an audit of the management and use of capital may also be carried out, but only under the circumstances that the background of the project construction has been closely followed. In carrying out RTA of special capital, the audit should focus on the raising, distribution, use, and performance of capital. In order to confirm the use of special capital, auditing can also be carried out of some selected relevant projects, but such audit should be carried out in the process of the use of the entire capital. In carrying out RTA of a policy, the audit should focus on the implementation and effect of the policy, as well as the formulation, implementation, and effect of supporting policies and measures. At the same time, auditing should be carried out of policy-related projects and capital in accordance with necessity, but such auditing is only for the purpose of confirming the implementation and effect of a policy.

CASE 5.2: **REAL-TIME AUDIT**

Since September 2008, with the aim of promoting smooth reconstruction and ensuring no big problems occur in the disaster-stricken area, the CNAO has been organizing audit institutions to audit reconstruction projects over the past three years in the Wenchuan area hit by a devastating earthquake. Some 11,648 auditors plunged into RTA on 27,902 reconstruction projects with planned investment of 767.8 billion yuan, and conducted final accounts auditing of 17,329 completed reconstruction projects. A total of 4,377 auditing reports were produced, alongside 14,680 audit bulletins. This helped promote the rehabilitation work.

 ## III. GRAND PATTERN OF FINANCIAL AUDITING

Financial auditing (FA), as an eternal subject and basic function of national auditing, is an important system arrangement to promote the improvement of national governance and safeguard democracy and the rule of law. Along with the deepening understanding of the nature of national auditing, audit institutions and auditors at all levels have kept improving the FA organizational mode, from auditing an individual project alone to auditing a number of projects combined. In view of probing into the grand pattern of FA, more stress is laid on the integration of audit resources, on taking advantage of the strength of various professional audits, and on giving play to the effect of FA as an integral whole. FA work has made new progress, featuring considerable enhancement of the depth, magnitude, and tiers of auditing, thus performing the "immunity system" function in promoting the reform of finance and taxation and ensuring the healthy operation of the economy and society.

(1) Practice of Building a Grand Pattern of FA

As national economic activities, the organization of revenues, arrangement of expenditures, management of capital, and overall balance constitute a complete system of finance. Correspondingly, FA, taking national finance as its audit target, should be likewise a complete system, to promote the intactness of national finance through the intactness of FA. Therefore, building a grand FA pattern is closely linked with the integration of audit resources. In June 2003, the CNAO set up a leading group for coordinating FA to probe into FA unification and the integration of audit resources. In September 2005, the CNAO formulated the Opinions about Further Deepening FA Work, setting forth the "Five Unification" principle (i.e., FA should stick to a unified audit plan, unified audit program, unified audit implementation, unified audit report, and unified audit handling). In June 2008, the CNAO clearly stated in the CNAO Plan for the Development of Audit Work 2008–2012 that it is necessary to integrate audit resources and build a grand pattern of national FA. In March 2009, Auditor-General Liu Jiayi set forth the "four musts" at the CNAO-sponsored training class on FA projects: Audit plans must be integrated, audit resources must be integrated, different audit projects or categories must be integrated, and audit information must be integrated at the high levels of fiscal management institutions, systems, and performance. At the seminar on national audit work held in Dalian in July 2010, the National Audit Office clearly stated that it is necessary to "strive for building a grand pattern of FA featuring unified objectives, dovetailed contents, clear tiers, and interaction between the higher and lower levels" so as to further enhance the entirety of the macro- and constructive natures of FA.

In the FA for the year 2009, the CNAO started research on building a grand pattern of FA and probed into building a completely new FA working system. It achieved an initial result, enhanced the time-effect of auditing, upgraded the level of "two categories of reports," and avoided the phenomenon of repeated entries in one same entity. In the FA for the year 2011, the CNAO, taking audits of and investigations into governmental revenues and expenditures at the county level as the platform, arranged three supporting projects, establishing closer links among various audit projects.

TERMINOLOGY: TWO REPORTS—REPORT ON AUDIT RESULTS AND REPORT ON AUDIT WORK

Report on audit results refers to the report submitted annually by audit institutions in accordance with laws and regulations to government leadership at the corresponding level on the audit results of budget implementation and other fiscal revenues and expenditures for the previous year. Report on audit work refers to the report presented annually by audit institutions as entrusted by the government at the corresponding level in accordance with laws and regulations to the standing committee of the people's congress at the corresponding level on the audit of budget implementation and other fiscal revenues and expenditures for the previous year. ▪

(2) Connotation and Focal Points of Grand Pattern of FA

According to the practical experience of FA in recent years, the grand pattern of FA at the level of central FA refers to interactions among various professional audits, among bureaus dispatched by vocational departments, between vocational departments and dispatched offices, in such aspects as the planning, implementation, report, outcome utilization, handling, and punishment as well as rectification under the precondition of identical objectives, and with coordination of local audit institutions, realization of the leading roles of Ministry of Finance and NDRC in auditing, and the supporting role of other professional audits. Specifically speaking, it is necessary to do a good job in four aspects, as follows.

(a) Integration of FA Plans

Audit institutions at all levels should, in line with the central tasks of the government and the status quo of financial reform and management, make studies on and set forth the overall objective and a package project plan of FA in a specified period and gradually establish an assessment system after a major FA project has finished. In the arrangement of the annual audit plan, the CNAO presents the report on audit work to the NPC Standing Committee as entrusted by the State Council as the starting point and, in line with the audit objectives, makes overall arrangements, with the specific organization of the Ministry of Finance, for carrying out auditing of budget implementation by central departments, auditing of departmental budget implementation, auditing of key special capital, and so forth to ensure coordination of various FA contents and mutual support of views. In formulating an annual audit plan, it is necessary to take into consideration the overall objective of national FA, the audit contents, and focal points so as to avoid such situations as FA projects not being integrated, with each going its own way.

(b) Integration of FA Strength

Audit institutions at all levels should establish working mechanisms for leadership, organization, coordination, and communication, and specify equally and in a balanced way to various audit vocational departments the various audit projects incorporated into the overall plan for auditing budget implementation at their corresponding levels. It is necessary to step up overall coordination in the implementation process and strive for the issuance of one audit notification, and the organization of one audit team for one auditee so as to avoid the problem of repeated entries and repeated audits of an entity.

(c) Integration of FA Modes

It is necessary to insist on organic integration of various audit categories and modes according to the project features, and actively probe and popularize FA managerial methods of multiprofession integration, multiangle analysis, and multidirection combination, so as to intensify audit efforts to meet the multiple needs of economic and social development of auditing.

(d) Integration of FA Outcomes

It is necessary to integrate audit outcomes at the height of boosting fiscal management, promoting fiscal reform, and uplifting the level of fiscal performance, comprehensively reflect problems relating to institutions, mechanisms, and systems, and put forward counterproposals on policy. It is necessary to further enhance the macro and comprehensive substance of the "two categories of reports," explore and voice integral opinions on budget implementation and other fiscal revenues and expenditures, and strive for the integration of audit assessment, problems found in the audit, and the causes, handling, and rectification thereof into an integral whole so as to provide the government with a better basis to step up macromanagement and provide the NPC and its Standing Committee with a reference for their review of budget and final accounts and their supervision of budget implementation.

(3) Ways to Build a Grand Pattern of FA

Constructing the great pattern of fiscal audit must follow the principles of unified objective, connected content, distinct level, and connecting the National Audit Office with local audit offices, with comprehensive consideration given to working mechanism, plan management, and use of achievements, instead of simple super-position of several audit projects or the simple piecing together of different majors.

1. **Improve work mechanisms and establish leading and coordina-tive bodies for a grand pattern of FA.** Audit institutions shall earnestly enhance the authority and independence of leading and coordinative bod-ies, establish effective mechanisms for policy making and management, enhance the supply standards of coordinative bodies, and allocate profes-sional personnel and forces. And they shall intensify efforts in the train-ing of composite fiscal audit personnel, boost research on and analysis of economic situations, fiscal management, and fiscal policies. In day-to-day work, it is necessary not only to coordinate the relations among various professional audits, but also to handle the appeals of local audit institutions relating to guidance, technology, and coordination, and to strengthen coordination, cooperation, and mutual trust between audit institutions at higher and lower levels, so as to form an effective networking mechanism and enhance FA efficacy in earnest.

2. **Improve planning and management modes, set up dynamic audit project banks, and improve the mechanism for examination and assessment.** Under the idea of grand FA pattern, FA is a conglomeration of different audit projects. There exists a relationship of coordination and cooperation among these audit projects. It is necessary to establish an FA project pool reflecting the requirements of the situation in line with differ-ent FA objectives in different periods and formulate plans for audit projects in accordance with FA features. Establish scientific, rational, objective, and fair FA examination and appraisal systems to make assessment of units participating in audit projects achieve effective control of FA quality.

3. **Grasp the connotations of finance comprehensively, define FA scope completely, and promote all-inclusive budget management.** It is necessary to lay stress on the effect of financial management, finan-cial system, and financial policies, and incorporate into the FA scope all revenues obtained by relying on public authority and performing public functions. At present, it is necessary to step up auditing of public budgets, fund budgets, operational budgets of state-owned capital, and social secu-rity budgets, so as to promote the openness of budgets, enhance the effect of budget implementation, safeguard financial security, and build a complete financial budget system, laying stress on the lawfulness and authenticity of budget implementation while paying attention to the effect and openness of budget implementation.

4. **Build a system of FA methods, and comprehensively enhance FA capacity.** It is necessary to probe and build a system of FA methods with "macro policy—project (activity)—budget—capital—management—effect" at the core. Horizontally, step up the auditing of various elements such as national financial revenues, expenditures, and management, and pay attention to the linkage between various elements. Vertically, carry out auditing of various elements such as policy, project, budget, capital, management, and effect relating to different projects and pay attention to whether various policies are coordinated, whether budget distributions are fair and reasonable, and whether a project conforms to the trend of financial reform.

5. **Set up a platform for sharing audit outcomes, enhance totality of audit outcomes, and uplift the level of audit outcomes.** It is necessary to adjust the year of the FA project from calendar year to the report year, and enable the "two categories of reports" to become "road signs" leading the organization and implementation of FA and the main platform reflecting audit outcomes. Carry out "integrated" and "systematic" processing of various professional audit outcomes, make audit more integral and more macro, amass various outcomes into an organically connected system of audit outcomes, and uplift the level of FA outcomes.

CASE 5.3: **AUDIT OF THE CENTRAL BUDGET IMPLEMENTATION FOR 2013**

Audit of the implementation of the central budget revenues and expenditures and the draft final accounts. The audit was focused on the overall situation of central budget implementation and draft final accounts, to be verified with treasury fund collection and payment as well as capital allocation. As the central final accounts (draft) prepared by the Ministry of Finance shows, in 2013 the central public fiscal budget revenues totaled 6,119.848 billion yuan and expenditures totaled 6,969.848 billion yuan, with a deficit of 850 billion yuan, equal to the budget. The central governmental fund budget revenues totaled 508.659 billion yuan and expenditures totaled 417.946 billion yuan, with 90.713 billion yuan of surplus carried over to the next year. The operational budget revenues of central state-owned capital totaled 113.038 billion yuan and expenditures totaled 97.819 billion yuan, with 15.219 billion yuan of surplus carried over to the next year.

As the audit results show, the overall situation of the central fiscal budget implementation was good. The preparation for draft final

(continued)

(continued)

accounts was fairly up to standard. However, the differentiation of various kinds of budget revenues and expenditures was not very clear. The compactness and accuracy of budgets were yet to be improved. The prepared contents of draft final accounts were not sufficiently clear. The delimitations of public fiscal budgets, governmental fund budgets, and state capital operational budgets were not sufficiently clear. The state capital operational budget scope was not complete. Revenues from various categories of budgets for special use could not be planned as a whole for use. This was not conducive to bringing capital into effect in time.

Audit of Central Fiscal Management. In 2013 the Ministry of Finance, National Development and Reform Commission (NDRC), and other departments strictly implemented fiscal budgets and increased input in key areas, including the people's livelihoods. Their budgets steadily became more standardized and transparent. However, the right to and responsibility for budget capital allocation had not been completely streamlined. Some irregular problems still existed in the management and use of fiscal capital: Collection and warehousing of capital as well as approval for budget were not up to the norms; there was failure in streamlining purse-string power and duties; streamlining and integration of special transfer payment were not in place; part of fiscal capital was not properly allocated, with some irregularly used; sediment of capital at the treasury of each level hindered the capital from playing a full role in use; management of local treasuries was not adequate, and breaches of regulations existed in the financial management of some localities. In addition, auditing was also carried out of the management of investments by the Social Security Fund.

Audit of the Budget Implementation and Draft Final Accounts of Central Departments. The audit was focused on 38 central departments and extended to 389 units affiliated with these departments. The audit covered 154.238 billion yuan of budget expenditures, accounting for 33.38 percent of the total yearly budgets of these departments. As the audit results show, the budget implementation of these departments for this year was good in general. On average, budgets were in place at the rate of 96.95 percent at the beginning of the year. Fiscal appropriations for three public expenses (expenditures for official hospitality, purchase and use of official cars, and overseas visits for official purposes) and conference fees were down by 22.93 percent as compared with the previous year. However, up to the end of 2013, 14.14 percent of the departmental budgets had not been implemented. In addition, some departments and their subordinate units had failed to strictly implement the CPC Central Committee's eight-point decision on improving Party and government conduct and the State Council's three-point decision on curbing government spending. Some violated regulations of financial and economic systems.

IV. UNIFIED ORGANIZATION OF A LARGE-SCALE AUDIT PROJECT

The unified organization of a large-scale audit project refers to an audit project jointly carried out by lower-level audit institutions in the whole country or whole province, or in a relatively large scope under the unified organization of higher-level audit institutions. In this way, through the audit of some major matters that the government cares for and attaches importance to and the general public are universally concerned about, by pooling together the strength of audit institutions at all levels, the synergy of audit supervision can be effectively brought into play and the integral, macro-, and constructive attributes of audit work enhanced. It is an important channel and anchor for audit institutions to practice scientific audit ideas, play the role of auditors and supervisors at a higher level, bring the "immunity system" of audit function into full play, and improve state governance. Over many years, the CNAO and local audit institutions carried out large-scale audit projects under a unified organization with positive effects and accumulated some experience in organization and management. For instance, in accordance with the arrangement of the State Council, the CNAO organized audit institutions throughout the country to carry out an audit of grain in 1998, screened the nationwide grain system for newly increased on-record financial accounts and irrational occupation of loans, and carried out an audit of the assets, liabilities, profits, and losses of grain storehouses that were to be upgraded to the central level, thus playing a significant role in promoting the reform of the nationwide grain circulation system. In 2011 and 2013, the CNAO organized audit institutions throughout the country to carry out an audit of local governmental debts in the whole country, gained a clear understanding of the base number, origin, and growing process of governmental debts in China, exposed existing main problems and hidden risks, and set forth audit recommendations, thus providing significant references for policy making of the central authorities to step up the management of local governmental debts and establish standardized mechanisms for local governments' borrowing and fund-raising. In 2012, a nationwide audit of social security was conducted, which provided a clear view of the overall situation of 18 social security funds, objectively evaluated the achievement of social security, accurately exposed problems, made audit recommendations, and played a very important role in further improving the Chinese social security system and maintaining the public's interests. The unified organization of a large-scale audit project has become an important mode for organizing audits by audit institutions in China at present.

(1) Features of the Unified Organization of a Large-Scale Audit Project

In comparison with audits of specific units and projects, the unified organization of a large-scale audit project has its own features, as follows:

1. **Big influence and sensitive audit task.** Large-scale audit projects under a unified organization are mostly audit tasks with a rather high-profile political nature, originated by the government, to which the leadership attaches importance. Take, for example, the audit of grain in 1998; it was a matter originated by the then premier Zhu Rongji in order to implement the spirit of the national conference on the reform of the grain circulation system. The audit of local governmental debts in 2011 was originated by the then premier Wen Jiabao in accordance with the arrangement of the central economic conference. It was written into the Report on the Work of the Government, and the State Council especially formulated and issued a program for audit work. In 2014, the audit of revenues and expenditures of land leasing and farmland protection was stated in the government working report. The contents of large-scale audit projects under a unified organization are mostly related to national economic and social security as well as the security of livelihoods and therefore are rather sensitive. For example, auditing local governmental debts involved issues bearing on national economic security. It was closely followed by governments at all levels, all circles of the society, and world opinion.

2. **Macro- and constructive audit objective.** The objective of an audit of a specific unit and project is mainly to exercise supervision over the truth, lawfulness, and effect of the auditee's fiscal and financial revenues and expenditures, with a focus on safeguarding national fiscal economic order and enhancing the effect of the use of fiscal capital, while a large-scale audit project under a unified organization focuses on a comprehensive audit of specific matters with overall, universal, and tendentious natures from a macro- and overall perspective. The latter pays attention to major institutional obstacles, systemic defaults, and management loopholes, and promotes the building of institutional mechanisms conducive to scientific development and the deepening of reform and system building. Therefore, the unified organization of a large-scale audit project, with more macro-objectives, can take better advantage of the constructive role of audit supervision and better serve macropolicy decisions at higher levels. For example, the objective of auditing local governmental debts throughout

the country was not only to get a clear picture of the base number, but also to expose problems and analyze their causes. The fundamental objective was to promote the healthy establishment of a standardized mechanism of local governments' borrowing and fund-raising.

3. **Systemic and comprehensive audit contents and scope.** Since the unified organization of a large-scale audit project focuses on macro-objectives and the overall situation to serve macropolicy decisions, its audit contents and scope are more systematic and comprehensive than auditing a specific unit and project. The scope of audited capital generally covers the entire capital of a certain category or certain item. The scope of the audited region generally covers a whole province or even the whole country. The audit contents generally cover all links in the raising, management, distribution, and use of capital. It often takes a longer time, so as to reflect the situation and analyze problems in a more comprehensive, historical, and systematic way. For example, in 2011, the audit of nationwide local governmental debts covered the debts in eight years by all governments at the provincial, city, and county levels throughout the country. In 2012, the scope of the national audit of social security capital covered the capital of 18 items of 12 categories in three parts: the social security fund, social rescue capital, and social welfare capital. In 2013, the scope of the audit of nationwide governmental debts covered government at central, provincial, municipal, county, and township levels. The audited units included all departments and subordinates under the State Council, Xinjiang Production and Construction Corps, China Railway Corporation, the Export-Import Bank of China, the Agricultural Development Bank of China, the China Development Bank, Central Huijin Investment, and local government, institutions entitled to financial subsidies, government financing platform firms, and so on.

4. **Unified and coordinative audit organization.** The unified organization of large-scale audit projects involves extensive contents, wide scope, and big numbers of participating audit institutions and auditors. The audit results must be pooled together at each and every level. It is imperative to have tight organization, unified command, unified implementation, scientific management, unified preparation of the audit program, unified design of the audit statement, unified standards, unified vocational training, a unified audit report, a unified audit announcement, and integrated audit resources so that audit institutions at all levels will interact, collaborate closely, support each other, and coordinate to ensure the ultimate achievement of the audit objective.

5. **Wide-ranging and multitiered audit actors.** A large-scale audit project under a unified organization covers wide-ranging contents and involves governments at multiple levels; the audited matter involves long time span; and the audit must be carried out in the same organized time span. The pressing time and heavy task impose high demands on audit resources. It is necessary to pool the strength of audit institutions at multiple levels and give play to their integral synergy to accomplish the task. Therefore, the audit project involves big numbers of audit institutions and auditors. For example, the audit of nationwide governmental debts had the participation of 41,300 auditors from 18 of the CNAO's resident audit offices and audit institutions at the provincial, city, and county levels all over the country, and the audit work lasted more than two months.

6. **Wide-ranging and far-reaching audit impact.** Large-scale audit projects under a unified organization are usually major projects that the government cares for and pays great attention to and the general public is universally concerned about, involving multiple tiers of governments and units. It is necessary to produce audit reports to governments at various levels, to expose problems, analyze the causes, make recommendations, and set forth rectification requirements. The audit results are more systematic, comprehensive, and authoritative. Therefore, their impacts are far more wide-ranging than the impact of an audit of a specific ordinary unit and project.

(2) Significance of the Unified Organization of a Large-Scale Audit Project

The unified organization of a large-scale audit project can effectively integrate the human resources of audit institutions at all levels, give full play to the integral synergy of audit institutions, perform the "immunity system" of a national audit at a higher level, and promote the improvement of national governance.

1. **It is conducive to giving full play to the "immunity system" of audit function and promoting the improvement of national governance.** Along with continuous economic and social development and ever deepening reform and opening-up, all kinds of complicated and deep-rooted contradictions emerged one after another. It is all the more necessary for reform to achieve breakthroughs in key areas and at key links. Likewise the difficulty of reform in tackling thorny issues also increases. The

realistic national conditions objectively require the central authorities and localities to step up efforts on the overall arrangement of reform at higher levels, to truly uplift reform to the institutional, mechanism, and systemic levels. In order to bring into better play the audit function of supervision, national auditing, with inherent functions of prevention, exposition, and resistance, and as an "immunity system" in the large system of national governance, must suit the needs of reform and development and show its integral, macro-, and constructive attributes even better. It is necessary, in line with the audit functions and the requirements of superior levels, to start from major matters that the state cares for and attaches importance to, the general public is universally concerned about, and that bear on the overall situation of economic and social development, to lay stress on exposing problems, analyzing their causes, and making recommendations at the institutional, mechanism, and systemic levels, and to provide reform with reliable support to policy decisions, thus promoting the improvement of national governance. Therefore, the unified organization of audit institutions at various levels to carry out selected large-scale audit projects in line with the central tasks and focal points of national governance will inevitably become an important channel for national auditing to play the role of promoting good national governance and scientific economic and social development. It is conducive to performing the "immunity system" function by national auditing.

2. **It is conducive to bringing into play the audit institutions' superiorities of independence and freedom from interference.** Comprehensive, true, and reliable information constitutes the basis of reference for governments at all levels to make important decisions on deepening reform and improving systems. Because of imperfect institutions and mechanisms, dispersed management and partition of departmental interests as well as historical reasons, governments at various levels often find it difficult to have a comprehensive and accurate grasp of relevant information and situations. Audit institutions, as an exclusive department in charge of economic supervision as endowed by the Constitution of the People's Republic of China, have superiorities and features of independence, freedom from interference, and professional knowledge. First, its constitutional status endows national auditing with the power to get relevant information. Second, truth, lawfulness, and effect constitute the basic objectives of national auditing. Audit institutions can provide the government with accurate, reliable, and complete information and situations through audit supervision over the truth, lawfulness, and effect of

state fiscal revenues and expenditures. Third, independence and freedom from interference in national auditing constitute the important guarantee of objective and fair audit results. Therefore, the unified organization of a large-scale audit project can give full play to audit institutions' superiorities of independence, freedom from interference, and professional knowledge and their unique role, and provide governments at all levels with the basis for policy decisions. For a long time, China's local governmental debts had such problems as unclear base numbers and risks and unhealthy mechanisms for borrowing and fund-raising, which became a major hidden danger in China's financial security. Through the audit of nationwide governmental debts, the situation was ascertained, problems exposed, causes analyzed, and recommendations set forth, which provided the central authorities with true and reliable data information for policy decisions.

3. **It is conducive to giving play to the superiorities of the audit supervision system with Chinese characteristics.** As the Constitution of the People's Republic of China stipulates, the State Council establishes an auditing body to supervise through auditing the revenues and expenditures of all departments under the State Council and of the local governments at various levels, and the revenues and expenditures of all financial and monetary organizations, enterprises, and institutions of the state. The CNAO, as a component department of the central government, takes charge of the audit work throughout the country under the direction of the premier of the State Council. Audit bodies are established by local people's governments at or above the county level. They carry out audit work in their respective areas under the leadership of the government at the corresponding level and the auditing body at the next highest level. Exercising leadership of the higher-level auditing body over the lower-level auditing body is one of the superiorities of the audit supervision system with Chinese characteristics. Under this system, the higher-level auditing body will be able to organize and lead lower-level auditing bodies in carrying out large-scale audit projects, form synergy in auditing, and fully perform the audit supervision function.

4. **It is conducive to strengthening audit professional guidance and boosting communication and coordination among audit institutions.** It is stipulated in the Audit Law of the People's Republic of China that local audit institutions at various levels shall be accountable and report on their work to the people's governments at the corresponding levels and to the audit institutions at the next higher levels, and their audit work shall be

directed chiefly by the audit institutions at the next higher levels. It means that local audit institutions implement the "dual leadership" system. The unified organization of a large-scale audit project can boost the leadership of higher-level audit institutions over lower-level audit institutions in audit work, and give guidance to lower-level audit institutions in such aspects as audit objectives, trends of thought in audit work, organizational modes, and technical methods, enhance coordination, collaboration, communication, and exchanges between higher-level and lower-level audit institutions, thus uplifting the aptitude and capability of auditors.

(3) Difficulties and Challenges Facing the Unified Organization of a Large-Scale Audit Project

The unified organization and implementation of large-scale audit projects is more complicated and difficult due to extensive audit coverage, a long audit chain, and more participants and more levels needing coordination between upper and lower levels, as shown in the following aspects:

1. **Challenges facing the integration of audit resources.** The unified organization of a large-scale audit project requires scientific organization of auditors in a large-scale, full mobilization of the initiative of audit institutions and auditors at all levels and full play of the integral efficiency of audit institutions at all levels. This makes a very high demand on the integration of audit resources.

2. **High demand on organizational and coordinative work.** Under time pressure, the requirements of unifying the leadership and management of the audit project, setting up a highly efficient, vigorous, and tiered command center, and proceeding with policy decisions, directions, and process controls all constitute new and higher demands on the organization and management of audit work.

3. **Necessity for breakthrough in audit methods.** Large-scale audit projects are generally rather complex. Traditional audit technical methods and means often can hardly meet the requirements of the unified organization of a large-scale audit project. It is to be achieved through innovation of technical methods.

4. **Difficulty in the control of audit quality.** The large-scale, complex process, multiple tiers of quality control, long chain, and multiple control checkpoints add to the difficulties of quality control of the unified organization of a large-scale audit project.

(4) Procedures and Requirements for the Unified Organization of a Large-Scale Audit Project

The National Audit Office has gradually accumulated rich experience in the unified organization of large-scale audit projects and mastered the relevant operational procedures and basic requirements to some extent through long practice. Generally speaking, the procedures and requirements of the unified organization of large-scale audit projects are as follows:

1. **Mapping out good project plan.** There are usually two modes in determining the unified organization of a large-scale audit project: entrusted directly by the State Council and local governments; and initiated independently by audit institutions themselves. No matter which mode is adopted, audit institutions should make full analysis of and preparations for the project to be audited. In a self-initiated audit project, audit institutions should, proceeding from the requirements of national governance and in line with the central task of economic and social development, pay attention to such areas and aspects as the people's universal appeals, the implementation of macroeconomic policies, management of government-invested projects, ecological and environmental protection, the people's livelihood and social construction, and the operational mechanism of power. They should select projects on the basis of safeguarding national economic security, promoting the transformation of the economic development mode, safeguarding the people's fundamental interests, and serving the scientific development of economy and society. A project plan should be set forth on the basis of full investigations and analysis. At the same time, higher-level audit institutions should timely communicate and coordinate with lower-level audit institutions in arranging large-scale audit projects. Lower-level audit institutions should handle well the relations between projects assigned by governments at their corresponding levels and projects under the unified organization of higher-level audit institutions, so as to rationally arrange project plans and carry out work in a scientific and orderly way.

2. **Unification of audit work program.** Work programs for the unified organization of large-scale audit projects should be formulated and distributed in a unified way, so as to achieve the unification of objective, scope, contents, focal points, and requirements. The preparation of an audit work program should have a clear objective, distinct focal points, specific requirements, valuable guidance, correct orientation, and be easy to operate. In order to map out a high-quality audit work program, it is feasible to

select some areas for experimental audits to sum up experience and accumulate methods. In order to ensure the implementation of the audit work program, it is necessary to organize unified training, through which ideas are unified, understanding enhanced, trend of thought clarified, objective, task, and requirements identified, and audit participants familiarized with policies to master methods, thus laying a sound foundation for the smooth carrying out of audit work. All participating audit units should, on the basis of actual conditions, do a good job of multitiered training to enable every auditor be familiarized with and master the program, as well as the requirements for attaching annexes and filling in forms, guidance of audit work, and relevant policies and regulations. Audit institutions at all levels should formulate implementation programs and carry out work in strict accordance with the requirements in the audit work program formulated and distributed in a unified way.

3. **Unification of organization and leadership.** A large-scale audit project under a unified organization should have unified organization, unified leadership, and unified arrangement by the audit institution initiating the project. The initiating audit institution should set up a leading group for the audit work, under which there should be an office taking charge of the specific organization, implementation, command, and coordination of the audit project. In projects under the CNAO unified organization, it is necessary to have good cooperation between the resident audit offices of the CNAO and audit institutions at the provincial level. The CNAO resident audit offices and relevant audit institutions at the provincial level should jointly set up a coordination steering group to discuss major matters in their work and produce a combined audit report. Lower-level audit institutions should also correspondingly set up audit work leading groups, which will organize audit work according to their division of labor. Lower-level audit institutions are accountable to higher-level audit institutions. They carry out auditing in accordance with the unified organization, unified leadership, and unified arrangement of the initiating audit institution, through interactions between the higher and lower levels, concerted steps, and concentrated progress. At the same time, in carrying out a large-scale audit project under a unified organization, it is necessary, on the basis of clear division of labor, to ascertain the responsibilities of the office of the audit work leading groups, the principal leaders of audit institutions, the audit groups, and audit personnel. Responsibilities are undertaken and checks made at each and every level to ensure audit quality through strict implementation of the responsibility system.

4. **Unification of standard statement.** To facilitate pooling, it is necessary to design a set of attached forms (tables) covering the focal points of the audit work program in accordance with the requirements of the audit work program of a large-scale audit project under a unified organization. The attached forms are a concrete manifestation of the contents of the audit work program and a concentrated reflection of audit results. By putting the audit work program at one end and the audit results at another, they constitute the basis for lower-level audit institutions to write out audit reports and the important basis for higher-level audit institutions to pool audit reports. The design of forms should have clear objectives, be simple and clear, consist of all elements, and stress focal points and clear logic. The requirements for filling in the forms should be detailed and accurate. Relevant concepts should have specific interpretations. The scope of each form constituting the attachment should be clearly defined and each field given detailed explanation. Audit institutions at all levels must earnestly fill in the attached forms after serious examination and verification in strict accordance with the requirements for a unified scope, statement, standards, contents, and time limit. They shall not change or revise their own the relevant forms and indexes so as to ensure identical standards, statements, scopes, contents, and time limits.

5. **Unification of audit report.** The combined report on a large-scale audit project under a unified organization should be reported to the government by the audit institution initiating the project after unified pooling. In principle, audit reports by lower-level audit institutions should be produced by the lower-level audit institution that issued the audit notice. In cases involving "lower-level audited by higher-level," "cross audit," and audit groups under a unified organization, the audit report should in general be produced by the higher-level audit institution organizing the audit in a unified way, or be produced by lower-level audit institutions separately after examination and approval by higher-level audit institutions. The office of the leading group of higher-level audit institutions should, in close line with the objectives and contents specified in the audit work program, timely study and draft the framework of guiding opinions about the audit report, to be distributed to lower-level audit institutions as guidance for them to write out audit reports. In order to ensure the quality of audit reports, it is necessary to actively innovate new modes for pooling audit reports and, through carrying out prepooling and trial pooling, to timely discover and resolve problems existing in data statements, data reports, and pooling analysis, so as to lay the foundation for improving

audit reports, making advance analysis and assessment of audit results, pooling into an official report, and ensuring the quality of audit reports and complete success of the audit task.

6. **Unification of audit announcement.** A large-scale audit project under a unified organization involves a wide scope and extensive interest in society. The announcement of audit results is of great significance. In order to avoid misunderstanding and hype, the pooled audit situation of a large-scale audit project under a unified organization should be made public by the initiating audit institution in a unified way. Audit results by lower-level audit institutions should be made public after higher-level audit institutions make public the audit situation in a unified way and with the consent of local governments, or made public simultaneously in accordance with the unified arrangement of high-level audit institutions.

7. **Integration of audit resources.** The unified organization of a large-scale audit project should foster the concept of "one game of chess," to integrate well the various professional audits among audit institutions at all levels, to make overall plans, to echo each other in content, and to interconnect the implementation time. In audit organizational mode, it is necessary to adopt the "lower-level to be audited by the higher-level," "cross audit," or form a unified audit group to carry out auditing to ensure the independence and quality of the audit. It is necessary to mobilize the initiative of audit institutions at all levels, boost their communication, collaboration, and coordination in earnest, and give play to the synergy of auditing and supervision to the maximum extent. Audit institutions at all levels should break up the internal lines of distinction between and among their divisions and sections, rationally dispose audit personnel, actively cultivate a contingent of audit teams boasting capabilities in such aspects as reviewing problems, making analysis, and application of computers and audit management, to take advantage of the superiorities of personnel and structure of audit groups, to enhance combat capability and to upgrade audit quality, level, and efficiency.

8. **Reinforcement of process control.** The main purpose of process control is to ensure audit quality and pace, standardize audit conduct, and prevent audit risks. It is necessary to give full play to the role of the office of the leading group of higher-level audit institutions in the organization, direction, and coordination of audit work, to integrate program formulation, on-site implementation, quality checking, and accountability to ensure against deviation, variation, or impracticality. It is necessary to build a computerized command platform covering audit institutions at all levels

and highly effective mechanisms for conducting on-site direction and information sharing, to achieve all-inclusive, real-time, and interactive project management. It is necessary, through compiling and distributing audit work bulletins, to timely pass on the leadership's instructions, set forth requirements for work, stress discipline, supervise the pace, answer questions and doubts arising from audit work, transmit and exchange experience, and direct work with vigor. Leaders of audit institutions at all levels should go to the front line to make scientific policy decisions, set forth clear requirements, and give forceful direction. It is necessary to implement a division of labor and responsibilities, specify responsibilities relating to the deadline, quality standards, and requirements for pace and practical effect of work, to ensure that the responsibility for every item in the audit implementation is assigned to specific persons. It is necessary to strictly apply the audit standards of the state, standardize evidence collection for auditing, and, with stress on linkage, procedures, and facts, to form a chain of evidence to support the audit conclusion. It is necessary to step up the work on audit review and quality inspection, and review the process of audit implementation to enhance the effect of quality control. It is necessary to carry out systematic, regularized, and standardized processing of the data in the attached forms (tables) of the program, and develop multitiered examination and verification tools to ensure the truth, accuracy, and intactness of data. It is necessary to be strict with planning and management and tighten control over the timing of checkpoints to ensure synchronized steps of the upper and lower levels. Superior audit institutions should establish links with separate areas, provide guidance to the work there, and conduct on-side direction, supervision, and investigation. With regard to such problems as major incidents in quality, deliberate omission of relevant data, problems found in the audit, and major case clues in reports, as well as failure in the strict implementation of the audit work program, it is necessary to call to account the leaders and responsible personnel of relevant units accountable.

9. **Reinforcement of technological guarantee.** The unified organization of a large-scale audit project with an IT application must make full use of the means of information technology, create new technological methods, boost technological guarantees, and improve audit quality and efficiency. It is necessary to set up technical guarantee groups or teams composed of computer professionals and audit professionals. They should, in accordance with the demands of the audit work and the features of the large-scale audit project, make overall plans and do work well in the following

aspects: make systematic, regularized, and standardized processing of the attached forms (tables) of the audit program to lay a solid foundation for data pooling; formulate an overall program for audit data pooling and make use of an Excel or data bank for data pooling; develop multitiered examination and verification tools according to the demands of the audit work to earnestly ensure the truth, accuracy, and intactness of the audit data; and develop a "networking audit analysis system" to ensure coordinated, highly efficient, and accurate data pooling analysis.

10. **Strict observance of audit discipline.** A large-scale audit project involves a wide scope, high degree of policy mandate, and extensive public concern. Audit institutions at all levels and all of the participants must carry out the audit according to law and in a civilized way, strictly observe audit discipline, and implement the various regulations with clean and honest conduct. They are not permitted to attend the auditee's dinners, accept gifts, go sightseeing, or partake in other activities or arrangements not relating to the audit. It is necessary to strictly observe the discipline of maintaining confidentiality. Without the approval by audit institutions at the superior level, no unit and no individual shall disclose the audit situation and audit data. With regard to some sensitive audit projects, audit institutions at all levels should, in carrying out an audit, handle well their relations with the media and refrain from privately accepting interviews by the media without approval. Moreover, it is necessary to pay attention to the modes and methods of audit work, self-consciously safeguard social stability, and avoid the occurrence of mass incidents and petitions.

CASE 5.4: **AUDIT OF CHINA'S LOCAL GOVERNMENTAL DEBTS IN 2013**

From August to September 2013, the National Audit Office organized 54,400 auditors to conduct an overall audit of debt levels among the central government, 31 provinces (autonomous regions and municipalities) and five municipalities with independent planning status, 391 cities (prefectures, autonomous prefectures, leagues, and districts), 2,778 counties (county-level cities, districts, and banners), and 33,091 townships, according to the principle of performing the audit by transaction and item on the basis of inspecting involved personnel, accounts, and objects in person. The audit contents included the debts the governments were

(continued)

(continued)

responsible for repaying, the debts for which governments needed to perform their liability to guarantee when repayment was difficult, and the debts for which governments might undertake certain relief duty when repayment was difficult.[6] The audit involved 62,215 government sectors and institutions, 7,170 financing platform companies, 68,621 budget subsidy public institutions, 2,235 public utility institutions, and 14,219 other institutions, concerning 730,065 projects and 2,454,635 separate debts. For each debt, auditors performed verification and evidence collection and solicited the opinions of relevant authorities, institutions, and local governments at all levels respectively.[7]

V. ORGANIZATIONAL MODE OF AUDITING IN AN IT ENVIRONMENT

Audit organizational structure and audit organizational mode are crucial to effectively performing audit functions, giving play to the audit role and achieving audit objectives. Along with the rapid development of IT applications and an ever-deepening understanding of the essence of auditing, it is necessary to make corresponding adjustments and improvements of the audit organizational structure and modes in time.

(1) Basis for the Improving Audit Organizational Structure and Modes

Optimization of organizational structure is the precondition for the improvement of organizational modes. Organizational structure refers to the various internal elements constituting the structure and a kind of relatively stable mode of relationship among the elements. It manifests itself in a static basic structure and appropriate operational mechanism. An operational mechanism endows basic structure with contents and vigor, to ensure the attainment of the organizational objective. Modern theories on organizational structure regard organization as an open and dynamic system, stress research on the relationship between organizational structure and social environment, and emphasize that organization should do in accordance with the changing environment, and that appropriate organizational structure be established according to specific conditions.

IT applications and popularization in audit work have enriched the modes and methods of audit work and provided good conditions for more flexible and effective organization of audit implementation and better performance of the "immunity system" function. They are conducive to the transformation from static to dynamic, from on-site to off-site auditing, conducive to the pooling and use of cross-trade, cross-department audit data, conducive to the popularization and application of computerized audit methods featuring "overall analysis, discovery of doubtful points, scattered checkups, and systematic studies." For the sake of better integration of audit work with IT, it is necessary to improve the existing organizational structure to ensure that policy decisions and directions are in place in time, effective communication between off-site and on-site audits, highly effective and smooth allocation of manpower, and audit process control. In recent years, large-scale audit projects such as the audit of local governmental debts and fiscal auditing have paid more attention to integration of multiple professions, analysis from multiple angles, use of multiple methods, overall allocation of manpower, and organization of composite groups and teams to carry out work. This has accumulated useful experience for probing the improvement of audit organizational structures and modes.

(2) Specific Ways to Improve Audit Organizational Structure and Modes

Audit work can be divided into two categories: on-site work and off-site work. The former mainly performs the function of specific audit work, while the latter mainly performs the functions of policy decisions and control. For the sake of performing the "immunity system" function, it is necessary, in the basic organizational structure, to build an organizational structure with data analysis, information processing, scientific policy decision, work implementation, and intensified control as the functional contents by relying on IT application. At the level of implementation, it is necessary to build a digital audit mode consisting of "three centers"—an information study center, a data analysis center, and a work implementation center—as well as a "three-tiered framework" consisting of the leadership, audit group, and audit team, to use the audit project management platform and other policy-decision and management systems to intensify audit process control.

(a) Overall Arrangement

In on-the-spot audit, for the sake of implementing audit process control, it is necessary to set up organizational bodies in accordance with the "five plates": (1) policy decision and direction; (2) information studies; (3) data analysis; (4) work implementation; and (5) process control centering on the audit project.

It is necessary to carry out work by relying on the "three centers": (1) information studies, (2) data analysis, (3) and work implementation. It is necessary to dispose audit personnel according to the "three dimensions": (1) institution, (2) center, and (3) project. It is necessary to build "five platforms": (1) audit management, (2) information transmission, (3) quality control, (4) performance assessment, and (5) supervision of the improvement of the Party's work style and the building of a clean and honest government.

(b) Specific Ways

1. **Setting up a "five plates" organizational structure.** According to functional attributes, organizational structure can be divided into "five plates":
   1. Policy decision and direction
   2. Information studies
   3. Data analysis
   4. Work implementation
   5. Process control

   The first plate is composed of the leadership taking charge of policy decisions and the direction of all work. The second plate is composed of information research centers undertaking the planning, policy research, information, papers, and theory studies directly relating to the audit work. The third plate is composed of data analysis centers performing the functions of collecting, analyzing, and managing e-data. The fourth plate is composed of various vocational departments performing the functions of on-the-spot auditing and management of daily staffing, casting away the original division of labor in professional work. The fifth plate is composed of comprehensive departments undertaking project process control in such aspects as audit management, information transmission, quality control, performance assessment, and supervision of the building of a clean and honest government.

   Take the special dispatched offices of the CNAO, for example, and the sketch map of the "five plates" organizational structure as shown in Figure 5.1.

2. **Carrying out audit work by relying on "three centers."** The information research center takes charge of mastering frontline dynamics, caring for hot-spot issues, and setting forth a "strategic trend of thought." In the course of project auditing, it submits the trend of the thought and information spot to the data analysis center or the work implementation center for analysis and checkup, and to extract the audit outcome from the information in hand while coordinating the functions at higher and lower

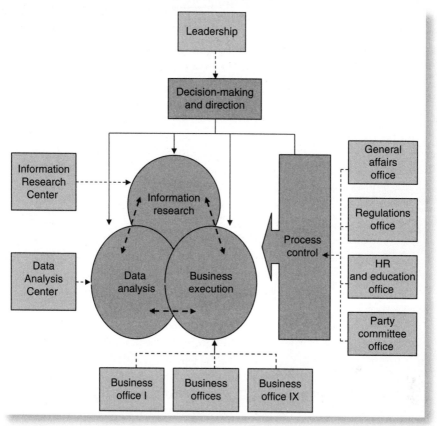

FIGURE 5.1 "Five Plates" Organizational Structure

---

levels. In the course of auditing away from the spot, it carries out research on the national economic central tasks and hot-spot issues, plans the trend of thoughts for audit work, and makes overall arrangements for information code standards.

The data analysis center takes charge of collecting and sorting out data, carrying out overall analysis, setting forth clues to doubtful points, and forming "precision guidance." In the course of project auditing, it cooperates with audit groups in collecting and analyzing data, submits clues to doubtful points to the work implementation center for on-the-spot extended checkup and verification while directly producing an audit outcome through data analysis. At times beyond the course of project auditing, it takes charge of the building, maintenance, and updating of the data bank; constructing all-inclusive data banks and an analogue audit laboratory; carrying out research on special subjects; probing cross-trade comprehensive analysis and use of data information; comprehensively pushing forward auditing with IT applications; and actively probing networking tracking auditing.

The work implementation center takes charge of on-site implementation, focal tracking, and extended checkups to materialize a "precision strike." In the course of project auditing, the center's various audit groups, apart from on-site audit checkups, pay attention to and check on the information spots provided by the information research center and the doubtful points and clues submitted by the data analysis center. At times beyond the course of project auditing, it carries out vocational studies and training.

The aforementioned "three centers" are technically supported by the audit information resources platform, the data analysis and application platform, and the audit project management platform respectively. The information resources platform is mainly supposed to collect the information of all categories of audit projects, research reports, work dynamics, and historical audit materials, analyze the collected information, and promote information sharing. The data analysis and application platform is mainly supposed to gather all kinds of data collected from relevant departments and units, and sort out, manage, and analyze these data. The audit project management platform is mainly supposed to use the input from the special audit network for transmission of audit documents, including announcements, audit diaries, and audit evidence, to achieve highly effective exchanges of on-the-spot data information and non-on-the-spot information, thus playing the role of audit management, policy decision making, and direction. The scheme map of the "three centers" carrying out audit work is shown in Figure 5.2.

3. **"Three-dimensional" disposition of auditors.** Auditors are disposed according to three dimensions of "profession, center, and project." In the dimension of "profession," it is necessary to build a platform to manage human resources, take full notes of the professional situation, and give full play to personal special skills in the disposition of personnel. In the dimension of "center," it is necessary to make overall arrangements for personnel deployment to meet the needs of the "three centers." In the dimension of "project," it is necessary to allocate audit forces according to the audit project plan, the special professional skills of audit personnel, and the demands of the project. The "three-dimensional" disposition of auditors

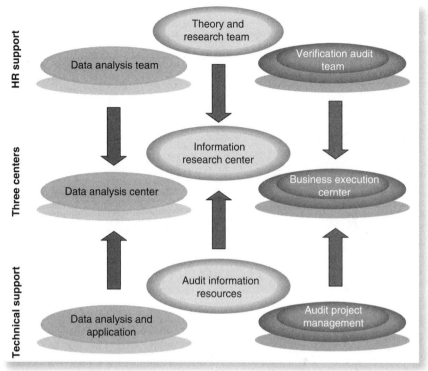

FIGURE 5.2   Scheme Map of "Three Centers" Carrying Out Audit Work

constitutes the key to integration of multiple professions, analysis from multiple angles, and integration of multiple methods.

The "three-dimensional" disposition of auditors is shown in Figure 5.3.

4. **Building "five platforms" to implement control.** First, build audit management platforms. Develop an audit project management platform relating to audit work, an institutional comprehensive management platform relating to institutional management, and multiple subplatforms relating to the circulation of documents, including a platform for the circulation of audit documents, with a view to achieving overall and unified management of the operation of audit work.

Second, build an information transmission platform. Build a networking information exchange platform through supporting systems including an "audit project management platform" to ensure that transmission of the various instructions of principal information is clear, levels and tiers

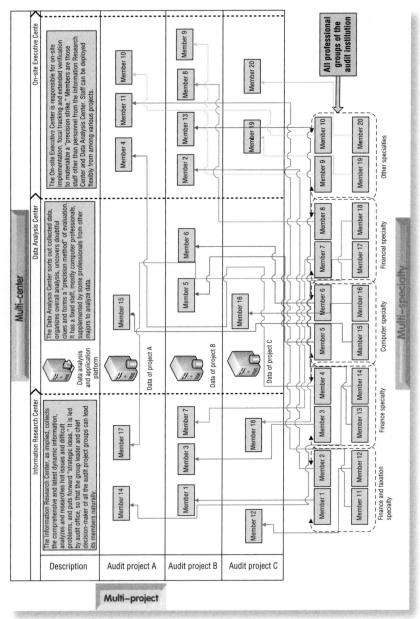

FIGURE 5.3 Scheme Map of "Three-Dimensional" Disposition of Audit Personnel

distinctive, transmission in place, and feedback in time (i.e., to achieve flat management).

Third, build a quality control platform. Intensify standardized management and control of audit quality, and step up real-time auditing and process-control of the project. Adopt the mode of "early involvement and entire-process real-time audit." Formulate and implement an audit gradation quality control system and carry out real-time checkups of the rectification of problems found in the audit.

Fourth, build a performance assessment platform. Implement a performance assessment platform centering on the audit project and individual performance. Link up performance assessment with the appraisal of the project and the employment, appraisal, and training of individuals to create an environment for competitive innovation and build an employment mechanism.

Fifth, build a supervision platform for building a clean and honest government. Explore new modes of building a clean and honest government. Implement a responsibility system for clean and honest conduct of the audit group.

(3) Key Links in Improving Audit Organizational Structure and Modes

1. **Appropriately handle the relations among vocational departments.** The setup of existing vocational departments stresses their professional functions while neglecting their coordination and cooperation. Under the "immunity system," national auditing should grasp all aspects of economic and social operations. It must enhance comprehensive and macroawareness, set up vocational departments according to audit objectives, stress the accomplishment of audit tasks under the guidance of objectives and tasks, stress the internal linkage among all vocational departments, and stress coordination and collaboration.

2. **Appropriately handle the relations between vocational departments and audit groups.** In order to ensure the orderly progress of the day-to-day management of auditors and various kinds of work, it is necessary to further clarify the division of responsibilities between vocational departments and audit groups, to ensure that all kinds of responsibilities are assigned to specific units and personnel, and to realize the normal linkage of relevant work in the courses of on-the-spot audit and off-the-spot audit.

3. **Appropriately handle the internal relations among personnel of audit groups.** It is necessary to have rational division of labor according to the auditor's characteristics and expertise, clarify the responsibilities for auditors at all levels, boost internal communication and exchanges among auditors, and give full play to the active role of each and every auditor and the overall synergy of audit group.

4. **Appropriately handle the relations among the "three centers" in the use and sharing of audit resources.** It is necessary to further improve the management regulations and utilization procedures of audit data and relevant information, to improve the functional contents of the "three centers," to make full use of the information exchange platform, and to boost coordination and collaboration to achieve the objective of the full share and effective use of audit resources.

BIBLIOGRAPHY

Chen, Zhigang. Carry Out In-Depth Audit Investigations by Drawing Experience from US Forward-Looking Audit. *Practice and Theories in Special Administrative Regions*, 2008 (1).

Jin, Xiaoguang. On the Real-Time Audit of Construction Projects. *Modern Economic Information*, 2010 (12).

Liu, Zhihong, Li Rongyi. A Few Points of Thinking on Carrying Out Real-Time Audit on the Implementation of Monetary Policy, *Audit Research*, 2012 (6).

Ma, Yiqun, Xu Gang. Building of Performance Audit Mode under the Large Pattern of Fiscal Audit, *China Audit*, 2010 (4).

NOTES

1. Promulgated by the China National Audit Office in February 2003; see www .audit.gov.cn.
2. China National Audit Office Announcement of Audit Results in 2012: "No. 6 of 2012: Special Audit Results of Construction of Rural Medical Care and Health Service System in 45 Counties."
3. Promulgated by the China National Audit Office in July 2008; see www.audit .gov.cn.

4. Promulgated by China National Audit Office in June 2011; see www.audit .gov.cn.
5. Answer by Auditor-General Liu Jiayi to questions from correspondents on February 19, 2009.
6. Responsibility falls into the category of government responsibilities or debts. The foregoing three categories of debts should not be added together.
7. China National Audit Office Announcement of Audit Results in 2013: "No. 32 of 2013: Audit Results of Nationwide Governmental Debts."

CHAPTER SIX

Study of Audit Management

M ANAGEMENT IS A PROCESS OF EFFECTIVELY achieving organizational objectives by planning, organizing, leading, and controlling resources possessed by the organization under certain circumstances. With the continual breakthroughs of science and technology, as well as new developments in management theories, modern management science that is based on operational research and behavioral science has been effectively applied to the operations of businesses, government agencies, non-profit organizations, and other entities. Based on the three basic features of organizations—namely, objectives, staff, and structure, China's audit institutions have been established according to the Constitution of the People's Republic of China as the component of national administrative organizations. In order to improve administrative performance and save social resources during the process of fulfilling their duties, audit institutions should undertake effective management of audit resources in accordance with the mandate by means of modern management theories.

I. DEFINITION OF AUDIT MANAGEMENT

Audit management refers to organizational and management activities conducted by government audit institutions in performing their duties. There is a wide range of audit management. From the perspective of historical development, audit management is an important factor concerning the scientific development of China's auditing, a key to achieving the legalized, standardized, scientific, and informationized process. Based on horizontal comparison, the management activities of government audit institutions, which are distinctly different from those of other institutions, focus on enhancing the independence and authority of government auditing and facilitating the effective implementation of audit projects. Good management can help audit institutions identify major violations of laws and regulations and the clues to economic crimes; conduct disposition and punishment; discover and analyze problems from various dimensions of systems, mechanisms, institutions, and policies; and provide audit opinions and recommendations. By these means the value of audit management will be reflected.

(1) Objectives of Audit Management

Following the guidance of scientific audit concepts, the overall objective of audit management is to improve the quality of government auditing and give full play to its function as an "immune system" in safeguarding the healthy operation of the national economy and society. Specifically, it seeks to strengthen the initiative of government auditing in serving the overall situation, to give play to the overall function of government auditing with a focus on scientific planning, to optimize the allocation of audit resources and strengthen control of auditing costs, to promote the standardization of auditing and enhance the quality of audit achievements, and to guarantee further development of auditing and building of qualified personnel.

(a) The Initiative of Government Auditing

In order to give full play to its function as an "immune system" in safeguarding the healthy operation of the national economy and society, auditing should establish itself as a complete scientific system with necessary means and conditions for the interaction between internal components and external environments. Audit management works with the contents of providing these conditions and means for such interaction, ensuring the smooth operation of the system as its function and focusing on strengthening the initiative of government auditing. It focuses on national economic development plans, major guidelines and policies, and macrocontrol measures of the Party Central Committee, and seeks to better integrate audit work with the building of a moderately well-off society in an all around way and strengthen audit supervision to deal with problems during the process of development. Meanwhile audit institutions should take the initiative to develop themselves to meet the demands of auditing. Auditing should face different expectations at different phases of economic and social development and require different management styles correspondingly. However, it is always the fundamental objective of audit management to enhance the initiative of auditing, which will play a great preventative role. Practice has proved that taking precautions and having a clear advance plan before action are far more effective than trying to remedy a situation that has already occurred.

(b) Full Coverage of Auditing

It is the statutory duty of audit institutions to bring all the public funding, state assets, and state-owned resources under examination to achieve the full coverage of auditing. Full coverage operates as an important way to improve the level and quality of audit supervision with a view to enhancing the impact and effectiveness of auditing through playing the role of "immune system" for the modernization of the state governance system and capability. Full coverage should be conducted in depth, with emphasis, and step by step. Auditing should focus on the central work of the Party and the government on the basis of the overall situation to determine key areas and matters of more concern. In the meantime, auditing should progress in a planned way and according to concrete conditions.

(c) Holistic Role

In addition to expanding coverage, auditing should pay more attention to major problems, conflicts, and risks concerning economic and social development from a higher level and a broader viewpoint in order to give full play to the function of the "immune system" and play a constructive role. Auditing of the public, the most fundamental and primary duty of audit institutions as laid down by legal provisions, should reflect the requirements of "national finance" and be governed by the idea that "all the money within the due management of government belongs to national finance,"[1] and thus focus on "budget implementation." However, the current artificial segmentation of public finance audit unfortunately restricts the holistic role of auditing. Based on the existing resources, audit institutions should undertake overall planning and systematic arrangement to allocate audit resources in a proper and balanced manner, strengthen the timeliness of planning and arranging of audit projects, refine such contents as audit objectives, scope, and milestones, and improve the timeliness of auditing, so as to play its holistic role.

(d) Optimized Allocation of Audit Resources

During the current period of rapid development and transition of society and economy, the conflicts between limited audit resources and audit demands are becoming more prominent. From the perspective of management science, the problem of resource scarcity can be solved in two ways: (1) Integrate internal resources of the organization, reduce costs, and improve work efficiency; and (2) coordinate internal and external resources to increase their availability. Audit plan management obviously includes the allocation of audit resources. To a large extent, the scientific nature of the audit planning is reflected by the optimization of resource allocation. Therefore, audit plan management should be strengthened to integrate both internal and external resources for a better allocation.

(e) Audit Procedures and Results

To strengthen audit management, audit institutions and auditors should follow auditing procedures and relevant provisions for each stage, perform their responsibilities and authority as conferred by laws, regulations, and audit standards, regulate audit reporting, and promote disposition and punishment according to laws to meet requirements and public expectations. Strict control over the auditing process is an important part of audit management, and a precondition of ensuring the quality of the audit. Audit results can provide leading organizations and related parties with the necessary information to understand the overall situation and achievements of audited entities in financial management, prominent problems, and their causes, as well as opinions and recommendations for solving the problems. Therefore, the application of audit results should be strengthened, and the supervisory role of society and public opinion should be given full play to promote rectification and reform in regard to problems uncovered by the audit.

(f) Implementation of the Party's Organizational Line, and Guidelines and Policies for Cadres

For better audit management, audit institutions should gradually establish and improve their human resource management system and mechanisms to satisfy the needs of scientific development of auditing, improve auditors' capability and audit quality, arouse the enthusiasm and creativity of auditors, and promote the development of personnel in an all around manner, so as to guarantee the scientific development of auditing from the perspective of personnel.

(2) Main Contents of Audit Management

From the organizational and managerial perspective, audit management covers many aspects, and the corresponding handling of these aspects constitutes the framework of the audit management system, which is directed by audit strategic management and guaranteed by audit quality and human resources management, with a focus on the management of the annual audit plan, audit results, and annual audit cost.

The framework of the audit management system is shown in Figure 6.1.

(3) Composition, Positioning, and Inner Link of the Framework of the Audit Management System

Activities of audit institutions can be divided into two categories: audit administration and audit practice. The former is to plan, organize, and allocate the

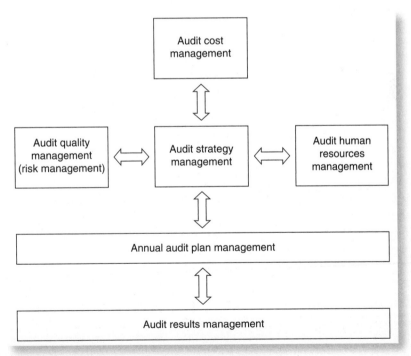

FIGURE 6.1 Framework of Audit Management System

staff, finance, and materials of audit institutions in order to ensure smooth completion of audit tasks. The latter refers to the execution of supervisory functions of audit institutions as an important part of state administration. Audit administration has a direct impact on the execution and effect of audit practice; while audit practice serves as the fundamental way to perform the duties and play the role of auditing.

The objective of audit administration is to ensure scientific, orderly, and efficient administration of audit institutions. It involves a hierarchy of three levels: the decision-making level, responsible for formulating the strategic plan of auditing and the annual audit plan, and determining audit projects; the management level, responsible for choosing appropriate audited units according to the annual audit plan and audit projects, and developing the audit work program; and the implementation level, responsible for drafting the audit implementation plan and directly conducting the audit. The decision-makers of these three levels are the top management of audit institutions, heads of audit departments, and the leaders of audit teams respectively. Since the characteristics, responsibilities, management objectives, and performance indicators at three levels differ from each other, the control content and methods for achieving efficiency and effectiveness vary widely.

Decisions at the decision-making level affect the management and decision making of lower levels. Therefore, in addition to ensuring correct work, decision-makers at this level must make overall plans and coordinate for lower levels. At the same time, an intention of higher level should be transmitted to the lower levels in a prompt, clear, and accurate manner. Therefore, organizational efficiency is vital in ensuring that higher levels play the role of organizing and coordinating the overall situation. There are three basic approaches: improving the leadership and decision-making mechanism of high levels to ensure the correctness, rationality, and feasibility of decisions made; establishing a system for efficient and smooth transmission of information to ensure a clear channel with a simple approach and reasonable methods; and establishing a mechanism by which lower levels can understand the decision-making intentions of higher levels and implement their decisions.

The management level plays a bridging role of communication between the decision-making and implementation levels, with its main work of processing the information from higher and lower levels, and works out concrete measures and methods to implement the high-level policies and plans. There are four basic ways to ensure the efficiency of middle-level management: ensuring a complete and reasonable middle-level work plan is available; ensuring the connection of measures taken by the middle and implementation level with high-level decisions; providing useful, accurate, and timely information and data for high-level decision making, including the feedback of earlier implementation of high-level policies and plans; and guiding and coordinating the implementation levels in a timely and accurate way.

The implementation level is the essential grassroots organization of an audit institution, comprising, as it does, the audit team. As for comprehensive departments, the implementation level is the functional department handling specific audit administrative affairs. Generally speaking, the implementation level undertakes only tasks assigned by superiors in accordance with auditing standards and operational guidelines. There are three main methods to manage the efficiency of the implementation level: (1) implementing related rules and guidelines strictly and efficiently, (2) providing useful information and data for the upper level's decisions in an accurate and timely manner, and (3) reporting problems or providing feedback as prescribed by procedures.

According to the different functions, the framework of the audit management system includes three parts: (1) the audit strategy management, acting as the commander-in-chief to conduct overall audit management; (2) the audit business management at the operational level (including the audit plan, audit program, audit results, and audit quality management), which plays the supporting role; (3) the resource management at the operational level (including the audit cost, human resources, and external audit management), which plays the security role.

There are six kinds of specific management activities under the framework of the audit management system as follows:

1. **Audit strategy management.** It mainly analyzes the organization's external environment, and identifies the main audit mission, development goals, and the key work areas within a specific period and makes clear the implementation of the development strategy and control measures. Based on the guiding principle and overall development goals of audit institutions and specific goals and measures of major work concerning the overall situation, audit institutions need to set specific goals to achieve objectives and clearly identify the plans, systems, and their mutual relationships within the framework of the audit management system.
2. **Annual audit project plan management.** This determines how to steadily realize the goal of work determined by the audit development strategy in accordance with the central work of the Party and government of the same year and the results of studying the socioeconomic situation. Annual audit projects could be determined in accordance with the departmental

budget and available audit resources. Audit institutions exercise planned management over annual audit assignments. All audit assignments are subject to the annual audit plan. Taking the leading position in audit business management, audit plan management is an important means and core part of integrating audit resources. Its main task is to bring together all audit resources to cover the field supervised by auditing, achieve full coverage, and improve audit quality.

3. **Audit quality management (risk management).** This pertains to business management and provides support for the implementation of the entire audit strategy. Audit institutions should annually review the work of audit quality management (risk management), change the business requirements and control environment in accordance with the external environment, and analyze the main risk level of prioritized work defined in accordance with the organizational development strategy to identify corresponding solutions.

4. **Audit result management.** Attention should be paid to the results and outcomes from audit work and to its presentation forms, such as the audit report, audit information, and the "Two Reports," so as to ensure better audit results with a lower input of audit resources—that is, maximization of audit results.

5. **Audit cost management.** Audit costs are resources used by audit institutions to carry out their audit duties. They include all controllable, uncontrollable, external, and internal costs incurred by audit institutions over a given period. Audit cost, in a narrow sense, refers to the monetary expression of all the expenses actually incurred by an audit institution, and is equivalent to the annual departmental budget to a certain degree. Therefore, the annual departmental budget mainly aims to provide financial support for implementing various management activities with an organizational development strategy at the core. However, it should be emphasized that the capital arrangement as well as the expected output and results of departmental performance assessment should be listed in the departmental budget.

6. **Audit human resource management.** This refers to adjusting the existing system to cope with the needs of any situation, and to cultivate innovative personnel so as to provide intellectual support and an organizational guarantee for the development of the audit cause by revising and improving the existing human resource management system. It aims to realize audit strategy management goals.

The six organic components of the audit management system interact and jointly promote a more scientific approach to the organization and management of audit institutions. Currently, although management of Chinese audit institutions overall involves these six aspects, there are three shortcomings: a lack of systemization—offices fail to carry out various audit management activities from an overall system perspective; a lack of internal relationships and support—management activities that should be supporting each other are actually hindered by internal conflicts; and a lack of effective management and control over the activities—a lack of periodic control and adjustment for the implementation of mid- and long-term strategic plans.

II. PRINCIPLES OF AUDIT MANAGEMENT

Audit management should be conducted in accordance with certain principles as follows:

- Overall consideration and focus highlighting
- Improving efficiency and performance
- People-oriented
- Risk control
- Emphasizing the usage of audit results

(1) Overall Consideration and Focus Highlighting

The Constitution defines the extensive objects and scope for government auditing and supervision. However, audit institutions are not able to bring all targets within their jurisdiction under supervision in the short term due to restrictions imposed by organizational deficiencies, personnel quality shortcomings, conflicting demands, and so on. Therefore, we should emphasize overall consideration and highlight specific focuses. During the process of making overall arrangements for annual project plans of audit institutions, we should firstly consider whether the audit task is necessary and determine the order of audit priority while considering the requirements of overall audit coverage. Secondly, we should assess the possibility of finishing audit projects—that is, to grasp the quality of the personnel in a scientific manner, to estimate the workload and quality requirement of the audit tasks, and to deploy under the principle of working within the existing capability while leaving enough room for adjustment. We should do a good job in organizing professional training for audit personnel so as to ensure the sustainability of their audit ability. In terms of arranging the audit plan, a specific focus should be highlighted. On this basis, we should audit major industries and funds in a planned way, focus on projects involving large amounts of money, a large scope, and a big impact, and make a project plan focusing on the integration of point and sphere. We should highlight the changes of focus and emphasize auditing and supervision of key sectors, departments, and funds. On the premise of enlarging audit coverage, we should keep a balance between comprehensive audit and key focuses.

(2) Improving Efficiency and Performance

The resources of audit institutions, including human resources, expenditure, and technical equipment, are limited. It is of great importance for audit management to achieve good audit results by making use of the available limited resources. Therefore, when formulating project plans, we should fully consider how to enhance work efficiency, guarantee audit quality, and bring the overall effectiveness of available audit resources into play through effective resource integration methods. Optimizing the allocation of audit forces directly impacts work efficiency. Therefore, we need to analyze the personnel structure, skill hierarchy, work level, and requirements of audit projects; we need to adopt the best project organization method to enhance work efficiency and "yield twice the result with half the effort." In accordance with economic theory, if the input of a project is greater than its output, such a project is uneconomical and is not worth implementing. The same applies to an audit project. The standard of measuring audit work performance is to reduce the cost so as to achieve the maximum performance on the basis of enhancing audit quality and efficiency. The audit work performance is reflected by the proportion of the sum of economic and social benefits arising from the audit to its cost. Achieving maximum audit work performance lies in realizing cost minimization, on the basis of achieving maximum economic and social benefits; or on the basis of the same audit cost, thus realizing performance maximization. Therefore, we should measure the audit workload in a scientific way and fully consider the audit resources needed.

(3) People-Oriented

Auditors ultimately are the ones to realize the maximization of audit work performance. We should stick to the principle of being people-oriented in audit management, focusing on improving the comprehensive quality of auditors, stimulating their subjective initiative and work enthusiasm, and encouraging them to enhance their audit work efficiency. First, we should promote the development of personnel by taking work characteristics into consideration. Second, we should recommend and appoint people based on their abilities. Building talent teams is a fundamental guarantee for the development of the audit cause, and thus we need to further establish and improve the scientific audit work performance evaluation system, to stimulate auditors' internal motivation, and to enhance their professional sense of honor. We need to recommend talents with broader vision, a higher perspective, and a greater breadth of spirit, and to cultivate and employ excellent auditors throughout the country. Third, we should be committed to bringing auditors' potential into full play and paying attention to their integrated development. Development of the audit cause will be impossible without the improvement of auditors' comprehensive quality, humanistic quality, and cultural level; auditors' integrated development and comprehensive quality enhancement depend on audit institutions to create equal development opportunities and an environment conducive to developing people's talents and wisdom. When carrying out audit management work, we should consciously bear the responsibility of creating an environment where people can develop in a harmonious environment, so as to promote the comprehensive improvement of auditors' quality, maintain the advance of the audit cause in line with the times, and promote continuous development.

(4) Risk Control

Audit risk refers to auditors undertaking social and legal responsibility for their work. It is closely related to audit quality. The better the quality, the lower the risk. Internationally, audit institutions of various countries constantly explore and take effective measures to lower audit risks—that is, to strengthen control, to deepen understanding of audit danger spots, to strictly abide by the professional standards and requirements of professional ethics, to implement quality control, and to pay attention to the management of auditors in regard to their discipline and resistance to corruption. Audit risk control is systematic. It needs to be strengthened at all stages and links of the audit work, including but not limited to making the audit project plan, audit work program, and audit implementation plan, auditing, obtaining audit evidence, formulating the audit working paper, submitting audit information, issuing audit reports, and issuing audit decisions. If management at any level of risk is insufficient, major quality problems may occur.

(5) Emphasizing the Usage of Audit Results

Audit results are the products of audit work and act as an "immune system" of audit by providing public products necessary for Party committees, governments, legislative bodies, executive authorities, audited units, society, and the masses. From the perspective of audit practice, the bodies in need of audit results include:

- **Audit department.** As for the internal division of labor in audit institutions, the audit operating department handles the audit results; the comprehensive department does the work such as processing and transferring the original audit results provided by the operating department, promotes the use of audit results, and oversees their transformation into programs for productivity and executive ability.
- **Audited objects.** As the main body using audit results, audited objects mainly use audit results to correct problems, strengthen management, and improve the overall system.
- **Party committees, governments, and other departments.** With in-depth development of the audit cause, Party committees, governments, disciplinary inspection organs, judicial organs, comprehensive management departments, and competent departments at all levels pay increasing attention to the use of audit results. They make use of them to fight against corruption, strengthen the construction of a clean and honest administration, and improve mechanisms as well as the management level.
- **Public.** Publicizing audit results is an important way to fulfill the public's right to know and the right of supervision. The public can use audit results mainly to monitor the duty performance of government departments and state-owned enterprises as well as the safety and effectiveness of public funds.

Different bodies have different demands for audit results. In the process of audit management, we should adhere to the demand-oriented principle and choose different vehicles, different expressions, and different transmission methods in order to provide useful audit results. We should adhere to the macrocontrol principle and provide high-level audit results; we should adhere to the principle of deep analysis and provide in-depth audit results; we should adhere to the stringent quality principle and provide high-quality audit results.

III. AUDIT STRATEGY MANAGEMENT

Generally speaking, this refers to management activity to achieve strategic objectives and implement policies and guidelines in a certain period and audit scope. It is developed and organized by the supreme decision-making body to be implemented in audit institutions and is an important management activity concerning the overall development of the audit cause.

The objectives of audit strategy management are to promote socioeconomic scientific development, deepen reform, accelerate the construction of the democratic legislative system, safeguard national security, combat corruption, and uphold integrity, as well as improve national governance, based on the major central policies and guidelines, national economic development plans, and macrocontrol measures.

The audit strategy management activities should concentrate on the overall development of the economy and society in different regions and nationally, and highlight work priorities, on the basis of conforming to the development law of auditing, and adapting to the resources status of audit institutions. Audit strategy management should be based on the following factors: First, the macroeconomic and social development plan, such as the five-year plan and regional development guidelines that were made over the same period. Audit work should contribute to and be subject to national and regional development plans and be consistent with socioeconomic scientific development. The second link is the key work of Party committees and governments, such as the spirit of the national and regional economic meetings, major reform measures of economic and social development, and the central and major tasks of national economic and social work. Development of the audit cause should be synchronized with the central tasks decided by Party committees and governments. Thirdly, audit work should take into account hotspot issues and difficult problems closely related to immediate public interest and social management, such as social security, poverty alleviation, issues of agriculture, farmers, and rural areas, and environmental protection. When developing audit strategic plans, we should strengthen auditing and supervision in these areas.

(1) Audit Strategy Management Is of Great Significance to Audit Work

Audit strategy management is based on establishing the guiding ideology, overall development objectives, specific objectives, and measures of key work in regard to the overall situation. In line with the overall development objectives it needs to make clear the various plans and systems as well as their interrelationship under the audit management framework.

(a) Scientific Audit Strategy Management Contributes to Improving the Allocation Efficiency of Audit Resources

Actually, the scientific development of the economy and society is to realize the scientific allocation of social resources. The quality and scale of the resource allocation determine the development quality and speed of socioeconomic progress. Under the condition of limited resources available in a certain period, scientific resource allocation is the key to propelling sound and fast development of the economy and society. Likewise, under the condition of limited audit resources, we should allocate them by projects and give play to the leading role of project arrangement in resource allocation, to ensure completion of key tasks; we should clarify the audit objectives and specific key work in detail, share audit results, consider coordinated arrangement of audited units, give play to the coordination and leading functions of fiscal, environmental, and economic accountability audits, improve audit coverage, and optimize the allocation pattern.

(b) Scientific Audit Strategy Management Contributes to the Construction of Audit Cadre Teams in a Comprehensive Way

The audit team is of utmost importance to the audit cause. To conduct scientific audit strategic management, we should adhere to the principle of "putting people first," pay close attention to the improvement of legal audit abilities and audit level of auditors, deepen the reform of the cadre and personnel system, strengthen the construction of auditor specialization, strengthen training for high-level professional auditors to build a talented core team of high quality, and broaden the training channels for cadres in order to constantly improve the overall quality and hands-on background of cadres.

(c) Scientific Audit Strategy Management Contributes to Improving Audit Plan Management

We should guide the audit project plan through audit strategy management, and ensure this through the annual project plan. We should arrange audit projects in a reasonable way, and clarify audit objectives, audit scope, allocation of audit resources, and the arrangement of key time nodes in detail. We need to lay emphasis on improving the timeliness of plan and task assignments, while strengthening plan guidance, improving integration of audit institutions at all levels, and strengthening the authorization management of audit business.

(d) Scientific Audit Strategy Management Contributes to Improving the Audit Quality Control System

We should further improve the Chinese audit law system, and promote auditing in accordance with the law. Pursuant to audit laws and regulations as well as national auditing standards, we should use the advanced experiences at home and abroad for reference and systematically develop audit guidelines and vigorously carry out the examination work of audit projects, based on Chinese audit practices. We should explore a postresponsibility system for audit quality control, enhance quality inspections, improve the evaluation level of outstanding audit projects, and improve the overall quality level.

(e) Scientific Audit Strategy Management Provides a Platform for the Exploration and Innovation of Audit Methods

On the basis of the in-depth summary of practical audit experience in China, we should focus on building a large pattern of financial auditing and improve the level and standard of audit work reports and audit result reports. We should improve the effective combination of various audit types, establish and improve the system of performance audit evaluation, endeavor to create new audit organizational forms, and realize informatization of audit methods.

(2) Five-Year Plan for Audit Strategy Management

The "plan" refers to a relatively comprehensive and longer-term development plan, being a complete blueprint for considering, discussing, and designing activities covering holistic and fundamental issues. Later development plans of the same unit for different periods involve improvements based on previous documents. Plan management with a cycle of five years is the main method with Chinese characteristics for the macromanagement of economic and social development, and also an effective management strategy proven by audit practice. The five-year plan for auditing is essentially the external form of audit strategy management, a strategic plan for considering, predicting, and analyzing audit development trends in the coming period and a major guide for audit institutions to fulfill their responsibilities. The contents of an audit strategy management plan should mainly define the primary tasks, overall objectives of audit institutions, specific objectives of key tasks, and corresponding action measures.

Currently, in order to give play to the function of audit work in promoting scientific development and accelerating the transformation of the economic development mode, audit institutions at all levels should make five-year plans for auditing based on their own practical audit work, pursuant to the middle and long-term guidelines for national economic and social development fulfilling the key work requirements of the Party Central Committee and the State Council.

(a) Evolution of National Audit Work Plans

In 1991, the National Audit Office of the People's Republic of China (hereinafter referred to as "the CNAO") promulgated and implemented the National

Audit Work Outline (1991–1995) as the country's first medium-term audit plan following its founding. Since 1998, the CNAO has successively issued several plans, including the National Audit Work Outline (1999–2003), National Audit Work Plan (2003–2007), National Audit Work Plan (2006–2010), National Audit Work Plan (2008–2012), and the 12th Five-Year Plan for National Audit Work. In the light of local social and economic situations, audit institutions at various levels work out their respective audit plans.

(b) Major Features of the 12th Five-Year Plan for National Audit Work

The 12th Five-Year Plan for National Audit Work contains the basic spirits of previous regulations. Meanwhile, in the light of the situation, it also contains new requirements and new experience gained in audit work over the years. It outlines new audit regulations based on audit work, achievements, and development, plus new regulations with regard to economic obligations auditing and changes in basic audit work. Major features are as follows.

First, the plan determines more clearly the auditing guiding ideology. The National Audit Work Plan (2006–2010) summed up the role of state auditing in the new period and called for efforts towards the better role of the "immune system" of audit work in socioeconomic operations in three aspects: to better serve socioeconomic development, promote the deepening of reform and democracy construction, and defend state security and fight corruption, thus making fresh progress in deepening reform and promoting more effective state administration; to achieve fresh progress in doing audit work according to law and in a more standardized, scientific, and informationalized way; and to improve China's audit theory and system construction in accordance with the Chinese situation and the needs of China's socialist market economic development.

Second, the plan highlights the need to take more initiative and be broader in vision and constructive in auditing. The plan stresses the need to show concern for major problems confronting state economic and social operations. Special efforts should be made to analyze these problems so as to propose suggestions for the solution of general problems, and measures that should be taken to prevent the occurrence of these problems and improve the system. These will prove to be informative for decision making. It is necessary to conscientiously make audit work an important part of national economic and social development, promote democracy and rule of law, defend national security, guarantee national interests, and promote coordinated sustainable development of China's social and economic development.

Third, the plan works hard to innovate the auditing organization mode. The plan stresses the need to strengthen cooperation within the system and coordination of various audit resources, and promote the audit organization mode featuring professional integration, profound analysis, and multiple integration so as achieve overall efficiency. There is also the need to do a better job with the finance audit in a planned way. Efforts will therefore be made to plan finance audit projects, with special management exercised over audit goals, special fields, audit resources, and results so as to upgrade the level of audit work reporting and the audit result report.

Fourth, the plan strives to optimize and upgrade auditing techniques. The plan stresses the need to build up and improve the electronic audit system for increased data concentrated efforts, realize the informationized audit method, and actively study ways and means for the realization of data mining, intelligent information processing, big data, cloud computing, and other advanced technology, for intelligent auditing and risk assessment.

Fifth, the plan seeks more comprehensive construction of the audit infrastructure. The National Audit Work Plan (2006–2010) proposed to strengthen auditing in three basic aspects: conducting scientific audit management, audit control, and audit technology. It also stressed the need to strengthen infrastructure construction in five aspects: vigorous promotion of the building of the audit team, audit legalization, audit informatization, audit theory construction, audit culture construction, and consolidation of the foundations for the sustainable development of the audit cause.

(3) Creation and Implementation of the Audit Work Plan

(a) Creation

The audit work plan is also called the audit strategy management plan. To formulate a good plan, it is necessary to use the knowledge of strategic management, process related information, explore audit rules, predict future audit trends using scientific methods, study and judge the ideal state of auditing, comply with system theory requirements, and rely on certain technical approaches. The essence of the audit work plan is to seek and establish optimal strategic development goals as a whole.

There are four stages:

1. **Analyze and study various types of information to determine strategic objectives.** Make clear the objectives for the period to be covered,

identifying dominant objectives and their relationship with subordinate objectives, and opportunities and threats in the process of achieving them.

2. **Study alternative measures and methods for achieving strategic objectives.** On the basis of predicting the external environment and internal conditions of audit work, study the ways of achieving goals and identify options. The external environment refers to the social, political, and economic situation directly influencing and restricting audit work, and is the basic premise of carrying out audit work and the main basis for determining audit focus and tasks. Internal conditions refer to the audit institutional environment, and quality and quantity of personnel, materials, and equipment essential to accomplishing the strategic goals.

3. **Predict the possibilities and results of achieving the audit strategy management goals determined in various plans.** Whether audit strategy management goals can be achieved depends on their scientific quality, the applicability of audit resources, and the validity of audit methods and ways. When setting audit strategy management goals, we should be able to predict the possibility and effect of various plans, and their potential contribution in achieving primary and secondary goals, and intermediate and ultimate goals. Only then can we determine specific plans.

4. **Conduct assessment and reach decisions.** The audit strategy management plan is validated and approved by the decision-makers of audit institutions on the basis of scientific assessment.

(b) Implementation

After the development of an audit strategy management plan, the internal and external agencies of audit institutions should implement specific measures according to their own situation, create annual and rolling plans, determine the respective departments or personnel in charge, designate clear responsibilities, strengthen process control, and try to meet all planning requirements. In the process of achieving strategic planning objectives, audit institution should arrange to inspect the implementation of plans, conduct general studies, and offer suggestions for work improvement, to ensure the implementation of the audit strategy management plan and specific requirements.

The National Audit Work Plan (2008–2012) is a guideline and strategic plan for the specific period. Significant results have been achieved in practicing the guiding ideology and achieving fundamental tasks and goals as stipulated. The 12th Five-Year Plan for National Audit Work more accurately reflects the new audit requirements proposed in the Outline of the National 12th Five-Year Plan, new achievements of the tracking and performance audits, and new provisions regarding the accountability audit, and also sums up the new experience of audit work, practical achievements in the coordinated approach to the public finance audit, and changes of basic audit work, thus becoming a more scientific and operational guide for overall audit work. Since the implementation of the plan, the audit project organization mode featuring varied professional fields and profound analysis has become the norm. In particular, audit institution has organized unified auditing of the local government debt, the national social security fund, the national government debt, stock funds, the national land transfer payments, and cultivated land transfer payment and expenditure, with great results.

 ## IV. AUDIT PLAN MANAGEMENT

As the sum of the activities related to the audit plan, audit plan management is the central thread integrating audit resources. Audit plan management sets performance targets for an audit institution during the plan period and determines the audit tasks and the needed audit resources. Making an audit business rolling plan is essential for the management of audit plans, which should make clear the steps for achieving the overall objectives set in the audit work plan, and also the measures for decomposing and achieving performance goals. Making an annual audit plan is a process of determining each project plan, and also allocating audit resources.

Procedures of audit plan management in chronological order are as follows: investigate and collect audit demands, conduct feasibility studies, identify alternative audit projects and priorities, assess and allocate audit resources, prepare, issue, and adjust the audit plan, manage the audit work plan, and check and evaluate the implementation of the audit project.

In recent years, audit plan management has undergone changes in five aspects: (1) improving the efficiency of planning by adjusting the planning year and planning period; (2) putting forward and implementing a coordinated approach to public finance audit by strengthening integration of audit resources, and meeting the requirements of audit work reports and audit result reports; (3) doing a good job of resource integration, making effective exploration in building a resource integration platform, and making scientific exploration in audit resources allocation; (4) unifying the national audit work, and organizing the implementation of a number of large national audit projects; and (5) enhancing the level of information management of audit planning, and, by exploiting available software installed in various audit institutions' statistical software in national audit institutions at all levels, collecting and analyzing audit results of audit institutions at various levels with regard to audit project arrangement, execution, resource input, and audit results.

(1) Management Objectives

Audit plan management is an integral part of audit management, so objectives of plan management should be included. Audit management aims to make audit better play its "immune system" role of safeguarding the healthy development of the economy and society. Audit plan management also aims to ensure limited audit resources are allocated to the most urgent projects on the basis of available audit resources, and in accordance with the principles of working within one's capabilities, overall planning, and being reasonable and balanced. It also aims to bring into full play the overall effect of audit resources by leaving room, avoiding repetition, and reducing overlap. Audit plan management should focus on preparation, implementation, summary, and assessment of project plans. The specific objectives for management are as follows:

- **Objectives of planning management:** All audit plan contents should be true, scientific, and reliable, and the audit focus should be determined according to the major work plans of the Party and governments, and reflect the principle of comprehensively auditing and highlighting the main focus; audit plan procedures should be compliant and reasonable; audit plan tasks should be assigned to and implemented by related departments and personnel; and clear targets and requirements should be set for each plan task, and targets and requirements should be consistent and balanced.
- **Objectives of plan implementation management:** In view of the complexity of audit work and the unpredictability of economic activities of the audited unit, the objectives are to master progress, understand information, study and seek to expose the defects and shortcomings in plan implementation, undertake measures in a timely way, and adjust plan contents to ensure the smooth implementation of the audit plan.
- **Objectives of plan results management:** The objectives are to inspect and assess the rationality of audit projects, and audit the implementation of quality control measures, project implementation quality, the progress of achieving audit objectives, and cost control; undertake measures to further improve plan management through inspection and assessment, and sum up lessons and experience.

According to the requirements for management objectives, the following shortcomings should be overcome: insufficient connection with audit strategy management; contradiction between audit work and available audit resources; and business-oriented sectors of audit institutions failing to meet the need of the new organization mode.

(2) Management Contents

Management controls mainly include audit plan management and audit work program management.

(a) Audit Plan Management

An audit plan refers to the arrangement made by audit institutions in accordance with the statutory audit responsibilities and the audit jurisdictional scope, and covering projects that need to be audited in a certain period. By project type, audit plans can be divided into unified audit plans, authorized audit plans, and customized audit plans. The unified audit plan is made by an audit institution to better perform its audit responsibilities, conduct unified planning and arrangements for the audit tasks within the audit jurisdiction, and organize audit groups or audit institutions to jointly implement an auditing project or implement similar programs. The authorized audit plan is one under which the superior audit institution delegates projects under its jurisdiction to a subordinate audit institution, and is a necessary supplement to the unified audit plan and an effective way of expanding audit coverage. The customized audit plan is the arrangement made by an audit institution upon entrustment of relevant departments, according to the actual conditions of local economic and social development and the resource situation, to meet the requirements of Party committees and governments.

An audit plan mainly includes the following contents: audit project name; audit objectives—namely, expected tasks and results; audit scope—namely, the unit, the various matters, and the period involved in the audit project; audit focus—namely, the contents and activities needing attention in the audit process; the unit organizing and implementing the audit project; and audit resources, including human resources, funds, equipment, and other elements. Audit institution can prepare the annual audit plan in the form of a text, a table, or in combination. A true, scientific, and accurate basis and reasonable procedures are necessary for making the audit plan, and clear objectives and requirements, and audit resources, should be available for various tasks.

Audit institutions conduct extensive research, collect audit demands, and initially select projects by understanding, mastering, and studying the trends of macroeconomic information and policies, visiting relevant departments, including the people's Congress, the people's Political Consultative Conference, Organizational Department, Discipline Inspection Commission, Development and Reform Commission, and the Finance Department, convening a consultation meeting of experts and scholars, seeking the opinions of internal and subordinate audit agencies, and so forth. In the process of collecting audit demands, preliminary selection of audit projects mainly involves: national and regional financial revenue and expenditure, related economic activities, major government work, audit requirements of administrative heads and related leading organs of the local government at the same level, matters a superior audit institution arranges or authorizes, matters that a related department requests audit institutions to check and audit, matters reported by the public, and matters needing audit after analysis of related data.

Audit institutions should conduct the feasibility study of audit projects preliminarily selected to determine audit objectives, audit scope, audit priorities, and other matters. The feasibility study of audit projects should focus on relevant laws, regulations, and policies, the management system related to the audited unit and its organizational structure, main businesses and operating situation, financial revenue and expenditure, relevant information systems and electronic data, previous annual audits, relevant management and supervision bodies, and the situation and the results of supervision and inspection.

On the basis of the feasibility studies, audit institutions should carry out grading on alternative audit projects according to their importance to national economic and social development, the extent of the concern expressed by administrative heads, related leading organs, and the public, the scale of funds and assets, and other factors. It also needs to assess the risks of projects according to factors such as project scale, management, and control status, objectively judging the expected effect of an audit, and comprehensively determine the audit project priorities by referring to previous audit frequency and coverage, and audit resource requirements. Audit institution should draft its audit plan according to priorities and available resources. If necessary, it can organize experts to check the draft plan. After seeking the opinions of various parties and obtaining approval in accordance with working procedures, audit institutions should submit the draft plan to the administrative head of the local government at the same level for the purpose of approval, report it to the superior audit institution, create a formal plan, and finally distribute this to the unit assigned to implement the audit project.

Upon issuance of the project plan, the implementing unit should strictly follow instructions, ensure completion, and make no changes without permission. Due to the complexity of audit work and the unpredictability of economic activities of the audited unit, the plan inevitably will have to be adjusted during implementation. This should be subject to the principle of "he who issues, adjusts" (i.e., the audit institution issuing the audit plan will make adjustments in accordance with working procedures).

In order to ensure implementation, audit institutions should conduct the all-dimensional and whole-process management of any audit plan, and strengthen planning and implementation control. The audit institution implements the system of reporting the audit plan—that is, the implementing unit should report the project implementation situation to the audit institution issuing the audit plan. The latter should regularly check the situation of implementing the annual audit plan, and assess performance. Apart from the regular progress checks, audit institutions should also strengthen the inspection and assessment of the entity being audited and the eventual audit results.

(b) Audit Work Program Management

The audit work program refers to the planning and arrangements made by audit institutions to smoothly complete the audit tasks and achieve the expected audit objectives. It is a written instruction for guiding an orderly and effective audit. For a unified audit project, the audit work program as the refined audit plan is the intermediate link between plan and actual audit. It is prepared by the business department of audit institutions and is implemented by the relevant audit institution or audit team. It is often issued as a formal document and generally consists of two parts: text and form. After preparing the audit work program, the business department will submit it for approval by the responsible leader of audit institution, and then distribute it to the audit team or subordinate audit institution undertaking the actual tasks. The program for an important audit project should be audited by an audit business meeting or the responsible person of audit institution.

When preparing the audit work program, the business department should conduct further investigation according to the audit needs of annual audit plans to determine audit objectives, scope, focus, and project implementation, as well as other elements. In the process of preparing the work program, the business department responsible for organizing and implementing the audit project should conduct extensive investigation and research according to the annual audit plan, select representative projects for trial audit if necessary, and then prepare the final audit work program. In drafting, the business department should solicit opinions of relevant departments to ensure the plan is scientific, rational, and highly operational.

The audit work program includes: audit objectives, audit scope, audit contents and focus, audit organization and arrangements, and audit requirements. It must be approved pursuant to prescribed procedures. Before approving the audit work program, audit institution may, as needed, organize experts to run a test. Prior to the starting time of the audit as stipulated in the annual audit plan, audit institutions should distribute the program to the unit undertaking the audit tasks. The latter may apply to adjust the program according to changes in the related audit situation, but must obtain approval.

(c) New Situation of Audit Plan Management

Audit plan management is closely related to the external environment. To consciously incorporate auditing into overall economic and social development, it is necessary to pay attention to changes in the external environment on the premise of maintaining audit independence. This is an essential feature of auditing, but one-sided emphasis on it will affect and possibly harm the relationship between the audit and the external environment. Audit practices in recent years show that the audit work cannot be separated from the external environment. To make an audit more effective, it is necessary to pay close attention to changes in the external environment.

For the purpose of achieving a better audit, it is necessary to strengthen audit plan management, effectively integrate audit resources, improve audit modes, and continuously expand the depth and breadth of the audit process. Judging by the practice of the two government debt audits, if work is done in accordance with the role played by original audit institutions, it is difficult to fully understand the government debt scale structure, and objectively evaluate the risks. This fails to serve decision making. In the practice of central budget implementation auditing and local government fiscal revenue and expenditure auditing, an audit institutions break the traditional division of work by working together and, at the same time, pay attention to the central and local government departments in their allocation, management, and use of funds for environmental protection, agriculture, forestry, and water conservancy. This gives full play to the role of audit institutions in a constructive way.

V. AUDIT QUALITY MANAGEMENT

(1) Connotation of Audit Quality Management

Audit quality management refers to the organization, control, and supervision activities carried out by an audit institution and individual auditors to achieve audit objectives and ensure audit quality according to prescribed standards. This definition involves the three connotative levels:

1. **All those involved are the subjects of audit quality management.** Although people's congresses, governments, and other organizations may raise audit quality requirements, relevant departments, the audited units themselves, and even the public can also evaluate and monitor audit quality. Fundamentally, however, it is the auditing profession that should undertake the necessary active measures.

2. **Audit quality management mainly focuses on complying with prescribed standards and achieving required audit objectives.** Audit quality is mainly reflected in two aspects: (1) Whether the auditors comply with national laws, regulations, and standards in regard to auditing responsibilities, authorities, procedures, and business processes, and whether the auditing work is normalized; essentially, this is a procedural requirement. (2) Whether the audit work and results meet expected objectives, and reflect the basic national requirements and the basic strategy of audit institutions; this focuses on the audit end result. These two aspects are interrelated and inseparable. Legal and standardized audit activities are conductive to safeguarding audit results, and good audit results can't be separated from normalization of audit behavior.

3. **It reflects the requirements for comprehensive quality management.** To achieve this, it is necessary to have the participation of all auditors and the comprehensive and whole-process quality management of audit operation activities. Before auditing, a lot of careful preparation is needed. In the process of implementing the audit project and reporting audit results, it is necessary to mainly control the quality of relevant activities, including audit plan preparation, acquiring and recording evidence, and audit reporting. After project auditing, it is necessary to inspect and supervise the overall quality, analyze any emerging problems, and ensure they don't recur.

(2) Objectives of Audit Quality Management

According to Chinese laws and regulations, and the requirements and expectations of all governments, leading institutions, and the public, the main objectives of audit quality management are as follows:

- **Complying with national laws, regulations, and auditing standards.** Participating auditors should implement relevant provisions and requirements of the audit procedures, work flow, and various links already laid down, perform duties, authorities, and objectives granted in accordance with laws, regulations, and auditing standards, and continuously meet the audit requirements and expectations of the state and the people.
- **Issuing qualified audit reports.** The audit report is the main product of audit work, reflecting the results in a concentrated way. Firstly, a qualified audit report should affirm that audit objectives have been fully achieved. It should reveal the problems that violate laws and regulations and affect performance, to maintain national economic security and strengthen construction of clean government. The audit report should also focus on revealing relevant system defects and problems of policy implementation and management, proposing improvement suggestions about systems, mechanisms, and institutions, and fully playing the constructive role and the "immune system" function of auditing. Secondly, it should also include necessary elements, meet basic requirements, have complete contents, clear facts, and correct conclusions, and be submitted promptly.
- **Disposal and punishment according to law.** Chinese audit institutions have the right to dispose and punish audited units violating provisions related to financial revenue. In doing so, they should comply with procedures and requirements for audit authorities and relevant financial regulations on the conditions, nature, and scope of disposal and punishment as prescribed. On the other hand, audit institutions should analyze the nature of any problems and amounts involved, consider subjective and objective causes and the historical background and environment, and analyze and study the impact of problems on the audited unit and social economic development, so as to conduct fair disposal and punishment.

(3) Main Contents and Ways of Audit Quality Management

To reflect the concept of and requirements for comprehensive quality management, global audit organizations and those of western countries including the United States have put forward six essential requirements for audit quality management: (1) They stress the leadership responsibility for audit quality. The leadership of an audit institution should rationally divide internal management responsibilities, develop a quality management system, and build a quality-oriented audit culture through demonstration and information transmission. (2) There is the aspect of audit ethics. Audit institutions should establish appropriate policies and systems and maintain independence and abide by audit ethics, thus forming the audit value guarantee for audit quality management. (3) There is a focus on audit arrangements. Audit institutions should fully understand the audited objects, and take audit resources and time into full account in determining audit tasks, so as to achieve high-quality audits. (4) There is the vital aspect of human resources. Auditors should have appropriate professional competence and service quality. (5) There is the actual audit implementation. Auditing should be conducted in accordance with laws, regulations, and auditing standards, and a qualified audit report should be issued. (6) There is the aspect of quality control. Through regular supervision, inspection, and external peer review, quality management policies and systems should be implemented appropriately and effectively. These six elements are the main contents of audit quality management. Audit institutions should establish specific quality management systems and conduct quality control based on the actual situation.

The means of achieving audit quality management are: The leadership responsibility for audit quality can be performed mainly through establishment and improvement of relevant rules and regulations, and leadership behavior; audit ethics can be cultivated mainly by establishing and improving the professional codes and rules, strengthening auditors' self-accomplishment, conducting typical demonstrations, establishing an ethics evaluation and education system, and so on; better audit task arrangement can be achieved mainly through strengthening audit plan management; better use of human resources can be achieved mainly through hiring auditors and external experts, conducting continuous education, strengthening training and practices, and establishing a quality-oriented performance evaluation, assessment, and incentive system; operations can be conducted smoothly mainly through controlling the audit process, audit behavior, and audit results; quality monitoring can be achieved mainly through various supervisory, inspection, and quality responsibility investigations.

Audit plan management has been elaborated in Section IV of this chapter; the leadership responsibility for audit quality and the audit ethics will be described in, respectively, Chapter 7 and Chapter 9, and human resources will be discussed in Section VIII of this chapter. This part focuses on the main content and specific approaches in regard to operations and audit quality control.

(4) Audit Quality Management

Audit services mainly include auditing and forming audit results. This part will mainly describe the key work and management measures for controlling the quality of preparing the audit plan, collecting audit evidence, and forming audit results.

(a) Audit Plan Quality Management

To achieve audit objectives, the audit plan should include the contents, ways, and persons of audit, and key work of quality control.

> **Step 1: Accurately determine the audit items and objectives.** A guiding and operational audit plan should make clear specific audit items. The more concrete and refined the audit items, the clearer the audit contents. These audit items may cover certain business activities of the audited unit, one or several funding incomes and expenses, and certain problems. Meanwhile, we should point out audit directions by item, make clear any questions and possible results, and determine audit objectives.
>
> **Step 2: Select the appropriate audit steps and methods.** After audit items are determined, it is necessary to select the audit paths and breakthrough methods. An audit item might require identifying multiple paths and methods for implementation; we should select the most efficient, easiest, and most economical paths. For some other audit items, regular audit methods may not be applicable, and specific breakthrough methods will then be brought into play.
>
> **Step 3: Rationally allocate the audit team's resources.** The team should rationally divide the work according to the characteristics of the audit items, as well as auditors' knowledge, ability, and experience, and fully consider the audit progress so as to allocate sufficient funds and time.

The key work of quality control mentioned earlier should be carried out mainly through the following management measures:

1. **Fully understanding the relevant situation of the audited unit.** Based on the audited unit's organization structure, business activities, industry status, financial and fiscal management system, balance of payments, the situation of implementing relevant laws, regulations, and

policies, and of previously receiving audits and supervisions, audit institutions should analyze possible problems and then develop a clear understanding of the conditions of the control environment, risk assessment, control activities, information sharing and communication, control supervision, internal control and implementation, and information system and electronic data construction. On this basis, audit institutions should analyze whether the internal control conditions of the audited unit are enough to prevent possible problems from appearing, and to lay a firm foundation for determining audit items and objectives. Further investigation of the audited unit will contribute to more accurate audit items being determined and more instructive audit plans emerging.

2. **Assessing possible important problems.** If problems emerge in the audited unit found after investigation and analysis, the audit team needs to hold group discussions, and possibly recruit experts to assess their importance from the perspectives of nature, amount, and specific environment so as to make clear the specific audit scope, items, and objectives.

3. **Determining audit response measures.** After audit items and objectives are determined, it is necessary to consider the actual situation of the audit team and the audited unit according to the audit objectives, and determine audit steps and methods item-by-item. As to important audit items, experienced auditors and adequate audit time should be allocated, and experts can be hired if necessary. For the audited unit subject to information system auditing and electronic data analysis, audit institutions should allocate competent staff or experts, and determine specific methods for inspection and analysis. For problems that may constitute major violations of the law or suspected economic crimes, special arrangements should be made in terms of inspection scope, method, personnel allocation, and audit time.

4. **Adjusting the audit plan in a timely way.** The quality of the audit plan depends on the degree of understanding of the audited unit's situation. In the short term, it is difficult to deeply understand a large audited unit with complex businesses or the business areas with which auditors are not familiar, and the process of "practice/cognition/repractice/recognition" will then be necessary. Therefore, the investigation, understanding, and cognition of an audited unit usually run through the whole process. Audit institutions may then need to update, revise, and refine the original audit ideas and adjust the audit plan. The audit team head can handle this in a timely way according to the investigation situation, except in the case of major adjustments of audit plans or programs for major projects. The audit

team head should record the plan adjustment situation in a convenient and efficient way.

(b) Audit Evidence Quality Management

Collecting evidence is one of the main tasks of audit work. Auditors implement an audit plan, collect audit evidence, draw audit conclusions, and finally draw up audit reports. The highlights of audit evidence quality control are as follows:

- **The sufficiency of audit evidence is a quantity measurement indicator.** Every audit conclusion must be supported by audit evidence, without subjective assumption; audit evidence collected must be sufficient to prove all elements of the audit item and draw correct audit conclusions.
- **The appropriateness of audit evidence is a quality measurement indicator.** Audit evidence should be relevant—that is, be substantively linked with audit items and objectives; and it should be reliable, true, and credible.

The highlights of audit evidence quality control are mainly subject to the following management measures:

- **Selecting the appropriate mode and method of collecting evidence.** The auditor must select a method that can obtain effective evidence for each audit item. Meanwhile, the auditor, according to the needs of audit conclusions, may investigate and collect evidences for all audit items or some specific items, or obtain sufficient audit evidences through the audit sampling mode.
- **Collecting audit evidence for elements of the audit conclusions.** Generally speaking, four elements should be present to draw an audit conclusion: criteria—namely, what it should be; and fact—namely, the actuality (the difference between the displayed fact and the required standard will constitute an audit problem); influence—namely, consequences; and causes—namely, why the problem has occurred. The auditor should collect audit evidence linked to these elements and ensure it is closely related to the audit conclusion.
- **Taking further measures to deal with conflicting evidence.** This should be consistent and mutually provable. If evidence of different sources and different types conflict, at least some of it may not be true. In this case, the auditor must remain on high alert, and take further measures to ensure reliability of audit evidences.

- ▪ **Guiding, reviewing, and supervising evidence collection and audit recording.** During auditing, the auditor should continuously evaluate the sufficiency and appropriateness of evidence. The audit team head should guide members to obtain evidence and then review it, organize research and discussion, or consult external experts. The audit team head should guide members to draft the complete audit plan in a timely manner, and then check audit processes, evidence, and audit, and review the audit draft.

(c) Audit Results Quality Management

Audit results are conclusions reflected in an audit report or other form. The highlights of the audit result quality control are as follows:

- ▪ **Accuracy of audit facts.** Audit conclusions should be based on facts. The facts and data must be accurate and consistent with the objective facts. Secondly, audit facts must be clear and complete, making clear the major parts of important items, and reflecting the relevant facts completely based on the four elements previously listed—criteria, facts, influences, and causes.
- ▪ **The focus must be on the correctness of audit conclusions.** These include comments on audit items, opinions or suggestions on disposal and punishment regarding violations of the laws and regulations, and suggestions for improving the system and performance and strengthening management. Audit institutions should put forward proper audit opinions based on facts, relevant laws, regulations, and standards, and according to the actual situation.
- ▪ **These must involve normalization of audit document formats.** Audit documents reflect the audit results and conclusions, and are binding upon the audited unit, affecting its interests. Standard audit documents are conducive to the proper understanding and implementation of the audited unit.

The highlights of audit result quality control are mainly due to the following management measures:

1. **The audit team brainstorming system.** After the end of an on-site audit, the team will discuss the audit situation and give opinions, which are the basis of forming audit results and an important guarantee for improving their quality. The audit team should evaluate the situation of achieving audit objectives, the sufficiency and appropriateness of audit evidence, and the importance of any problems uncovered, put forward opinions on

disposal and punishment, as well as the overall evaluation opinions and audit suggestions, and finally form audit reports and other documents.

2. **Business department review system.** The business department establishing the audit team, or to which it belongs, guides and supervises the field audit, and controls the audit results quality from an overall perspective and higher level. The review by the business department should be comprehensive, and cover all audit documents, as well as audit evidence, audit draft, and audited unit feedback.

3. **The audit project review system.** According to the requirements of "establishing and improving the power structure and operation mechanism featured by the interaction and coordination between decision-making, executive, and supervisory power" raised in the Report at the 17th Party Congress, the National Audit Work Plan (2008–2012) proposed to make the audit plans and implement and review the system for managing audit items that separate and constrain each other. On the basis of past experience, the audit project review system was established in 2010. The Regulations for the Implementation of the Audit Law of the People's Republic of China and the National Auditing Standards of the People's Republic of China treat this system as an important audit quality management system. Under it, the specialized review agency independent from the audit, based on the audit plan, focuses on the audit processes and results, comprehensively reviews audit information, and listens to the opinions of audit institution, to make an independent judgment and put forward opinions or suggestions on disposal and punishment. Audit review is audit process supervision, and is essential to form audit results. The review agency should review the audit procedure execution situation, the audit plan and its implementation situation, the sufficiency and appropriateness of evidence, integrity of audit records, factual accuracy of audit documents, and the correctness of applicable laws and regulations. In addition, it should propose review opinions, directly propose or modify the disposal and punishment opinions of audit institution, directly modify and form audit documents, and report to the responsible person of audit institution for approval.

4. **The system of examining and approving audit results by the responsible person of audit institution.** This person, on behalf of an audit institution, examines and approves audit results, and signs and issues audit documents. According to the importance of the audit results, he or she can examine and approve audit results by directly examining and approving or deciding to convene a conference.

(5) Audit Quality Supervision and Inspection and Accountability

In addition to the quality management of audit processes and results, ex-post external supervision and inspection should be strengthened, and major audit quality problems exposed.

(a) Internal Quality Inspection System of audit institution

Many foreign audit institutions have established a peer review system, under which an audit institution invites other audit institutions or audit agencies to regularly supervise and inspect its audit quality management situation. According to audit management system requirements and actual conditions, China's audit institutions implement an internal quality inspection system, under which the audit quality management department not involved in auditing independently checks the audit quality of those involved in the actual audit, puts forward inspection opinions and suggestions for the audited unit to correct and rectify problems, and promotes strengthening and improving audit quality management.

The main contents of audit quality inspection are: Inspect the situation of establishing and improving the audit quality management system, and expose major shortcomings and obvious disadvantages of the quality management system. Inspect the implementation of the audit quality management system, expose major problems of failing to strictly comply with laws, regulations, auditing standards, and internal rules of audit institution on audit quality management, and analyze the causes and impacts. Check the completed audit items, expose major problems of failure to implement the audit plan, obtain sufficient and appropriate audit evidence, reveal the outstanding problems of the audited unit or dispose and punish according to law, and finally put forward measures for correction and disposal.

(b) Internal Hierarchical Audit Supervision System

China's audit institutions are responsible for leading subordinate agencies in audit work. In accordance with the Audit Law of the People's Republic of China and its implementation regulations, audit institution supervises the operations of subordinate audit agencies, requiring them to modify or cancel audit decisions violating relevant state provisions, or directly change or revoke the decisions. The Outline for Promoting Law-Based Administration in an all-around way promulgated by the State Council in March 2004 also provides for the superior audit institution to innovate a hierarchical supervision system, and establish and improve the system of regular supervision, especially the specific administrative acts of subordinate audit agencies. Through quality inspection, the application of the audited unit for reconsideration, or appeals, media coverage and public reporting, or any other channel, the superior audit institution can find major quality problems of subordinate audit agencies in regard to disposal and punishment, correct them according to the law, and strengthen supervision.

(c) External Audit Supervision System

External supervision of audit quality is achieved mainly in four aspects: Firstly, supervision by the NPC and government through instruction and requirements for strengthening audit quality management, and handling administrative reconsideration or judgmental matters. Secondly, there is supervision by relevant functional departments, such as judicial offices through the hearing of administrative litigation cases, and supervision through investigating and handling audit transfer matters. Thirdly, supervision can be performed by the audited unit by raising objections to the draft audit report, taking relief measures, or lodging complaints if disagreeing with the audit decision. Fourthly, there is public supervision, the media's critical reporting, and so on.

(d) Audit Quality Accountability System

In case any auditor causes a major quality accident due to willful misconduct or gross negligence, violation of laws, regulations, auditing standards, and other regulations, he/she shall be investigated for criminal responsibility, which is an important guarantee for implementing an audit quality management system, and also a necessity for administration by law. Many auditors usually jointly implement an audit plan and form audit results. The following work should be done for implementation of the audit quality accountability system: making clear the management duties of the audit team head and its members, personnel from the business department to which the audit team belongs, the personnel from the review agency, and the responsible person of the audit institution; according to the division of auditing duties, providing definitions of direct responsibility, review responsibility, and leadership responsibility, and determining procedures for the disposal of responsible personnel; and when a major quality accident is discovered through audit quality inspection, administrative audit reconsideration, administrative litigation, government arbitration, public reporting, and so on, dealing with the responsible auditors according to the law.

VI. AUDIT RESULTS MANAGEMENT

Audit results management is an extension of the audit and an important part of the whole audit management. Strengthening the management of audit results is an important method and way to enhance the audit efficiency and audit results, and is of great significance to prevent the loss of audit results, improve the audit level, and enhance the effect of audit supervision.

(1) Connotation of Audit Results

Audit results reflect the effects or benefits of audit—that is, finding out the real situation and existing problems, putting forward suggestions for improving the work and system, promoting problem solving, and eventually converting into administrative power and productivity. Basically speaking, auditing is an "immune system" to safeguard the healthy development of the national economy and society, and the audit results reflect the "immune system" functions in three aspects: handling and correcting problems in violation of laws and regulations, promoting income increases and cost savings, improving fund usage efficiency, and directly reflecting the economic benefits of audit; improving the systems and strengthening management to create a good system for economic development, and indirectly reflecting the economic benefits of auditing; and providing real and reliable information to governments and the public, standardizing management, urging all walks of life to pay attention to, participate in, and supervise national financial revenue and expenditure activities, promoting administration according to the law and making government affairs public, and improving the credibility and executive force of government departments, thus reflecting the social benefits of auditing.

From the perspective of management, audit results usually are divided into two categories. Firstly, audit results can be further divided into two categories by content: (1) Major problems found during auditing that need to be solved by relevant parties, including the problems concerning the audited unit, and problems affecting normal audit, such as audit resistance, lack of audit forces, mismatching of audit laws and regulations, and large audit risks. This is one of the most important audit results, and embodies audit operational results in a centralized way. For such problem results, audit institutions should analyze the causes and propose a solution. (2) Experience results—namely, various experience and practices generated or revealed during auditing, including the advanced experience and best practices of an audit institution and the audited unit. Secondly, audit results can be further divided into four categories by carrier: (1) decision results, such as audit decisions; (2) report results, such as audit reports, audit investigation reports, audit results reports, audit work reports, special audit reports, and audit results announcements; (3) suggestion results, such as audit proposals and audit transfer disposal documents; and (4) information results, such as key audit information, important information catalogues, audit briefing, information transfer letters, audit work correspondences, and audit dynamics.

(2) Objective of Managing Audit Results

Managing audit results must fully reflect the overall audit objective, and play a positive role in promoting and facilitating its implementation. Meanwhile, according to the principle of maximizing management benefits, the audit results should also be maximized.

- To achieve the overall audit objective, audit results management should meet three requirements: (1) allowing the superior audit agencies and related audit parties to understand the realities of the audited unit, including the overall situation of financial management, achievements, outstanding problems, and the degree of seriousness, causes, and means for solution; (2) urging the audited unit to rectify audit problems; and (3) ensuring the public understands the audited unit's financial management status in order to form powerful social opinion supervision, and urge the unit to enhance its responsibility for its performance and strengthening its management.

- To improve audit performance, audit results management should maximize the audit results (i.e., achieve greater results with fewer audit resources). Specifically speaking, audit institutions should combine audit results management with audit organization: focusing on the problems involving the large amount, hazard, and impact on the basis of analyzing and studying the audited unit; and playing a constructive and proactive role—audit institutions should have both micro- and macroviews, and focus on putting forward specific opinions and suggestions to improve systems and policies, so as to fundamentally solve problems. Audit institutions should improve efficiency, integrate and use internal and external resources through scientific management methods and advanced technologies, highlight rectification and reform, and promote openness, so as to maximize the utilization of audit resources and results.

(3) Usage of Audit Results

At present, usage of audit results is as follows:

1. **Audit reporting system.** For projects organized by theCNAO, the comprehensive audit report should be submitted to government after the audit results are summarized. For problems concerning the major special projects found in the audit, the special audit report should be submitted to government.
2. **System of annual audit results report and work report.** The CNAO conducts audit supervision on central budget performance and other financial revenue and expenditure situations and makes an audit result report to the Premier. Local audit institutions at various levels conduct audit supervision on corresponding level's budget performance and other financial revenue and expenditure situations and report results to the local people's government and audit institution at the upper level. At the same time, audit institutions at all levels annually produce an audit work report of the corresponding level's budget performance and other financial revenue and expenditure to the corresponding Standing Committee of the local people's congress, upon the entrustment of local governments.
3. **Audit results announcement system.** Audit institutions make public the audit results while ensuring the safety of state secrets and the business secrets of audited units according to law, and abide by the relevant regulations of the State Council.
4. **System of disposing matters in violation of rules.** For financial revenue and expenditure as well as related behavior in violation uncovered by an audit, audit institutions should take care to stay within their legitimate authority and the laws in making decisions on disposal and punishment. For matters needing to be transferred to the competent authorities or units to correct, dispose, and punish, or needing investigation of the responsibility of relevant personnel, audit institution must issue a letter of audit transfer and handling.
5. **Audit information reporting system.** For the clues to major cases concerning violation of laws and rules, and universal and emerging problems found in the audit, audit institutions need to submit relevant information to governments individually.
6. **System of correcting problems found in the audit.** According to the Audit Law, governments at various levels should report the rectification and disposal results of problems detailed in the audit work report to the

Standing Committee of the local people's congress. If the stipulations concerning financial revenues of higher authorities performed by the audited units violate laws and rules, audit institutions should suggest correction by the competent authorities. If the relevant authorities do not handle them properly, the audit institutions can refer the matter to the institutions having the right to handle them according to law.

7. **System of transferring clues to cases and disciplinary violations.** During the investigation and treatment of illegal acts, if they seem to constitute a crime requiring investigation of relevant personnel for criminal liability, the audit institutions transfer the matter to the public security or procuratorial organs in a timely way according to relevant regulations. If involved personnel have to be investigated for administrative responsibility for illegal acts, the case should be passed to the supervisory organ in a timely way according to relevant regulations. Problems concerning surpassing the limits of authority of audit disposal and punishment should be transferred for investigation by the relevant administrative departments in charge according to regulations.

(4) Contents of Audit Results Management

Audit results management is important to enhance the audit effect. To process audit results deeply through audit results management, and provide more quality products with high technology contents and high-end products meeting various needs, audit institutions must determine the highlights of the expected audit results around the economic and social development priorities, constantly improve the quality and effectiveness of audit results, strengthen macro-analysis and integrated analysis, and improve the global and forward-looking nature of audit results. Specifically, audit results management involves four aspects.

(a) Standardizing Audit Results Carriers

In modern society, information is an important part of management activities, and indeed their ultimate purpose. That is to say, managers' ultimate goal is to obtain all sorts of valuable social, political, economic, scientific, technological, and cultural information. Audit institutions should try to build an audit results platform, with "two reports" as the core, and audit reports and audit information as the basis. Audit institution should strengthen unified management of audit projects, and comprehensively understand the situation of the audited unit, which helps master the situation systematically, reflect universal problems, improve the pertinence of the audit report, and provide extensive, comprehensive, and systematic materials for government decision making. In this way, even without an increase of audit resources and forces, audit institutions can better play their role of audit supervision. To this end, the following two aspects are important: firstly, striving to improve the quality and level of audit reports. Audit reports include the report issued by audit institutions after auditing, and the report issued after the special audit investigation.[2] Audit institutions should pay close attention to the standardization of audit reports, prepare and review them in strict accordance with the Audit Law of the PRC and implementation regulations, national auditing standards, and related provisions, and create a report characterized by complete contents, clear facts, correct conclusion, appropriate words, and standardized formats. Special audit investigation reports should focus on the problems regarding macro-aspects, universality, policies, institutions, or mechanisms according to specific objectives, and encourage suggestions for improvement. In addition, the audit report should also present comments on authenticity, legitimacy, and efficiency according to different audit objectives and the audit facts affirmed, on the premise of preventing audit risks, and in accordance with the principle of importance. Secondly, there is a need to improve the audit information work. Audit institutions should further improve and standardize the audit information management, make better overall planning of audit information, strengthen information transfer and feedback between superior and subordinate agencies, and enhance systematization and the initiative and timeliness of information work; seriously implement information accountability, better control quality, and ensure a report has clear facts, accurate nature determination, refined contents, specified format, and timely reflection. It is also vital to strengthen integrated analysis, improve the macro- and comprehensive level of information, and increase information of importance, high quality, large impact, and good effect.

(b) Improving Utilization of Audit Results

Audit results management must be strengthened: firstly, enhancing macro-awareness, with comprehensive, systematic, and dialectical thought, and conducting integrated use of audit results through summary, analysis, and integrated refinement. Secondly, it is vital to summarize common and regular problems according to concrete and microeconomic phenomena, grasp tendentious and sensitive issues, and offer valuable proposals in a timely manner for strengthening management, remedying system defects, and resolving social conflicts. Thirdly, it is necessary to broaden and deepen the use of audit results horizontally and vertically, and achieve multiple results for one audit and multiple uses of one result; standardize and educate a number of audited units through one audit; and improve the level of serving overall economic and social development by deeply mining the audit results.

(c) Expanding Channels for Use of Audit Results

At present, the audit results are reflected mainly in the form of an audit document and information briefing. The audit results are shared only by superior government departments and audited units, and liquidity is weak; thus their role cannot be fully displayed. Audit institutions can expand the channels for utilization of audit results in three aspects: firstly, expanding the scope of information disclosure, and forming joint forces supervising and managing an audited unit. On the premise of keeping national secrets and the commercial secrets of relevant units, audit institutions should send copies of audit opinions and audit decisions to the competent department of the audited unit, and report the related audit situation to the departments of Party committees, and discipline inspection and supervision, so they will understand in a timely way the related situation and will strengthen the management and supervision of audited units and other relevant departments accordingly. Secondly, there is a need to resolutely implement the system of announcing auditing results, and gradually standardize the forms, contents, and procedures of such announcements. The system of announcing auditing results is implemented to promote the rule of law, administration according to law, and development of the audit cause. It is necessary to announce the results of all audits and audit items except those involving national secrets, commercial secrets, and other information that cannot be disclosed to the public; release audit results information by taking full advantage of TV, newspaper, network, and various news media; guide the public to conduct indirect supervision of the audited units; urge audited units to exercise audit decisions through strong social opinion powers; and maximize the sharing and use of audit information (results). Thirdly, it is now necessary to accelerate the electronic dissemination of audit results and resources, and establish an audit information resource database; this needs the establishment of an information-sharing platform based on the government information network to share audit resources, promote in-depth application of audit results in the fields of administrative supervision, law enforcement supervision, cadre management, and macromanagement through more levels and channels, explore the approach of recording audit results in anticorruption databases and the personnel files of leading cadres from the audited unit, and regard them as the basis for assessment, promotion, communication, job transfer, and demotion.

(d) Enhancing the Effect of Utilizing Audit Results

The effect of utilizing audit results can be enhanced mainly through three measures: (1) strengthening quality control of audit results. Quality of audit results is the basis and prerequisite of determining their effect. Audit institutions should strictly regulate audit conduct, strengthen audit quality control, constantly improve the ability of auditing according to law, and ensure audit results are characterized by clear facts, accuracy, proper disposal, easy implementation, and operation. (2) It is necessary to establish an audit results track and inspection system and promote their transformation. Auditing aims to reveal problems and resolve them, which is more important. Whether the auditing decisions are effectively implemented determines whether the desired effect of audit supervision can be achieved, and whether the solemnity and authority of the audit supervision can be maintained. Therefore, audit institutions should strengthen the conversion of audit results, promote their application, supervise and inspect the situation of implementing and adopting any audit decision, audit opinion (audit report), or audit suggestion, track, analyze, and evaluate the situation of utilizing audit results and rectification, conduct follow-up auditing if necessary, and assist in correcting related problems found after auditing. (3) It is important to strengthen organizational leadership, improve systems, and make responsibilities clear. It is necessary to strengthen the cooperation with relevant departments during the application of audit results, and establish a sound reporting system, a system of supervision and inspection, an accountability system, and an information disclosure system for effective utilization of audit results. In addition, audit institutions should explore the establishment of a mechanism for coordinated utilization of audit results and the long-acting mechanism for rectification, improve the efficiency and effect of utilizing audit results, and further promote the role of audit supervision.

VII. AUDIT COST MANAGEMENT

The ultimate requirement for scientific auditing is to reduce audit costs, save audit resources, and maximize audit benefits, all to be achieved through scientific management.

(1) Connotation of Audit Costs

In a broad sense, cost is an economic concept, referring to the resources occupied or used by people for specific purposes in economic activity. In a narrow sense, cost is a value concept, referring to the entire fiscal expenditure for a certain activity. Audit cost also can be explained through use of both perspectives. In a broad sense, audit cost refers to the resources occupied or used by an audit institution in exercising its auditing duties, including all external and internal costs controllable and also uncontrollable by an audit institution within a certain period. In a narrow sense, audit cost refers to all fiscal expenditure an audit institution can control or influence. The following audit costs involve this latter sense: labor costs, such as basic staff costs and various expenses involved in staff training; daily public expenditures, including office expenses and other costs incurred by an audit institution; project expenditures, such as the expenditure for implementing an audit project; and other costs for resource occupation and consumption in exceptional circumstances, under the *force majeure* concept, such as accidents and natural disasters.

(2) Objectives of Audit Cost Management

Audit cost management refers to a series of approaches and measures taken by an audit institution to reduce audit costs and better perform auditing duties and functions by law. The ultimate goal is to reduce audit costs on the premise of improving audit quality and efficiency, so as to maximize the effect. Audit efficiency is the comparison between audit costs and the sum of economic and social benefits produced by the auditing results. So-called audit efficiency maximization means minimization of audit costs while maximizing economic and social benefits, or the maximization of audit efficiency under the condition of matching audit costs.

To better achieve the specific objectives of audit cost management, attention should be paid to the following two aspects: (1) It should not only focus on minimizing the costs; audit cost refers to the resources occupied and consumed to achieve an expected audit result. If minimizing the audit cost is the only goal, it may have an adverse impact on audit work and reduce quality. For example, some audit institutions and individual auditors may lower the audit objectives, thus increasing audit risks; some auditors may simplify the audit evidence-collection procedures, which lowers the pertinence and sufficiency of audit evidences; some auditors may use inappropriate audit methods, thus causing an erroneous audit judgment. (2) It should be combined with utilization of audit resources, innovation of audit technologies and methods, and integrated use of audit results. It is necessary to promote integration of audit resources, and maximize their utility through optimization of different auditors and audit departments; audit institutions should use more advanced, scientific, and economical audit ways and methods to improve audit efficiency; and they should promote integrated utilization of audit institutions and auditors, and in-depth development of audit results.

(3) Content of Audit Cost Management

This will be decided by factors of affecting overall audit cost. Audit work by nature can be divided into two categories—namely, audit administration and audit operation. The former refers to a series of activities for planning, organization, control, and distribution of labor, finance, and materials to guarantee a smooth audit operation. Audit operation refers to specific professional work as an important component of state power. Audit administration is a guarantee for an audit operation, and its level is directly related to the degree and effect of the latter; audit operation is the fundamental way of bringing into play the full audit function and role. Therefore, audit cost management mainly covers the cost and efficient management of audit administration and audit operation, aiming to improve the efficiency and effect of an audit institution in performing its supervisory duties.

(a) *Cost and Efficiency Management of Audit Administration*

This mainly aims to ensure an audit institution functions in an efficient and orderly way through administrative management, and seeks to reduce audit costs and enhance audit supervisory efficiency. As mentioned earlier, audit administration involves decision making, management, and implementation. Because different levels have different characteristics, duty ranges, and management objectives, the contents and methods for management of cost and efficiency should also differ.

(A) Cost and Efficiency Management of High-Level Organizations The efficiency of a high-level organization is mainly embodied in its organizational efficiency (i.e., improving the overall effect and saving audit resources through overall organization and coordination). Cost and efficiency management involves the following: improving the high-level leadership and decision mechanisms, ensuring the correctness, rationality, and feasibility of high-level decisions, and ensuring the plans and arrangements reflect clear objectives and proper coordination; establishing a system for efficient and smooth information transfer, and ensuring smooth channels, shortest paths, simple ways, and scientific and reasonable methods; and establishing a mechanism to ensure subordinates can understand and implement high-level decisions.

(B) Cost and Efficiency Management of a Middle-Level Organization   This mainly embodies organizational efficiency. Cost and efficiency management involves: guaranteeing the completeness and scientific efficiency of work plans; ensuring implementation measures are connected to high-level decisions; providing useful information and data for high-level decision making in a timely and accurate way, including feedback on the implementation of earlier high-level plans and policies; providing executive-level staff with guidance or coordination services in a timely and accurate way; strengthening integration of audit resources; and reducing audit costs through optimized allocation of resources.

(C) Cost and Efficiency Management at the Executive Level   This is mainly embodied as mechanical efficiency, and involves the following: establish and improve relevant operating norms and guidelines; strictly and efficiently implement relevant norms and guidelines; provide useful information and data for high-level decision making in a timely and accurate way; report or provide feedback on problems uncovered in accordance with stipulated procedures; and strive to achieve the purpose and requirements of the senior level.

(b) Cost and Efficiency Management of Audit Operation

Audit institutions meet social need through specific economic supervision. After the establishment of audit organizations, continuous operations are carried out. Any audit result is achieved by the input of certain audit costs. Audit results reflect the economic supervision functions of audit institutions in a concentrated way, and also comprehensively reflect the audit management effect. Audit operation benefits mainly consist of economic and social benefits. Therefore, the cost and efficiency management of audit operations is mainly embodied in the management of economic and social benefits.

(A) Management of Economic Benefits of Auditing   This refers to the proportion between an audit institution's input in time, labor, and funds, and the role of auditing in making up for economic losses and maintaining healthy economic development. Economic benefits of audit cannot be simply quantified; both quantitative and qualitative measurement must be adopted. By calculating and assessing the workload per unit of time, audit institutions can achieve a basic evaluation of audit efficiency, and then analyze the inputs and outputs for each audit item, so as to achieve the best audit effect and audit benefits with minimum input of labor, material, and financial resources and time. Currently, audit work focuses on central economic tasks, and economic benefit

management mainly involves the following aspects: concentrating resources and forces on important audit projects; optimizing work arrangements efficiently to save time and handle various audit problems quickly and accurately; paying attention to the integration of audit technologies and methods; and forming standardized operational procedures and technological methods.

(B) Management of Social Benefits of Auditing   This refers to the social contributions of the audit in promoting scientific and technological progress, protecting natural resources and the ecological environment, safeguarding national and social security, and improving national defense capabilities, people's material and cultural life and health conditions, and national governance. Social benefits are more difficult to quantify. The main audit function is supervisory, so as to promote democratic and political reform and socioeconomic development and safeguard stability. Therefore, it is necessary to maximize the social benefits of audit supervision, and effectively bring into full play the role of audit supervision in promoting political, economic, and social development. This mainly involves: first, focusing on strengthened detection of major violations of laws and regulations, an important means of utilizing the deterrent role of audit supervision—over the years, through detection of major violations of laws and regulations, especially detection of major cases, social influences of audit supervision have been significantly enlarged with better results; second, revealing the problems and improving systems and mechanisms simultaneously. Revealing problems is only a temporary solution, the fundamental approach being to identify defects and weaknesses in the control links and systems, and promote the establishment and improvement of systems, so as to fundamentally improve the social benefits of audit work. The third item is ensuring the objectivity and fairness of audit. Audit institutions need to promote a sound ethical approach, demonstrating overall professional ethics. By revealing problems and handling them objectively and fairly, audit institutions can help an audited unit to carry forward adherence to laws, and being honest, trustworthy, and upright for greater social benefit.

(4) Measures for Strengthening Audit Cost Management

(a) Strengthen Innovation of Auditing Technologies and Methods

Science and technology are the primary productive forces, and innovation is the driving force. Currently, audit institutions at all levels should constantly improve the technical contents, level of audit, and the innovation of audit methods and techniques, reduce consumption of audit resources, and improve audit efficiency through science and technology. The main measures are: to promote digitization of audit management, apply digital technologies to all aspects of administration and audit quality control, gradually establish and improve the national audit information fast channels and sharing platforms, and improve the overall digitization level of audit management; to vigorously promote computer audit technologies, explore the establishment of a networking track audit system characterized by online audit and real-time auditing, and strengthen the unified management of major projects, and real-time monitoring of field audit; and to improve the construction and application of a professional audit database according to the principle of "building and auditing simultaneously," and study and explore the exchange and sharing of professional audit data.

(b) Strengthen System Construction and Implementation, and Control Audit Costs at the Source

In a broad sense, "systems" refer to the political, economic, and cultural systems and mechanisms established under certain conditions. In a narrow sense, the term refers to work procedures or action guidelines formulated by a system or unit that all members should abide by. Systems are the standards for maintaining collective behavior, and work procedures or action norms. Good management systems and implementations can better promote the realization of audit objectives. The establishment and implementation of audit systems can be strengthened mainly through the following three measures: firstly, strengthening system construction and establishing long-term mechanisms; promoting the abolition, modification, and establishment of audit cost management systems; establishing sound operational management systems focusing on audit decision making, financial management, and business specification; achieving the goal of "having laws to abide by, having rules to follow, and having evidence for review"; paying close attention to the implementation of systems; strengthening supervision and inspection; and handling affairs in strict accordance with rules. Secondly, it is necessary to actively promote scientific decision making and democratic decision making. For major financial matters and project expenses, audit institutions at all levels should adhere to the principle of "collective leadership, democratic centralism, case-specific consultation, decision making by meeting," and strictly follow procedural rules and decision-making procedures; for capital construction projects subject to tender, proper tendering activities should be carried out; and materials and equipment subject to government procurement provisions should demonstrate clear, procedural transparency. The third aspect is to strengthen financial management and budget binding, strictly conducting budget management, striving to achieve scientific preparation of the budget plan, strengthening project planning and management according to the budget and avoiding idle budget funds, strengthening basic accounting work, striving to strictly handle expenditure examination and approval procedures, standardizing accounting and asset management, exploring the establishment of a saving incentive system, and improving auditors' enthusiasm for participating in cost control.

(c) Strengthen Audit Organization and Promote Integration of Audit Resources

Audit cost control is a means to achieve the audit objective through the rational allocation of resources and the smallest audit costs.[3] Integrated management aims to control costs and improve efficiency. The quality of utilizing audit resources directly determines the audit costs. Therefore, an important means of cost control is to adhere to comprehensive auditing, stress key points, strengthen audit organization and management, and promote the best allocation of audit forces and audit objects. Currently, the optimization of audit organization and the integration of audit resources are achieved mainly through the following five aspects: firstly, enhancing project plan integration, achieving coordination and linkage between annual project plans and long-term development plans, establishing a dynamic project library, preparing a rolling project plan, and strengthening integration of various annual projects to avoid overlapping and fragmentation. The second aspect is strengthening integration of auditing contents. According to the requirements for establishing an integrated audit mode with Chinese characteristics, audit institutions should first study the financial revenue and expenditure situation of the audited unit, focus on responsibility performance, integrate the compliance and performance audit, and comprehensively consider the audit benefits, efficiency, and effect from the perspectives of policy implementation, funds usage, resource utilization, and administrative efficacy. Third, there is a need for strengthened integration of auditing methods. Audit institutions should scientifically select the best way to carry out the audit investigation and follow-up audit according to project characteristics, actively exploring and promoting management modes, including multiprofession integration, multiperspective analysis, and a combination of multiple methods. Fourth, we have to strengthen the integration of human resources. Audit institutions should focus on audit projects, strengthen the unified allocation and integrated use of various professionals, pay attention to the use of external auditing forces, optimize the allocation of human resources, and strengthen the coordination and cooperation between the CNAO and local audit institutions, bringing into full play the overall advantages of audit supervision. Fifth, it is necessary to strengthen integration of audit procedures. The more complex the audit procedures, the higher the audit costs tend to be, so the former must be strictly controlled to cut costs. It is necessary to study and design audit procedures according to the overall audit requirements, avoid overlapping, ensure the planned nature of audit procedures, promote the effective operation of procedures, determine costs, and simplify audit procedures.

(d) Strengthen Auditor Style and Ability

To reduce audit costs, establish economical audit institutions, and improve audit efficiency and effect, we should cultivate auditors' cost control awareness and a frugal style, and improve their ability to perform their audit duties. This can be done mainly through three measures: firstly, vigorously promote and carry forward the style of hard work and thrift. At present, the problem of shortage of audit funds is still prominent in some places. Audit institutions at all levels should try to save funds and other audit resources and resolutely combat extravagance and waste according to central government requirements for building a conservation-minded society. Secondly, promote a style of being realistic and pragmatic, precise, and meticulous. Audit institutions should be realistic and pragmatic, precise, and meticulous. Thirdly, audit institutions should improve the expertise and performance capabilities of individual auditors to achieve better audit quality and efficiency.

VIII. AUDIT HUMAN RESOURCE MANAGEMENT

Human resource management (HRM) and organizational structure are inseparable. To improve organizational performance, rational positions should be set for the design and optimization of the organizational structure; the right personnel should be appointed to each post, and human resource management is needed to ensure this. The organizational structure is the "hard environment," while human resource management is the "soft." The two depend on each other, forming the operational system of an organization. Organizational structure and human resource management are influenced by the external environment and internal organization development strategies at the same time; thus, audit institutions need to adjust in accordance with the changing environment and organizational development. As the carrier for human resource management, the organizational structure exerts direct influence, so it makes no sense to study human resource management without studying the organizational structure.

(1) HRM Framework in Audit Institutions

Human resource management involves the integration of management procedures, including employment, allocation, development, examination and evaluation, incentive, and guarantee in accordance with relevant laws, regulations, and provisions conducted by an audit institution's personnel department, to ensure smooth development of the audit cause and effective performance of supervision responsibility, and to bring the "immune system" function of audit into full play. It can be seen from the foregoing definition that HRM involves six interacting parts—employment, allocation, development, examination and evaluation, incentive, and guarantee. Newly hired public servants provide a guarantee for human resource allocation; examination and evaluation create the criteria for measuring personnel for allocation; the incentive mechanism serves as a driving force for personnel allocation; development provides the optimization method for personnel allocation; and guarantee (including salaries, insurance, and health security) provides stable dependency for the personnel allocation.

The framework of audit institutions' human resource management is shown in Figure 6.2.

On the whole, it is systematic, combining dynamic and static management, in which the internal and external environment blend and interact; it is an organic combination whereby internal management procedures influence and interact with each other.

(a) Dynamic Nature of HRM in Audit Institutions

In Figure 6.1, the time axis presents dynamic changes. That is to say, changes will occur in both the internal and external environment that audit institutions face as time passes, and the internal environment should be adjusted in accordance with the changing external environment. Therefore, the HRM practices of audit institutions should be dynamic, focusing on the long-term development of the audit cause and the sustainable development of individual auditors, continuously helping to revise, adjust, and even change the organizational structure and concrete management behavior based on changing audit demand and the external environment.

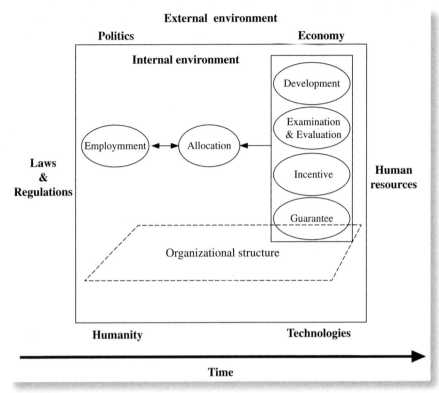

FIGURE 6.2 Framework of Audit Institutions' Human Resource Management

(b) Static Nature of HRM in Audit Institutions

Since the dynamic state is composed of multiple single-stage, static states, the audit environment is relatively stable within a given period. As a subsystem of the nation, the audit system inevitably will be influenced by the internal and external environments. As a component of audit work in audit institutions, HRM should be based on the internal situation and in consideration of external environment as well. The political, economic, cultural, technological, human resources, and legal factors in external environment will relatively affect the operation of HRM.

As for the internal environment, organizational structure serves as the foundation and platform for HRM. It determines the number of departments, hierarchical structure, and departmental division of work within an organization, and also determines the number of personnel, personnel structure, ranks, and management mode. That is to say, achieving the ideal state of human resource management initially lies in establishing a scientific organization structure. This should be one in which the powers and responsibilities for functional departments are well defined. This will ensure that orders can be smoothly sent to the lower level from the upper level and information can be successfully released to each other. Functional departments can cooperate and communicate with each other effectively and share their information in a timely manner, and personnel transfers can be conducted smoothly among departments. Second, audit institutions should allocate existing auditors and newly employed public servants in a scientific way in accordance with the demand of the organizational structure. When scientific allocation of human resources fails to work with existing personnel, new personnel should be hired in accordance with the demands of scientific human resource allocation. That is to say, the scientific allocation of human resources will affect the number of newly hired personnel and the qualities they should have. If auditors are allocated scientifically, management processes including development, examination and evaluation, incentive, and guarantee will decide their performance. Audit work will be conducted in an orderly and efficient way only when a relative balance is maintained between a scientific organizational structure and the scientific allocation of human resources. However, this balance is not static, and a new balance will have to be established by continuously improving the organizational structure and human resource allocation. Accordingly, due changes should be made in the management process of employment, development, examination and evaluation, incentive, and guarantee.

(2) Human Resource Management Strategy of Audit Institutions

This involves seven aspects:

1. **Establishing a scientific human resource concept.** This involves being people-oriented, just and equitable, with dynamic allocation, good system management, optimization of labor organization, and a virtuous cycle. Scientific human resource concepts should be firmly established before implementing human resource management, and should be used to guide the work.
2. **Two tasks for optimizing the organizational structure.** In accordance with the principles of optimizing the organizational structure defined by theory, human resource quality evaluation and supporting

technologies and methods should be further strengthened. Specifically, an audit institution should first clarify the responsibility of human resource quality evaluation and set quantitative evaluation criteria. Clear responsibility contributes to defining rights and liabilities, so that everyone has due responsibility and the shirking of responsibility can be avoided. Quantitative evaluation criteria contribute to forming objective and just results that are comparable. Therefore, the personnel departments of audit institutions should make sure that the internal organizations concerned undertake responsibility for human resource quality evaluation based on the principles and requirements set down and can refine criteria where necessary. Secondly, audit institutions should establish and improve their joint expert consultation organizations to offer suggestions on technical methods. These are of obvious importance to audit work as advanced methods can enhance the pertinence, effectiveness, and quality of audit work. Audit institutions should provide technical method support and guarantees for auditors, and expert guidance should be given if necessary.

3. **Optimize the allocation of human resource step by step.** Scientific organization structure is the foundation for the scientific allocation of human resources. The organizational structure tends to be relatively stable in a given period after optimization. However, human resource allocation should be adjusted by stages using scientific procedures in accordance with clear audit objectives. In the process of adjustment, audit institutions should creatively use various allocation methods, including rationally combining leading personnel with backbone personnel; combining personnel with different professional backgrounds; exploring ways to establish and implement the auditor profession access system; making full use of external audit forces prudently; and so on. In line with the requirements of human resource allocation theory, the following goals should be achieved: audit human resources and audit tasks should be well matched; auditors should have due abilities for their positions; teams and groups should ensure that their respective advantages complement each other; and a rational hierarchical age structure of the same rank should be maintained to ensure the balanced promotion and stability of cadre teams and to stimulate auditors' working enthusiasm.

4. **Establishing a human resource evaluation mechanism.** Human resource evaluation is the premise and basis for conducting HRM. Audit institutions need to understand their own current human resource situation through evaluation, so as to determine the focus and direction of its management. Before conducting evaluation, audit institutions must

establish a multilevel evaluation index system, consisting of the individual personnel evaluation index system and the evaluation index system for human resources of different levels. Step-by-step evaluation should be conducted based on which audit institutions should be able to analyze the common and individual problems of staff, so as to determine any weaknesses in the overall human resource allocation and to make rational decisions about employment, allocation, and development of human resources.

5. **Improving approaches for human resource development.** Audit institutions should tap the potential of the existing and the newly employed auditors through innovative approaches, enhance their abilities in auditing by law, and focus on cultivating integrated and high-level auditors who are experts in one area but also good in many others. Such approaches include career planning for auditors, devoting greater efforts to cultivating auditors in practice, encouraging internal and external communication within the audit cadre system, conducting training in accordance with the demands of audit work and auditors' development, setting up an audit experience learning and sharing mechanism, establishing an effective integrated personnel training mode, and so on.

6. **Establishing a good personnel selection and employment mechanism.** This is the key link in human resource allocation to select and employ the right leading cadres. Audit institutions should further deepen the reform of cadre and personnel system, eliminate old concepts of giving top priority only to seniority in selection or seeking to be perfect, and adhere to and innovate the mechanism of selecting and employing the personnel who have abilities and integrity and are recognized by the masses. Audit institutions should improve the system of taking up a job through competition so that excellent personnel will tend to stand out; improve the evaluation system, and make better use of evaluation results; organically combine the application of evaluation results, feedback, selection of cadres, training, education, management, supervision, incentives, and constraints so that excellent personnel can be placed in important positions, personnel with potential can be cultivated, and those who are lagging behind can be encouraged to try harder. Audit institutions should improve cadre promotion policies, select both the right leading personnel and the nonleading personnel, and create broader space for the career development of audit cadres.

7. **Create a good cultural and working environment.** Organizational management theory studies suggest that within an organization, members' satisfaction and loyalty to the organization is in direct proportion to

its cultural and working environment, which, in turn, is closely related to the improvement of members' working efficiency. Therefore, audit institutions should endeavor to create a good internal cultural and working environment with profound cultural connotations, a good climate for learning, and harmonious interpersonal relations, where cadres enjoy good physical and psychological health, cherish their posts, and devote themselves wholeheartedly to their work. In this way, auditors' creative thinking can be developed, their professional qualities and cultural accomplishments can be continuously improved rapidly, and audit institutions will be able to retain talent.

BIBLIOGRAPHY

Buo, Guil. On Optimizing Organization Structure of Governments. *Chinese Public Administration*, 2007 (5).

Dong, Dasheng, Chief Editor. *Auditing Techniques*. Beijing: China Modern Economics Publishing House, 2005.

Dong, Dasheng, Chief Editor. *Chinese Government Audit*. Beijing: China Modern Economics Publishing House, 2005.

Du, Xingqiang. Brand New Thinking of Audit: Strategic System of Audit Pattern. *China Audit*, 2003 (7).

Financial Director. The Eight Annual FTSE350 Audit Fees Survey. 2005 (1), www.financialdirector.co.uk.

Gao, Xiaoping. Scientification: Innovations of Human Resource Management of Public Sector. *Chinese Public Administration*, 2004 (2).

Guo, Qun, and Sun Fangjiang. On Integration of Government Audit Human Resources. *Audit Digest*, 2008 (2).

Hao, Juncai. Discussion on Values of Audit Results. *Zhongzhou Audit*, 2002 (6).

Hao, Zhiyuan. Establishing the Audit Human Resource System Meeting Demands of Scientific Development. *Auditing and Finance*, 2008 (10).

Hou, Wenkeng. *Vocabulary of Auditing*. Shenyang: People's Publishing House, 1992.

Hu, Xianzhi, and Yu Qian. From the Government Employee System to the Public Servant Appointment System—Improvement and Innovation of Human Resource Management System of Public Sectors. *Journal of Jiangsu Administration Institute*, 2009 (5).

Liao, Hong, and Bai Hua. Study on Auditing Fees of United States Certified Public Accountants. *Chinese Certified Public Accountant*, 2001 (8).

Liu, Jie. On the Enhancement of Audit Efficiency from the Perspective of the Relation between the Audit Quality and Audit Efficiency. *Northern Economy and Trade*, 2004 (10).

Liu, Yinglai. Seminar Overview on the Audit Plan Management and Audit Field Quality Control. *Audit Research*, 2005 (6).

Ramos, Michael. Section 404 Compliance in the Annual Report. *Journal of Accountancy*, 2004 (10).

Ricchiute, David N. *Auditing Concepts and Standards*. Nashville: Southwestern Public, 1982.

Song, Bin, and Xie Xin: Concepts and Trends of Human Resource Development of Governmental Departments. *Chinese Public Administration*, 2002 (11).

Song, Hongyin, Ding Quana, and Wu Xiangrong. Reflection on Integration of Audit Resources. *Shaanxi Audit*, 2003 (S2).

Tang, Yunwei. *Modern Audit Management*. Shanghai: Lixin Accounting Publishing House, 2001.

Wang, Qianhua. Make Better Use of Audit Results and Bring Audit's Due Function into Play. *China Audit*, 2002 (5).

Wang, Xinguang, and Yu Jianghong: Reflections on Integrating Audit Resources [J]. *Shangdong Audit*, 2003 (7).

Xiao, Yingda, and Zhang Jixun. *International Comparative Auditing*. Shanghai: Lixin Accounting Publishing House, 2000.

Xu, Shuping: Organizational and Structural Design of Local Governments' Super-Ministry Reform. *Administrative Tribune*, 2010 (3).

Xu, Zhengdan, Xie Rong, Zhu Rong'en, and Tang Qingliang. *Audit Research Front*. Shanghai: Shanghai University of Finance and Economics Press, 2002.

Yang, Yu. Research Overview and Outlook of Governmental Human Resource Management. *Journal of Gansu Institute of Administration*, 2004 (3).

Zhang, Jie. Discussion on the Present Situation of China's Audit Human Resource and Integration Plan. *Audit Monthly*, 2007 (4).

Zhang, Xin. Research Overview on the Comparison of Government and Enterprise Human Resource Management. *Chinese Public Administration*, 2008 (12).

Zhang, Yuanlun. Measures to Strengthen the Management of Audit Cost. *Audit Information and Technique of China*, 2000 (8).

Zhao, Jinsong. Statistical Analysis and Reflections on Audit Surveys to China's Governments Conducted from 1990 to 2003. *Audit Research*, 2004 (3).

Zhou, Yingliang. Cost Control and Performance Improvement of Governmental Audit. *China Audit*, 2005 (14).

Zhu, Yanli. Discussion on How to Strengthen the Usage of Audit Results. *China Audit*, 2003 (20).

NOTES

1. Cited from the speech delivered by Mr. Jiayi Liu, auditor general of P.R. China, at the training on the auditing of public finance held by the National Audit Office in 2009.
2. See the National Auditing Standards of the People's Republic of China promulgated by the National audit Office of P.R. China on September 1, 2010 (No. 8 decree).
3. Yunwei Tang, *Modern Audit Management*, Shanghai: Lixin Accounting Press, 2001.

CHAPTER SEVEN

Research on Audit Standardization

AUDIT STANDARDIZATION THEORY REFLECTS the rules that audit activities shall follow. According to differing content, audit standardization can be divided into two categories: (1) the rules on the relationship between audit offices and auditors and the outside world in regard to audit activities; such rules are achieved mainly through legislation and other means of external regulation; (2) the business operating rules within audit offices, including auditor qualifications, job requirements, auditing rules, audit quality control rules, and so on. They are achieved mainly through formulation of internal regulations, such as auditing standards.

I. MEANING AND SIGNIFICANCE OF AUDIT STANDARDIZATION

(1) Basic Concepts: Audit Standardization

Audit standardization. Audit standardization refers to rules of conduct by which audit activities should abide, including audit laws, regulations, standards, guidelines, manuals, and so forth, which regulate the activities of audit and provide a code of conduct to be followed by audit offices and auditors.

The government audit standardization system includes: the government audit law system, government audit regulations, government audit rules, auditing standards, and the ethics of auditing. According to different features, content, and binding forces, audit standardization can be divided into audit legal norms and a code of ethics. Audit legal norms are prescribed or approved by authorities, have legally binding forces, and are guaranteed by coercive force. The code of ethics is gradually formed by auditors in the long-term audit practice, and maintained by people's inner beliefs, social opinions, and other means to promote compliance. The code of ethics usually presents certain ethical ideals, opinions, customs, criteria, and so on. From the practice of establishing *Government Audit Standards*, the requirements for the code of ethics have been integrated into auditing standards and issued in the form of departmental regulations, being one integral part of the legal norms.

Basic concepts: Auditing standards. Auditing standards refer to the qualifications and professional requirements about how audit offices and auditors perform their statutory duties. They are basic requirements for performing audit business and the codes of conduct when creating implementation plans, collecting and using evidence, preparing working documents, evaluating and reviewing issues, drafting and approving reports, making decisions, and publicizing results. Auditing standards are an important part of audit standardization. They are formulated or revised and published by the audit office in accordance with prescribed procedures.

Basic concepts: Audit guidelines. This is the guidance document based on the audit regulations and standards, suitable for certain aspects of the government audit services to guide and regulate their operation. It is the best auditing work scheme and auditing requirements proposed for specialized audit areas, and is a guideline for good auditing practice with strong guidance and operability, yet not legally enforceable, serving only as reference to the work.

Basic concepts: Audit standardization. This mainly refers to formulating unified operational norms for the internal audit scheme, quality standards, technical methods, work management, and other aspects. Conducting auditing strictly in accordance with established rules can avoid subjective arbitrariness, and the audit work could be conducted normatively. Establishing the auditing standard system and improving the legal system of audit supervision and auditing standards can address the problems of legal basis and behavioral codes in auditing. Therefore the audit offices and auditors have laws and rules to follow. To fully and correctly implement the audit laws, regulations, and auditing standards, audit offices should continue to regulate audit operations and management work to strengthen audit law enforcement and audit quality supervision and inspection.

(2) Significance of Audit Standardization

This is embodied in the following five aspects:

1. **Standardization is an important prerequisite for auditing by law.** Executing audit power and regulating audit behavior by law are an important guarantee of high audit quality. Achieving standardization of audit business means to refine work processes and unify procedures and standards. Then every audit project has a unified model to implement, such as an audit objective, content and scope, work process and operating mode, embodiment of the audit result, formation mechanism and presentation of the audit report, release of the audit conclusion, and handling and punishment of problems. It prevents the randomness of auditing activities. With unified standards, auditors know what they should audit, how to audit, what criteria the audit should meet, and what responsibility they should bear. In this way, the audit can follow procedures, with evidence and records, and be reviewable, and auditors can receive rewards and punishments, thus achieving auditing according to the law.

2. **Audit standardization is an important way to promote administration by law.** To implement administration by law and build a government of law, audit offices as government departments should first follow the Constitution, the Audit Law, and its implementation regulations to conscientiously perform their supervision responsibilities. Audit standardization defines the specific ways in which audit offices perform their duties according to law. The Constitution establishes the government audit system; the Audit Law specifies the constitutional provisions for audit supervision, and makes more comprehensive provisions for the basic content of the government audit system; and the Regulations on the Implementation of the Audit Law provide more specific guidance. The focus of audit legislation work is to specify the responsibilities, authorities, and audit procedures of audit offices and to regulate the audited entity's responsibility to avoid impeding the audit and violating financial regulations. As for the development of professional norms, such as government audit standards, the Audit Law and its implementing regulations are further implemented into various audit categories. Using professional norms to plan, implement, and report every audit project, the audit offices and auditors can effectively perform their duties in accordance with the law.

3. **Audit standardization is a necessary requirement to improve audit quality.** Audit quality is the lifeline of the audit. Continuing to regulate audit conduct and improve audit quality in accordance with the law is an inherent requirement and an objective need for long-term development of the audit

cause. Government auditing is an administrative supervision behavior, and also a kind of professional public service. Audit quality evaluation is mainly the evaluation of auditors and their professional conduct. Audit standardization, especially audit standards, provides a scale for audit quality assessment. An objective assessment of audit quality can be made by developing professional standards and following them to supervise and confirm whether audit offices and individual auditors are effectively complying with the professional standards, so as to promote the continuous improvement of audit quality.

4. **Audit standardization is an important factor of the leadership system of audit offices.** The leadership system of audit offices is an important part of audit management. Achieving audit objectives and maximizing the audit role are the starting point and destination of leadership activities. The leadership structure system mainly includes core values, management philosophy, independence, strategic planning, risk management, and other factors. Auditing standards cover the corresponding provisions of the foregoing factors. Therefore, the development and implementation of auditing standards can improve the leadership system, and enhance the role of the leadership system, especially the leading role of the National Audit Office for national government audit work. As audit offices belong to governments, local audit offices are in a dual leadership system. They are under the leadership of administrative heads of governments at the corresponding level and audit offices at higher levels. With the National Audit Office formulating auditing standards, and the local audit offices following, the leadership of the National Audit Office for local audit offices can be achieved.

5. **Audit standardization is the foundation of improving audit offices' business management.** To improve internal management, assure audit quality, and improve audit efficiency, audit offices must base themselves on scientific, rational, and clear audit standardization. Developing and conducting audit standardization is necessary to provide guidelines for the behavior of auditors and evaluate their performance. Standardization and rationality of audit activities can be guaranteed by formulating audit offices' various audit management systems on the basis of audit standardization, thereby enhancing their internal management level.

II. AUDIT STANDARDIZATION PROCESS

After the reform and opening up of China, the audit standard system has been gradually established and developed in accordance with the requirements for audit supervision for building the socialist market economy. Thirty years of development has basically formed an audit standards system with Chinese characteristics and basically achieved audit standardization. Government audit standardization mainly includes the construction of audit laws and regulations and the audit standard system.

(1) Process of Audit Laws and Regulations Building

The formulation of China's audit laws and regulations mainly passed through three stages.

(a) Foundation Stage of Audit Legal System Building (1982–1988)

In December 1982, the Constitution was adopted at the Fifth Session of the Fifth National People's Congress. It specified the government audit system in China, established the legal status of audit supervision, specified the principles of the audit system and supervision, the basic powers of audit offices, and the legal status of the auditor-general. It laid the foundation of audit legal system building. The Central Government issued the Provisional Regulations of the State Council on Government Audit Work in August 1985, and the Audit Regulations of the PRC in November 1988. They specified audit supervision principles outlined in the Constitution, and the audit work was gradually integrated into legal system building.

CASE 7.1: **CONSTITUTION ADOPTED IN 1982 ESTABLISHED THE LEGAL STATUS OF AUDIT SUPERVISION**

A total of seven articles in the Constitution directly relate to government auditing. Article 91 stipulates that "the State Council establishes an auditing body to supervise through auditing the revenue and expenditure of all departments under the State Council and of the local governments at various levels, and the revenue and expenditure of all financial and monetary organizations, enterprises and institutions of the state, . . . under the direction of the Premier of the State Council, the auditing body independently exercises its power of supervision through auditing in accordance with the law, subject to no interference by any other administrative organ or any public organization or individual." Article 109 stipulates that "Auditing bodies are established by local people's governments at and above the county level. Local auditing bodies at various levels independently exercise their power of supervision

(continued)

(continued)

through auditing in accordance with the law and are responsible to the people's government at the corresponding level and to the auditing body at the next higher level." Articles 62, 63, 67, 80, and 86 stipulate that "the Auditor-General shall be a member of the State Council, be nominated by the Premier of the State Council, be decided by the National People's Congress or its Standing Committee, and be appointed and removed by the President." The audit supervision system stipulated in the Constitution laid the cornerstone of the development of China's auditing cause.

(b) Initial Stage of Audit Legal System Building (1989–1994)

In January 1989, the Audit Regulations of the PRC were officially implemented. To coordinate and ensure its implementation, the National Audit Office successively formulated the Rules for the Implementation of Audit Regulations of the PRC, the Provisions of the National Audit Office of the PRC on Internal Audit Work, the Provisions of the National Audit Office on Social Audit Work, the Provisions of the National Audit Office on the Implementation of the Audit Work Procedures, and other regulations. On August 31, 1994, the Ninth Meeting of the Eighth National People's Congress Standing Committee adopted the Audit Law, which took effect on January 1, 1995. On the basis of summarizing more than 10 years of auditing experience and learning from the beneficial content of foreign audit legislation, it provided comprehensive regulations of the basic system for government auditing, including the basic principles of Chinese audit supervision, audit offices, and auditors, responsibilities and authorities of the audit offices, audit procedures, and legal liabilities, and established the high-level legal status of audit offices. The adoption and implementation of the Audit Law symbolized that the government audit stepped onto the track of legal system building.

CASE 7.2: **ISSUANCE OF THE FIRST AUDIT LAW**

In 1990, the National Audit Office was entrusted by the State Council to draft the Audit Law. In 1991, the Audit Law was officially listed in the Eighth Five-Year Plan for Legislation.

In October 1992, the 14th CPC National Congress was held. The Congress put forward the strategic target of establishing the socialist market economic system. The Congress pointed out that strengthening the legal system building, especially speeding the formulation and improvement of the laws and regulations guaranteeing reform and opening up, strengthening macroeconomic management and standardizing microeconomic behavior was vital in building the socialist market economy system.

On August 31, 1994, the Audit Law was approved at the Ninth Session of the Eighth Standing Committee of the National People's Congress.

(c) Development and Improvement of Audit Legal System Building (1995 onwards)

After the Audit Law was implemented, the State Council successively issued the Interim Measures for Audit Supervision on the Central Budget Implementation, the Regulations on Implementation of the Audit Law, the Interim Provisions on Accountability Audit of Leading Cadres below the County Level in Their Terms of Office, the Interim Provisions on Accountability Audit of State-Owned Enterprises and State Holding Enterprises' Leaders in their Terms of Office, the Regulations on Punishment for Illegal Fiscal Acts, and so forth. Formulation and implementation of these audit laws and regulations further improved the legal system of audit norms and ensured that auditing had laws to abide by.

With the gradual establishment and improvement of the socialist market economy, society has undergone profound economic changes, creating a number of new tasks and requirements for government auditing. On February 28, 2006, the Twentieth Meeting of the Standing Committee of the Tenth National People's Congress adopted the Decisions on Modifying the Audit Law of the PRC. Later, the Regulations on the Implementation of Audit Law of the PRC were also revised. On December 8, 2010, the General Office of the CPC Central Committee and General Office of the State Council issued the Regulations on Accountability Audit of the Main Leading Cadres of Party and Government and Leaders of State-Owned Enterprises, which provided new assurance for regulating accountability audit work.

CASE 7.3: **PROMULGATING REGULATIONS ON ACCOUNTABILITY AUDIT OF MAIN LEADING CADRES OF PARTY AND GOVERNMENT AND LEADERS OF STATE-OWNED ENTERPRISES**

The accountability audit is an audit type with Chinese characteristics. In May 1999, the General Office of the CPC Central Committee and General Office of the State Council issued the Interim Provisions on Accountability Audit of Leading Cadres below the County Level during the Term of Office and the Interim Provisions on Accountability Audit of State-Owned Enterprises and State Holding Enterprises' Leaders during the Term of Office (hereinafter referred to as the "two Interim Provisions"), marking the implementation of the accountability audit as a supervisory system.

In December 2010, the General Office of the CPC Central Committee and the General Office of the State Council distributed the Regulations on Accountability Audit of Main Leading Cadres of Party and Government and State-Owned Enterprise Leaders. The Regulations, consisting of six chapters and 44 articles, explicitly stipulates that local party committees, governments, judicial and procuratorial organs at all levels, major persons-in-charge of central and local party and government departments, institutions, and people's organizations, and other units at all levels, and the legal representatives of state-owned and state holding enterprises are accountability audit objects. The Regulations defined the direct responsibility, supervision responsibility, and leadership responsibility of leading cadres, and formulated procedures, contents, evaluation, reporting, application of results, and other aspects of accountability auditing. This is an important achievement of the accountability audit legal system building.

(2) Process of the Auditing Standards System Building

Construction of government audit standards also went through the process of start-up, deepening, and basic establishment.

(a) Coexistence of Auditing Standards and Administrative Provisions

In the early days, constrained by the level of development of government auditing, many aspects were difficult to fully regulate according to scientific criteria, and were made only administrative requirements. Some of these normative documents related to auditing standards, while others were rules, methods, and regulations. In 1995, the National Audit Office proceeded to develop auditing standards. By the end of 1996, it had issued 38 audit regulatory documents (referred to as the 38 Regulations). They played a positive role in promoting audit infrastructure, regulating audit behavior, ensuring audit quality, and improving efficiency.

(b) Parallel Phase of Hierarchical Auditing Standards and Quality Control Method

From 1999, on the basis of the aforementioned 38 regulations, the National Audit Office began to establish the system of auditing standards. From 2000, it successively issued 20 auditing standards, including the Basic Principles of Government Audit with four audit orders. The standards system consisted of three levels: The first level was the basic criteria of government auditing, mainly stipulating the basic principles of audit offices and auditors performing the audit, and proposed the principal demands for the key links and elements of audit activities. It undertook promotion of the Audit Law and other relevant regulations, and unified the specific audit guidelines. The second level was the specific auditing standards and professional auditing standards. Specific auditing standards regulated the main elements and actions of audit activities, including audit scheme guidelines, audit evidence standards, guidelines for auditing working documents, audit report standards, and audit review guidelines. Professional auditing standards regulated the activities of professional auditing, such as the auditing standards of national construction projects. The third level was the audit guidance. It is the guidance document on the specific operations of the government audit business, such as the Guidance of World Bank Loan Project Audit, Guidance of Commercial Bank Audit, Guidance of Central Department Budget Implementation Audit, and so on.

To further improve audit quality, the National Audit Office issued the Measures for the Quality Control of Audit Projects of Audit Offices (Trial) (Audit Office No. 6 Order) in February 2004, which made provisions for the whole process of quality control, including the preparation of the audit scheme, collection of audit evidence, compilation of the audit diary and auditing paper, issuing of the audit report, arrangement of audit files, and so forth. Thus, the Chinese auditing standards formed a situation wherein the hierarchical auditing standards coexisted with quality control measures. In the course of the subsequent actual implementation, quality control measures replaced the auditing standards.

(c) Stage of Single National Auditing Standards

As China's economic and social situation has undergone profound changes, audit work has seen more thorough development, which makes the task of revising auditing standards more urgent. First, after the Audit Law of the PRC and its Implementing Regulations were amended, the original auditing standards needed to be revised accordingly, in order to make them consistent with the Law and Regulations. Secondly, audit offices at all levels established the concept of scientific auditing, increased audit supervision, innovated audit supervision ways, and accumulated a lot of experience, which needed to be summarized and fixed through the development of standards. Thirdly, some provisions of the original standards could no longer fully meet the development requirements for audit practice. The complexity of the original standards system also produced some overlap, needing revision.

On July 15, 2008, the National Audit Office issued the Notice on the Establishment of the Government Audit Standards Advisory Panel and Revision Working Group, officially launching the start of the revision process. After two years of work, the Government Audit Standards of the PRC were adopted at the auditor general meeting on July 8, 2010, issued with the 8th order and implemented from January 1, 2011.

At present, China has basically built up the audit standardization system composed of different-level regulations, including the Constitution, the Audit Law and its Implementation Regulations, the Government Audit Standards of the PRC, and various audit guidance.

CASE 7.4: **IMPLEMENTATION OF GOVERNMENT AUDIT STANDARDS**

On July 8, 2010, the Government Audit Standards of the PRC were promulgated by the National Audit Office (Order No. 8), with implementation from January 1, 2011. The Standards, consisting of seven chapters and 200 articles, provide detailed and specific provisions in such aspects as audit institutions and auditors, audit plans, audit implementation, audit reports, and audit quality control and responsibility, providing an important safeguard for strengthening audit quality control and improving standardization.

III. SYSTEM STRUCTURE AND MAIN CONTENT OF AUDIT STANDARDIZATION

Audit standardization is an integrated whole with different-level regulations. The whole is the audit standards system.

(1) System Structure of Audit Standardization

It has two classification methods: (1) It can be classified according to different standardizing matters, which could be called the internal structure system of audit standardization; (2) it can be divided according to the different manifestations of audit standardization. The system consisting of different levels of regulations according to this method is called the external structure system of audit standardization. The internal structure system of audit standardization is mainly embodied in the content of all types of audit standardization, which will be discussed separately later. The following is the external structure system of audit standardization.

The external structure system of audit standardization is formulated in accordance with certain procedures by the state legislature and other agencies with power to formulate laws and regulations, and composed of standardizations with different legal effects.

Chinese audit laws and regulations include the code of ethics. Professional audit ethics is a basic professional requirement for auditors performing their government audit supervisory duties. Therefore, the Audit Law of the PRC and its Implementing Regulations as well as the Government Audit Standards of the PRC clearly delineated the professional audit ethics of audit offices and individual auditors.

In accordance with different formulating bodies and legal effects, the government audit laws and regulations can be divided into government audit laws, regulations, and rules (including auditing standards). Audit laws refer to the government audit provisions involved in the Constitution formulated by the NPC and its Standing Committee and in the various laws. Audit regulations refer to the government audit provisions involved in the administrative regulations formulated by the State Council and the local laws and regulations by local people's congresses and standing committees. Audit rules mean audit regulations and government audit standards issued by the National Audit Office, and also include the government audit provisions of administrative regulations promulgated by other departments of the State Council and local governments.

Adapting to the characteristics of Chinese legislative system and audit norms, the external structure system of audit standardization is composed mainly of the following categories:

1. **Constitution.** The 1982 Constitution specified that China implemented the government audit system, and set out the basic principles of auditing and supervision, setting and leadership system of audit offices, basic

duties of audit supervision, the auditor general's position, appointment, and removal, and so on, which are the basis of the Chinese audit standardization system.

2. **Audit law and other laws related to government audit.** The Audit Law of the PRC, promulgated on August 31, 1994, and amended on February 8, 2006, is the special law regulating government auditing and the core of the audit standardization system. It provided comprehensive regulations for the basic principles covering audit supervision, audit offices, and individual auditors, the audit offices' authorities, auditing procedures, and legal responsibilities. In addition to the Audit Law, a number of other laws have provisions for government audit work. For example, the Budget Law of the PRC, the Accounting Law of the PRC, the Law of the PRC on the People's Bank of China, the Securities Law of the PRC, and the Commercial Bank Law of the PRC all have audit provisions in their respective areas. In addition, some laws about the national administrative supervision, such as the Administrative Procedure Law of the PRC, the Administrative Punishment Law of the PRC, and the State Compensation Law of the PRC, also apply to government auditing. Therefore, these laws are also an important part of the audit standardization system.

3. **Administrative regulations on government auditing.** There are two types of administrative regulations. One is the special government audit administrative regulations promulgated by the State Council, such as the new Regulations on the Implementation of Audit Law of the PRC adopted in 2010, and the Interim Measures for the Central Budget Implementation Audit Supervision in 1995. The other involves administrative regulations with government audit content or related to government auditing promulgated by the State Council, such as the Regulations on Punishment for Illegal Fiscal Activities issued on November 30, 2004.

4. **Departmental regulations on government auditing.** Departmental regulations on government auditing are mainly the government audit regulations lawfully issued by National Audit Office and the ministries and commissions under the State Council, such as the Government Audit Standards of the PRC, the Regulations on Safekeeping Material and Assets by Audit Offices published by the National Audit Office, and so forth. The Government Audit Standards of the PRC are special administrative regulations promulgated by the audit offices with binding forces on audit offices and auditors, and normalizing audit business.

(2) Main Content of the Audit Standardization System

(a) Main Content of China's Audit Legal Norms

Chinese audit-related laws and regulations stipulate the organization, work, and reporting systems of government auditing. They comprise audit organizational norms, entity norms, and procedures. Their core content is most directly related to implementation of the audit business, including responsibilities, authorities, and procedure requirements for audit offices.

First, they stipulate the main responsibilities of audit offices. The basic principle in determining the responsibilities of audit offices is that any units and individuals involved in the use of state financial capital, possession and use of state-owned assets, and the management of public funds and other public resources are subject to audit supervision. According to the provisions of the Constitution and the Audit Law, the State Council sets up audit offices to supervise the financial revenue and expenditure of its various departments and local people's governments at various levels, as well as the country's fiscal and financial institutions and enterprises. This determines the wide responsibilities of audit offices.

Second, they stipulate the main authorities of government auditing. Relevant laws stipulate the audit offices' authorities to fulfill their duties and perform audit supervision. They have such powers as access to information, to check and investigate (including the power to check public funds for personal money), to require assistance, to punish, to recommend (including the power to transfer), to notify and publicize audit results, and to take administrative enforcement measures. And administrative enforcement measures include the authority to stop, to sequestrate, to notify concerning the suspension of disbursements, to require deductions and payments, and so on.

Third, they stipulate the statutory procedures of government auditing. Government auditing is a kind of administrative activity. In accordance with the requirements for administration according to law, the relevant laws and regulations made strict rules for audit schemes.

(b) Main Content of Auditing Standards

Auditing standards prescribe mainly audit offices' and auditors' qualifications and job requirements. They are the codes of conduct for developing annual project plans, preparing audit schemes, obtaining audit evidence, making audit conclusions, and managing audit business. They cover the following:

Qualifications of audit offices and auditors. These mainly cover audit offices and auditors' basic conditions and requirements for performing audits, the basic ethical principles of auditing, independence, professional competence, the professional relationship with the audited entity, and so on.

Audit types and work objectives. This means to scientifically classify audit activities within the statutory duties of China's audit offices. Government auditing can be classified as auditing, special audit investigation, and accountability auditing. And the objectives of these types are clearly stipulated.

Audit plan. This mainly covers the main content and formulation procedures of the annual audit plan, the main content and preparation requirements for audit schemes, tracking, inspection, and statistics of the annual audit plan implementation and results.

Audit process execution. This means to regulate the audit project implementation process. The main content includes: (1) standards of the audit implementation scheme, which stipulate the main content and formulation procedures; (2) standards of the audit evidence, which mainly stipulate the meaning of audit evidence, quality requirements for audit evidence appropriateness and adequacy, models, methods and requirements for obtaining audit evidence, and requirements for the use of expert advice and work results of other agencies; (3) standards of audit records, which mainly stipulate the scope, objectives, and quality requirements for producing audit records, classification and content, review of auditing papers, and so on; and (4) standards of the inspection activities of major violations, which mainly stipulate the characteristics of major violations and the special procedures and countermeasures for their inspection.

Audit findings. These mainly include five aspects: (1) standards of the form and content of the audit report, which stipulate the basic elements and main content of the audit report and special audit investigation report, special features and contents of the accountability audit report, audit decisions, and the main content of the audit transfer and handling; (2) standards of the audit report editing, which stipulate the requirements for drafting, comments, review, hearing, approval, issuance, and handling of major violations found in a special audit investigation; (3) standards of the special report and comprehensive report, which stipulate the requirements for compiling the special audit report, newsletters, comprehensive reports, economic responsibility audit reports, and the report on budget implementation and other financial income and expenditure; (4) standards of the release of the audit results, which stipulate the information type, content scope, quality requirements, and approval procedures of published audit results; and (5) standards of the audit result follow-up examination, which stipulate the examination items, time, manner, test result reporting, and treatment measures.

Audit quality control and responsibility. This mainly includes establishing the goal of the audit quality control system, elements of audit quality control, all levels of quality control duties and responsibilities based on "quality responsibility," quality control responsibility of the audit file and filing content, audit quality checks based on "quality control," annual business assessment, and the system of outstanding audit project selection.

Auditing under an IT environment. Auditing under an IT environment should also comply with the relevant norms. The IT environment has special requirements for auditing. It mainly includes overall competence of the audit team; requirements for using data to analyze the results in the process of preparing the annual audit plan and using technical equipment; requirements for investigating and gaining knowledge of the information system and the electronic data of the audited entity when preparing the audit implementation scheme and for checking the validity of the information system; special requirements for audit evidence in electronic form, auditing papers, and audit files; the requirements for auditors focusing on the fraud potential in information systems, system vulnerabilities, and measures to deal with such problems; special requirements for the networking audit for audit scheme preparation and audit reporting; confidentiality requirements for publicizing the audit findings with regard to the technical details of information systems security control, system vulnerabilities, and so on.

Audit management. This means to standardize the system structure and main elements of audit management. Audit management practice includes four main aspects: (1) standards of the allocation and integration of audit resources, which mainly stipulate the way to develop the project plan, coordination, and connection between the annual project plan and long-term development plan, establishment of a dynamic project library, preparation of a rolling scheme plan, integration between the various annual projects, and so on; (2) standards of the audit model, which stipulate that each project shall explore starting from the audit of financial revenue and expenditure, focusing on responsibility performance and accountability, and integrating compliance and performance audits. The audit shall comprehensively consider the efficiency and effect of policy implementation, use of funds, resource utilization, and administrative efficiency, so as to meet the various needs of economic and social development through auditing; (3) standards of the audit methods, which stipulate that the selection basis and methods shall be considered with the project characteristics to scientifically select the audit, audit investigation, or real-time audit, and to actively explore and promote the management mode of the multidisciplinary integration, multi-angle analysis, and multiway combination; and (4) standards of handling the relationship between audit task, audit force, and audit risk, which specify the principles of the stressing the key point, acting based on capacity, specifying responsibility, and preventing risk.

(c) Main Content of the Audit Profession Ethics

This involves professional virtue, competence, liability, and so on. Its core principles include acting in strict accordance with the law, integrity and honesty, objectivity and fairness, diligence, and confidentiality.

Compliance with the law means auditors must conduct audit supervision and standardize their audit behavior in strict accordance with their statutory audit duties, powers, and procedures.

Integrity and honesty mean that auditors uphold basic principles and not yield to external pressure; neither distort the facts nor hide audit problems; practice self-discipline and do not use their powers for personal profit; and safeguard national and public interests.

Objectivity and fairness mean that auditors shall support the audit conclusions with appropriate and adequate audit evidence; realistically assess and address audit problems; and maintain an impartial stance and attitude, to avoid bias.

Diligence means that auditors conscientiously fulfill the duties of an audit; are meticulous and ensure audit quality; are efficient, completing audit business in a timely way; and maintain self-discipline and do not use their powers for personal gain.

Confidentiality means that auditors shall keep state, commercial, and work secrets while engaged in an audit; shall neither provide nor disclose information obtained from the implementation of audit assignments, audit records, and the relevant circumstances to the outside world without approval; and shall not use any information for purposes unrelated to the audit.

The roles of audit professional ethics are mainly reflected in three aspects. First, they are an important part of audit standardization, and a necessary condition for strengthening audit professional management and giving full play to the role of the audit as well as the important guarantee of the smooth completion of the audit task. Second, they are an important measure to establish a good audit image and maintain credibility, playing a positive role in fostering the formation of a good audit culture and industry morality. Third, they are a driving force to improve auditor quality through formation of morality and shaping the audit spirit.

IV. PROBLEMS AND AFFECTING FACTORS IN CHINESE AUDIT STANDARDIZATION

Although government audit standardization has made great achievements, there are still some problems due to the impact of various internal and external factors. From the perspective of the objective requirements for audit development, some aspects need strengthening and gradual improvement.

(1) Problems of Audit Standardization

Problems of audit standardization are mainly manifested in the following aspects:

Relevant standardization has not been completed, and the audit guidance system is not sound. An audit standardization system should consist of laws, regulations, auditing standards, audit guidelines, professional ethics, and so on. China's current auditing standardization system has completed the construction of audit laws, regulations, and guidelines, but the progress of audit guidance construction is still lagging behind. Although several guidelines have been formulated before the introduction of the new auditing standards, most professional auditing has no relevant audit guidelines. Some content of the existing guidelines is inconsistent with the new guidelines and needs to be revised. Therefore, the next key task of building the auditing standardization system is to strengthen the research and formulation of audit guidelines, and develop them for audit guidelines by major types of audits.

The standardization and scientific level of audit plans need improving. The audit plan provides the necessary foundation for audit projects, audit objectives, planned working time, resource investment, and so on. If the audit plan is not scientific or clear, or audit objectives are not clear, it will affect the unity and regulatory contribution of the actual implementation process. Currently, the main problems of audit plans include that the individual auditors' participation in plan formulation is inadequate, the evaluation of the plan for the required effort is not accurate enough, and audit objectives are too abstract.

The audit implementation plan is not specific, with inadequate operability. An audit implementation plan is used for guiding audit fieldwork, and includes the audit objectives, scope, focus, and content of the audit, audit measures and methods for all content, and so on. It is also the basis for on-site work, audit recording, and review. Audit recording includes the implementation process, the information obtained, and conclusions. At present, the audit implementation plans of the majority of the audit offices still cannot meet the required standards. Especially the relevant measures and audit evidence collection methods are not specific enough. This will largely influence the standard of fieldwork, and cause difficulties in audit recording and audit standardization. The problem of audit implementation plans not being specific and inadequate operability are key areas that need to be solved in Chinese audit standardization in the next period.

The reviewing system of audit projects is not fully implemented, and the audit quality assurance system is imperfect. The main purpose of establishing the reviewing system is to encourage the auditing business departments to exercise their authorities of audit supervision in accordance with the law and ensure audit quality. The main relevant contents stipulated in government audit standards include: whether audit matters determined in the audit implementation plan have been completed, whether the important problems found in the audit are reflected in the audit report, whether the main facts are clear, whether the evidence is appropriate and adequate, whether applicable laws, regulations, and standards are appropriate, whether evaluation, determination, handling, and punishment are appropriate, and whether audit procedures meet the regulations. Currently, the review system has not been generally adopted throughout the country, and it's hard to determine whether the audit implementation plan has been completed in field auditing.

(2) Factors Affecting China Audit Standardization

Internal and external factors affect China's audit standardization.

Contradiction between huge auditing demands and limited audit resources. The Chinese economic system with public ownership as the mainstay means many units are covered by government audit supervision. The social demand for audit supervision is also increasing. However, there are less than 80,000 government auditors in the whole country. The disparity between huge auditing demands and limited audit resources will exist for a long time. Therefore, audit offices need to focus on the priority areas, review the key problems, and reach conclusions. But they cannot comment on the financial condition and operation results of the audited entity like foreign government audit offices. The target and system design of China's audit standardization should differ from that of foreign countries.

Diversity of audit types and diversification of the audit goal. The Audit Law specifies that the audit types of the audit offices include: budget implementation auditing, auditing of financial revenue and expenditure, auditing of assets, liabilities, profit, and loss, auditing of construction project budget implementation and accounts, accountability auditing, and special audit investigations. Regarding the overall objectives of the audit, the Audit Law stipulates supervision over the truthfulness, compliance, and performance of financial revenue and expenditure. Each specific audit may focus on one or a few audit objectives. Among the different audit projects of the same type, objectives may differ. These audits reflect the diversity of audit project types and objectives of China's audit offices. For example, as for the budget implementation audit, it may target truthfulness, the budget implementation effect, or budget implementation compliance. And it may even be the comprehensive audit of budget implementation truthfulness, compliance, and performance. Because of this, China's audit system is not as easy to regulate as some foreign audit authorities or Chinese CPAs' audit involving giving opinions about financial statements. It is difficult to standardize all audit projects. Only some principled requirements can be raised, which increases the standardization difficulty.

The rapid development of the government audit creates new requirements for standardization. China's current audit is witnessing rapid development. Government auditing has developed from aiming at checking errors and preventing drawbacks to an "immune system" protecting economic and social soundness, and plays a role in national governance. As the essence of the audit, the immune system function is required to focus on the problems of systems and mechanisms found in the audit, and actively plays a constructive role. In practice, the organizational way has some new changes, such as real-time auditing, an extensive pattern of financial auditing, and a large project management platform. The audit standardization method for these new ways differs from that of risk orientation and internal control orientation. This means we shall design a new audit business operational system and organizational models, and build auditing business practices and management practices on the design. This puts forward new requirements for audit standardization.

The professionalization level of the auditors does not adapt to the requirements for standardization. The standardization level depends on the professionalization level of the auditors. Although China has implemented an audit professional qualification system, obtaining the qualification has not yet become the necessary condition for entering audit offices. The overall professionalization level of the audit team cannot fully meet the requirements for audit standardization. This can be truly achieved only by improving the specialization level and competence of auditors.

V. PRINCIPLE AND WAY OF CHINESE AUDIT STANDARDIZATION

Audit standardization is an eternal theme of audit development. Standardization has different requirements in different stages of development. At the beginning, the main task was to establish a standardized system, which has basically been done. Now, the level of audit standardization and audit quality needs to be improved by conscientiously implementing the relevant legal system and auditing standards, while combining with changes in the external environment of the audit and raising the quality level.

(1) Principles of Chinese Audit Standardization

China's audit standardization follows five principles in its construction and development.

1. **Combine socialist political, economic, and social features with Chinese characteristics.** Auditing is an important part of the national politics, economy, and society. To bring into full play the immune system function in ensuring economic and social soundness and effectively serving national governance, we must build a standardization system adapted to the political, economic, and social environment. The socialist system with Chinese characteristics determines that the leadership system of China's audit is the administrative system under the leadership of the State Council. The centralized system of the central and local relationship determines the dual leadership system of local audit offices. The economic system where public ownership plays the dominant role determines that government auditing has a wide range of responsibilities. An administrative type of system gives audit offices administrative supervision powers, including the power to deal with and punish in performing their duties. The people's congress system determines the form of reflecting the audit results when the audit offices report them to the government and are entrusted by the government to report the audit to the People's Congress. Therefore, the implementation of audit standardization must proceed from the actual condition of Chinese auditing. The immune system function can be brought into play by implementing the standardization system adapted to the socialist system with Chinese characteristics.

2. **Combine with audit practice to reflect Chinese characteristics and to enhance operability of standardization.** Standardization must take

full account of China's audit system features and administrative punishment power, and the emphasis on investigation and handling of major violations, as well as the unbalanced development status of audit offices at all levels in terms of personnel, organization, and the law enforcement environment. The standardization of operability can be enhanced by the combination of provisions and rules, and form requirements and substantive requirements, encouraging the development of supporting policies and measures, and so forth.

3. **Combine with the construction of auditors and audit culture.** Long-term audit work and the specific environment create a specific audit culture, which to some extent will influence the behavior of auditors. The cultural characteristics of the audit, such as advocating independence, focusing on evidence, professional care, professional skepticism, and caring about liability, must be reflected in the audit professional standards. Different audit cultures have different requirements for audit ways and quality. Western audit culture focuses on an audit opinion on the basis of professional judgment. Chinese audit culture focuses on the determination and handling of violations on the basis of audit evidence. Western auditing focuses on using overall inference on the basis of sampling. Chinese auditing focuses on collecting specific evidence. This cultural difference makes Chinese auditing significantly different from Western auditing in methods of obtaining evidence and judgment. China's audit standardizations are required to reflect the difference.

4. **Insist on combining with the level of audit technology development.** Audit standardization defines the way of auditing and the method of gathering audit evidence and making audit judgments and findings, which are dependent on certain audit techniques. Therefore, we must consider the technical level at a particular phase, and the development stage of audit techniques from the overall perspective and the development trend to decide how to regulate audit activities. If the standardization requires a higher level of audit technology, it may be difficult to achieve these requirements in the implementation process, creating a challenge to the seriousness of standardization. On the contrary, if the standardization requires a lower level of audit technology, it cannot lead to advanced audit technology promotion and application, thus hindering the progress of audit techniques and improving the efficiency of the audit.

5. **Adhere to the science and openness of audit standardization.** Audit standardization must comply with the rules of audit development and audit activities. Only by respecting science and standardizing audits according

to scientific requirements can we effectively raise the level of auditing and maximize its role. While meeting the current needs, we also need to take into account the changes in the audit environment and long-term development. For example, the development of audit practice requires increasing the standards of performance auditing, audit rectification, information technology environment auditing, and so on. This requires auditing standards to be forward-looking and open. By learning from mature and effective experience in foreign audit work and other types of auditing, we can meet the development needs of the audit, and constantly improve the level of standardization.

(2) Ways and Measures of Audit Standardization

There are three main ways to build audit standardization. The first is starting from constructing the system and following the audit process to build a system with a clear, standard, reasonable structure and complete functions. Then, based on the Audit Law and its implementing regulations, work is needed to improve the relevant provisions of the Government Audit Standards and the accountability audit, to fully carry out the construction of guidelines and to enhance a series of related regulations. In accordance with these regulations and guidelines as well as the reality, audit offices at all levels need to make efforts to establish a more specific system in line with their own characteristics. The second way is to strictly implement the system and strengthen supervision and restraint. To fully implement the audit review system, establish and improve the accountability systems of audit objectives and significant quality issues, and gradually institutionalize and regularize the audit quality inspection work. The third way is to uphold auditing by law and manners, pay attention to strengthening communication with the audited entity and relevant departments, and seriously handle opinions from all sides, conduct in-depth analysis to ensure that the audit results are true, reliable, impartial, and objective.

Standardization is an important prerequisite and foundation for audit offices to perform their duties effectively. To strengthen it, we must first improve audit regulations. Secondly, we must build an auditing standards system. On the basis of summarizing experience, we must improve existing auditing standards in accordance with audit career development and changes in the external environment, and thus build a government audit system in line with our actual audit and international practice. Through the development of audit guidelines, we should provide guidance for auditors to implement audit standards and carry out the specific audit business to comprehensively improve service standardization.

Strengthening standardization mainly includes the following:

1. **Constantly sum up experience and refine the effective practices to ensure that the audit norms will adapt to Chinese audit practice.** Since their establishment more than 30 years ago, Chinese audit offices have accumulated rich experience in the implementation of audit commitment, audit quality accountability, audit review, the audit business conference system for determining audit conclusions, the audit result announcement system, and so on. These experiences and practices can effectively improve work efficiency and achieve audit objectives, and can be accepted by the audited entity and society. Hence, we should summarize these experiences and practices, obtain common and rational principles, and standardize them in the forms of laws, systems, or guidelines as an integral part of audit professional standards. Professional standards generated from audit practice are in line with the actual situation, can really play a guiding role in audit practice, and reflect the characteristics of coming from practice and applying to practice.

2. **Strengthening theoretical study of the relevant standards, and learning from advanced experiences to build a high-level audit standardization system.** Building an auditing standards system needs to be supported by theory. Only by having a clear cognition of audit theory can we develop scientific auditing standards. The auditors who understand and master the audit standardization can effectively implement them in practice. Audit standardization should be based on the complete system of audit theory from the following aspects:

   1. The concept of audit, the auditor's core values and the establishment of audit ethics need to be guided by systematic theory. The general principles of the audit standard need to build on the theoretical foundations of the immune system.

   2. Regulating the audit conduct of audit offices and individual auditors needs to be theoretically guided.

   3. Standardized audit plans and implementation processes require theoretical support based on auditing technology.

   4. The standardized formation and submission of audit results require compliance with the relevant requirements for the audit report.

   5. The standardization of audit management activities should be guided by management theory, especially public management theory. In addition,

to build a scientific audit standardization system, we must learn from advanced experience at home and abroad. Foreign audit offices and social audit organizations have nearly a century of history in developing standardization. Chinese CPA standardization has also made progress. These experiences have significance for Chinese government audit standardization.

3. **Comprehensively improve the professional competence of auditors and enhance the level of standardization of audit work.** To achieve standardization of auditing, we must first build a scientific standard system, but more importantly, we must implement them through the practice of auditors. Auditors' professionalization determines their ability to perform audit services and behavior. For example, application of some auditing technology, maintaining due professional care, the use of professional judgment, cognition of the audited matters, internal control and audit risk assessment, and communication with the audited entity requires auditors to have professional competence. If the overall professional competence of the auditors is not strong and some important professional regulation requirements cannot be achieved in practice, it is difficult to achieve audit standardization. Currently, we should pay particular attention to the professional construction of auditors. Only by establishing a team that has high professional standards and can continue to maintain professional competence can we truly achieve standardization of auditing.

4. **Build a sound quality management system and strengthen supervision and inspection to ensure that audit standardization is effectively implemented.** Audit standardization serves as the criteria and benchmark of audit quality, and they are complementary. Audit quality problems are mostly due to violation of audit professional standards. The problems not only damage the interests of the audited entity and other parties, but also have a negative impact on audit work. Therefore, to achieve standardization of auditing, we must build a sound quality management system to ensure effective implementation of professional standards. Audit offices must establish and enhance the consciousness that audit quality is the lifeline, take a variety of measures to achieve the transformation of the audit quality management system, and strive to improve the level of standardization. The measures include establishing correct audit values, innovating audit quality concepts, management means and methods, and management elements and systems, combining the quality management mode and audit offices' performance management to change, innovating audit business processes and management means, and so on.

5. **Reform the audit management system, and enhance the audit standardization.** The audit management system covers audit plan management, performance management of audit offices, audit project cost management, administration affairs, and external relationship management. The management system is the basis and assurance for achieving audit standardization. For example, we need to ensure the implementation of auditors' qualifications through personnel management and the compliance with audit standards through quality management, to guide and regulate the behavior of auditors through performance management, to improve auditors' work efficiency through cost management, to standardize their audit evidence collection and working papers through record management, and so on. By building an effective management system, we can continuously improve the management level and the operation efficiency and level of audit offices in order to ensure the realization of audit standardization.

6. **Continuously improve the level of audit standardization through innovation.** Along with the continuous development of the situation, audit offices should seek to improve and enhance their work level to effectively fulfill their audit responsibilities. This requires constant innovation in working methods and means for improvement and change in auditing standards. The focus of the current audit standardization innovation must be: an audit reporting system, including the object to report, content, ways, and methods; audit techniques; and audit management way and content.

 BIBLIOGRAPHY

Dong, Dasheng, Chief Editor. *Chinese Government Audit*. Beijing: China Modern Economic Publishing House, 2007.

Li, Jinhua, Chief Editor. *Research on Audit Theory System*. Beijing: China Modern Economic Publishing House, 2005.

Xiang, Junbo. *Research on Legal System of Government Audit*. Beijing: China Modern Economic Publishing House, 2002.

8

Research on Audit Informatization

NFORMATIZATION REFERS TO THE TRANSITION process of applying information technology methods, such as sensing, communication, computerization, and control, to a certain field to comprehensively reengineer the business process, establish and improve the new production pattern, and enhance the capacity and level of management. It also refers to a state whereby information technology is greatly utilized, information resources are widely shared, and the traditional economy and social structure are moderately transformed and reasonably reshaped by information technology. Audit informatization means ensuring that audit practice embodies and applies information technology to the greatest extent through the transition process. As information technology develops at full speed, we must strengthen the audit informatization approach, and actively explore methods to apply big data technology to the entire auditing process to further comprehensively utilize data, so as to improve our ability to detect problems, evaluate judgments, and analyze in a macroscopic way, to effectively give play to the role of auditing.

I. DEVELOPMENT COURSE OF STATE AUDIT INFORMATIZATION

In the late 1990s, with the rapid development of information technology, computer technology was more and more widely applied in all walks of life, which brought unprecedented challenges to the audit profession, which also needed to upgrade its skill in examining account books and relevant economic activity materials. Without computer knowledge, the auditors were not able to open an accounting book, and thus failed to conduct audit work. In 1998, the National Audit Office began to plan for audit informatization and officially applied to the State Council for approval of its proposed system at the end of 1999.

In 1999, the National Audit Office, in the *Application for Approval of Audit Informatization System Construction Plan* submitted to the State Council, established the overall goal of an audit informatization system (hereinafter referred to as the Golden Auditing Project), which was to meet the demands of national economic management informatization and the electronic development of accounting information, drastically improving traditional audit methods through modern information technology, such as computers, databases, and networks, constantly expanding audit coverage, standardizing audit behavior, promoting audit efficiency and quality, and lowering audit risk, so as to better perform audit supervisory duties. The written reply from the State Council further clarifies the construction idea of "overall planning, unified design, overall promotion, implementation by step, popularization and application, strengthening guidance, being diligent and thrifty, and being rigorous and meticulous." Based on this consolidated goal and idea, the first phase of the "Golden Auditing Project" was started in April 2002, focused on "planning, infrastructure, and basic applications." After over three years, it passed the acceptance inspection of the National Development and Reform Commission in November 2005. The second phase began in July 2008, highlighting "initial establishment of the State Audit Information System" and improving "the capacity of audit supervision"; it was completed in June 2012. It initially achieved business collaboration, interconnection, and interworking and resource sharing in the central and local audit offices at all levels, raised audit efficiency, quality, and level and provided national e-government and national macroregulation decision making with audit information support. Currently, its third phase is under approval.

After more than a decade of construction and application practice, the overall framework of the national audit informatization was basically established, which consists of an application system meeting the needs of audit services and audit management, providing a number of data resources supporting audit services and audit management, a network system achieving interconnection and information sharing, a safeguard system maintaining information security and system operation, a service system safeguarding system maintenance and application promotion, and an audit team satisfying real-time informational needs. The completion of the first and second phases plays a decisive role in improving the internal and external environments of audit informatization.

(1) Research and Development and Promotion of Three Major Auditing Application Systems

The promotion and application of three major audit systems developed by the National Audit Office—namely, the audit management system (OA[1]), the on-site audit system (AO[2]), and the online audit system—contributed to audit informatization and digitization. It is used by all audit offices above provincial level—86 percent of municipality-level audit offices and 75 percent of county-level audit offices. The AO system was actively utilized in almost all the audit projects, restoring the ability of auditors to open accounting books. The applicability of the online audit system is being constantly enhanced, and many online audit systems of the initial version have been established by combining computer audit methods for budget execution, taxation, investment, and social security.

CASE 8.1: **CONSTRUCTION OF THE OA SYSTEM AND AO SYSTEM**

The first phase of the Golden Auditing Project focuses on the planning and construction of the OA system and the AO system, the wide-area interconnection of the National Audit Office and local audit institutions at various levels, training in computer audit skills, operation, and maintenance, and so on.

In September 2003, the OA system, with the function of auditing documents, plans, statistics, archives, personnel affairs, and application, had been deployed at the headquarters of the CNAO and 25 dispatched audit offices. At present, the OA system has been implemented at the National Audit Office, 37 provincial audit offices (including the municipalities with independent planning status, and Xinjiang Production and Construction Corps), 331 municipal audit offices (including 14 division-level audit bureaus subordinate to Xinjiang Production and Construction Corps), and 2,560

(continued)

(*continued*)

county audit offices. Metro-region and wide-area interconnections among the headquarters of the CNAO, dispatched audit offices, resident audit offices, and provincial audit offices have been achieved.

In July 2004, the AO system, with functions of audit project management, audit data collection and conversion, audit sampling and analysis, preparing audit working papers and audit reports, audit statistics, and electronic data archiving, was introduced to audit offices nationwide after pilot use. Currently, more than 100,000 copies of the AO software have been distributed to audit offices at various levels. Since 2004, the CNAO has organized the activity of collecting and selecting the best AO system application cases and IT audit methods. By the end of 2012, 15,661 AO system application cases and 4,726 IT audit methods had been included in the IT audit library.

(2) Establishment of a Nationwide Audit Information Network

The local area network for audit management and daily office work by audit offices was established in the late 1990s. Currently, the nonclassified four-level audit network established for the National Audit Office and provincial, municipal, and prefectural audit offices has become the main channel of collaborative management and data sharing. A case in point is the classified audit intranet, which links the Audit Office with special offices and bureaus and 37 provincial-level audit offices. In terms of transmission, the higher audit offices can send administrative documents to prefectural audit offices within a working day; lower audit offices can transmit the administrative documents to report a situation and apply for instructions to higher ones speedily. The security client system used in the National Audit Office and its special offices allows auditors to log into the local area network in different places. The classified network established by audit offices above provincial level effectively maintains state information secrecy. The Internet access network established by audit offices at all levels ensures that auditors can make full use of Internet resources; audit offices can announce audit results to the public in time, and accept public complaints and tip-offs through their portals. The wide application of the Internet and communication technology in audit offices has helped raise audit efficiency.

(3) For Audit Informatization, Application Is the Key and Talent Reserve a Guarantee

Audit offices firmly establish the concept of total staff participation, attach great importance to cultivating computer audit talents and information management talents, and have achieved good results after inputting a lot of human, material, and financial resources. The information technology training adhered to the combination of introductory training and advanced training, of professional computer training and audit practice training, and of universal training and specific training, thus building a multilevel and priority-based training system. A system featuring the combination of computer audit talents and information management talent, and of high-end research and development personnel and middle- and low-end application personnel, has been preliminarily established.

Audit institutions enhance their work through science and technology, advance the audit cause through talent cultivation, and significantly improve the capability of audit supervision, process control, and decision-making support as well as office affairs management. Mainly through computer audit software application, auditors accumulate experience, innovate, and improve their capabilities in problem checking, comprehensive analysis, evaluation, and judgment.

(4) Accumulating Rich Resources of Audit Data

The database application of audit institutions started with the retrieval of finance audit regulations, and the documents database was gradually accumulated in the process of the implementation of Office Automation software. In 1997, the National Audit Office started to train auditors to use Excel and Access. With the application of audit software and development of network-based auditing, the utilization of the auditees' database had entered a new phase. To achieve data standardization, the CNAO prepared national standards for accounting software data interfaces, standardizing the format of accounting software data output, opening an efficient data exchange channel, and eliminating audit data access "bottlenecks." The CNAO also formulated professional audit data rules according to basic data needs and by industry category, and developed the rules for data collection, analysis, and storage, achieving interactivity and comparability of audit data. It also developed basic data center rules, and standards for database building. It built the national audit data center and started pilot construction of provincial subcenters. With the establishment of 13 categories of databases—namely, audit management, audit practice, governmental budget implementation audit, tax auditing, customs auditing, financial auditing, enterprise auditing, investment project auditing, social insurance auditing, foreign capital auditing, agricultural auditing, accountability auditing of leaders and cadres, and special auditing—the data that audit offices can control and share internally has become increasingly abundant.

(5) Exploring Audit Methods and Ways in an Informatization Environment

Large-scale databases such as SQL Server, data storage technology, and disk array technology laid a strong foundation for data analysis and data mining, which provide technical support for auditing. In terms of data analysis technology alone, it has broadly passed through the following three development stages.

1. **Transitional stage from a manual to semi-informationalized state.** Auditors were more concerned about acquiring relevant knowledge regarding software, hardware, network, databases, operating systems, and so forth. The audit way evolved from reviewing account books manually to the combination of electronic and manual review. Auditors could export financial data of the auditees, and AO audit software connected effectively to financial data, representing an analytical mode in which financial data was placed first, followed by business data.

2. **"Independent" stage of data analysis.** With the construction of China's Golden Auditing Project, taking the auditing of various industries as the leading priority of informatization, auditing was carried out independently according to features of different industries. The principle was that those responsible for the auditing should be in charge of the storage and custody of data. This stage can also be referred to as the "data audit" stage. As to methods, auditing departments and affiliated agencies analyzed data and reviewed the results. For example, the financial and business data of the auditees, such as custom and taxation administrative agencies, were downloaded for public finance audit, while those of banks and insurance were downloaded for auditing of financial institutions. A batch of frequently used data analysis methods and audit cases formed references for the auditing of each profession. A batch of auditing software, such as data collection and analysis, generalized auditing, central government budget execution auditing, and customs business auditing software, was put into use in succession.

3. **"Integration" stage of data analysis.** Various types of audit data and systems were integrated, and a new model of informationalized auditing of "overall analysis, recognition of questionable points, verification dispersion and system research" was formed. New thinking in audit circles is to find an appropriate path and method for overall data analysis by summarizing audit experience, so as to precisely guide auditors in the field, eventually

summarize audit findings, systematically analyze causes, and make recommendations. In the integration process, audit offices worked to establish an audit data plan. For instance, auditing of financial institutions led the way in establishing a data storage platform for commercial banking, leading to the creation of a data analysis platform. It ensured the share of underlying data among commercial banks through the development of data standards. In the integration process, a model for data analysis was created through the establishment of a data analysis team. The follow-up audit of key commercial banks' new loans since 2010, the audit of local government debts in 2011, and the audit of national social security funds in 2012 were all supported by the data analysis team.

The comprehensive analysis of internal and external data as well as financial and business data frees the auditors from merely relying on account books and greatly enhances their ability to reveal problems and offer solutions. The audit profession plays a significant role in standardizing the management of public finance, improving performance, and safeguarding national economic security.

II. MAIN FORMS OF AUDIT INFORMATIZATION

This refers to a state in the audit process to which IT is fully applied; auditors are able to audit informationalized auditees and IT management is carried out when the audit project is implemented. The work is divided into five types, and the audit fieldwork digital management mode is also introduced.

(1) Electronic Account Book Auditing

Auditing of account books is the traditional work of the audit profession. Electronic account book auditing still treats accounts as the entry point for obtaining audit evidence, which represent "bookkeeping auditing" in conditions of informatization. Just like traditional account book auditing, the electronic type also needs to carry out the audit and examination of external forms. For example, it needs to examine whether the setting and application of the accounting ledger (a term of computerized accounting) follow the provisions and meet management and accounting requirements; it also needs to audit and examine the authenticity and legitimacy of accounting information, which is to examine whether the economic activities reflected by the accounting information can be considered authentic and legitimate, whether the relevant accounting items are recorded authentically, the account balance is calculated reasonably, the property and debts reflected by the account balance indeed exist, and so on; it also needs to audit and examine the rationality and effectiveness of economic activities—namely, to examine abstracts of the accounts to judge whether they reasonably and effectively reflect the relevant economic activities. In the three kinds of audits and examinations just mentioned, minute and repetitive research and checking can be completed entirely by the computer, along with the audit ways of thinking. Therefore, the efficiency of electronic account book auditing is much higher than traditional ways.

(2) Data Auditing

Data auditing is a new audit mode arising with informatization. Based on the internal control and evaluation of the information system, audit objectives are fulfilled through collecting, transforming, arranging, analyzing, and verifying electronic data. Compared with accounts-based auditing, which regards paper accounts as the entry point in obtaining audit evidence, systems-based auditing regards the internal control system used to control the economic business and its records as the entry point in obtaining audit evidence. This also applies to risks-based auditing, in which the whole course of risk analysis incorporates the internal control system and risk factors within the audit scope. Thus, data auditing regards not only the electronic accounts as the audit object but also the computer information system as the direct factor in evaluating internal controls. It aims at accounting data as well as business data, management data, and other nonfinancial data and also introduces external data to the audit process for comparison and analysis instead of relying only on internal data.[3] "Selection, comparison, and query"[4] in data auditing reproduces the methods of traditional manual auditing. However, its efficiency can be improved significantly. Provided with a standard, the computer can carry out auditing on a large scale. Moreover, "selection, comparison, and query" can be used together and carried out at the same time. The audit software adopts three techniques to carry out "selection, comparison, and query": first, an SQL query to access the data and inquire, update, and manage the related data system; secondly, multidimensional data analysis (also called OLAP) based on massive data input; and thirdly, data mining, which means that implicit, previously unclear but potentially useful information and knowledge are extracted from the massive, incomplete, noisy, blurry, and random data of practical application.

In recent years, according to the idea of "overall analysis, discovery of doubtful points, dispersed inspection, and systematic study," big data analysis was widely implemented in major projects related to social security funds, special financial funds, and land transfer funds organized by the CNAO, with outstanding results. Generally speaking, "big data" refers to massive and complex data that cannot be extracted, saved, searched, shared, analyzed, and processed with existing software. Typical features are: large volume, reaching terabyte (TB) magnitude; secondly, complex data sources, including the financial and business data of auditees and their internal data, as well as associated data of external units; and thirdly, rich data types, including structural data, and unstructured data, such as pictures, video, and location information. The utilization of big data by multidimensional data analysis is a new starting point for auditors, which greatly expands the breadth and depth of auditing. For example, for audits of social security funds, the CNAO, besides obtaining the business and financial data of various social security institutions, also collects massive external data from the departments of industry and commerce, public security, taxation, housing provident funds, and electricity suppliers; conducts associated analysis through the integrated data analysis platform; and analyzes doubtful areas from the perspectives of deposit, distribution, and receipt of social security funds. This not only expands audit coverage but also improves audit efficiency and precision.

CASE 8.2: **CHINA'S INFORMATIONALIZED AUDITING**

1. By associative analysis of bank financing system data, deposit system data, and stock trading system data, auditors discovered the senior executive of a certain company was involved in insider dealing, and this company was suspected of transferring equity income rights through trust products and bribing others, such as the senior executives of another listed company during preparations for a major asset reorganization. This discovery came about through deeply tracking and analyzing cash flows.

2. Auditors got relevant data about the withdrawal of enterprise employees' pension insurance from a social insurance agency and information on the registration of dead employees from the police household registration department and the civil administration

(continued)

(*continued*)

> bureau's funeral and interment department, or the population and family planning department. By establishing an analytical model, auditors were able to uncover the fact that pensions were still being paid to dead employees properly listed by the aforementioned organizations. Therefore, the auditors disclosed the illegal behaviors of pension insurance staff in a certain department who made use of the late workers' pension cards to transfer a large amount of funds for their own use.
>
> 3. Auditors did associative analysis of the date of finance, taxation, banking, social security, land leasing, water and electricity charges, and more in a national key monitoring enterprise in a certain province to see whether the central government's policy of eliminating backward production capacity was being properly implemented. The auditors found out that the consumption of power and water of these enterprises that should be eliminated was rising instead of dropping. The conclusion could be drawn that these enterprises were still in operation.

(3) Analytical Auditing

Based on shared data, analytical auditing is an audit mode in the third stage of China's Golden Auditing Project on the premise that the audit data plan of the second stage has basically been completed and data has been accumulated to some extent. It's mainly applied in two aspects.

1. The audit supervision of national public management by virtue of analytical auditing means the key evaluation indicators of management performance and fiscal and financial performance in regard to public finance, products, and services and the computer system of its related audit models of methods, standards, norms, and evaluations are established on the basis of the sufficient data. Audits were carried out based on these key evaluation indicators so as to reveal the potential problems existing in national public management and improve overall public financial management standards and performance.

2. The audit supervision of national economic security by virtue of analytical auditing means to establish various indicators in the important fields related to the national economic security. The goal is to establish audit models by combining national policies, external shared data, internal accumulated data of the audit system, and information on national

economic operation and macroregulation, study and analyze national economic security generally, reveal potential risks, and make macropolicy recommendations.

An important step in carrying out analytical auditing is the establishment of the audit simulation laboratory. Simulation is a way of converting the uncertainties specific to a certain particular level into determination of their influence on the target. The audit simulation laboratory was put into use in the second stage to provide technical support for audit prediction, allowing auditing to enter the digital application stage. To take advantage of the audit simulation system software, firstly the simulation model should be established and the methods to implement the simulation experiment should be developed, and then the computer can calculate the relevant data and come to a simulation conclusion. The simulation technology is a new method to improve audit work capacity, reduce audit risks, and enhance the credibility and availability of audit recommendations and opinions.

(4) Network-Based Auditing

In contrast with on-site auditing, network-based auditing has the same concept as a foreign audit mode, literally translated as online auditing. Compared with on-site auditing, the most important function of network-based auditing is to access databases, dynamic early warnings, and real-time verification of the auditees in real time or subreal time remotely. Auditors and audit information are separated in space, but auditors can access the data via network technology, and their audit offices can audit several auditees at the same time. If the auditee adopted the centralized accounting system, auditors can audit the subordinates in various regions without travel, thus enlarging audit coverage. At the same time, compared with past and relatively static data in a certain stage, the data from network-based auditing is relatively fresh and dynamic, and is drawn from the information system being used in the economic management, production, and operation of the auditees. The ability to store and reuse the electronic data helps audit institutions accumulate data from auditees more easily and conveniently. Although network-based auditing merely changes the way of accessing the audit data instead of the audit content, such a change can transform the audit from single on-site auditing into one combined with remote auditing, single static auditing being combined with dynamic auditing and single concurrent auditing into the one combined with ex-post auditing.

(5) Information System Auditing

Information system auditing is the process of collecting and evaluating the audit evidence to judge whether the information system can protect the security of assets, maintain the completeness of data, effectively fulfill the goals of the operation, management, and other auditees, and utilize their resources efficiently. It should focus on three key points—namely security, effectiveness (reliability), and economic efficiency. In light of the duty and task of audit offices and the actual situation of informatization and application of auditees, information system auditing should be carried out focused on the "security" of the network, equipment, operating system, database, environment, and other elements of the system, the "effectiveness" of standardizing management, improving efficiency, sharing information, keeping accurate data and other functional elements, and the "economic efficiency" of achieving organizational goals, investment income, cost performance, utilization coverage rate, and other elements of the project. Besides fiscal and financial revenues auditing and economic benefits auditing, audit institutions should audit the information system of auditees to reveal the information and economic security risks arising from defects in the information system, help auditees strengthen internal management and control, improve the benefits of informatization construction, guarantee the reliability and availability of the data needed in an audit, avoid "auditing the fake accounts," and reduce audit risk.

(6) Audit Fieldwork Digital Management

The implementation of audit fieldwork digital management is what on-site auditing should seek to attain when the computer application develops to a certain stage. In this state, all the data acquired and formed during the process of the audit operation and fieldwork management are transmitted, exchanged, stored, processed, and utilized in a digitized form in order to maximize the advantages of the computer technology. At the beginning of the IT audit, the lack of requirements for digitalized management led to a managerial form of the "manual workshop," ill-adapted to the informatization audit mode in audit fieldwork. Collection of audit data wasn't planned collectively, leading to repetition and omission of needed data and the scattered and poorly shared data that couldn't achieve the required data resource platform after being collected. This also caused auditors to work separately and to fail to promote their good ideas in time and mutually employ the working results, and caused leaders and chief auditors of audit teams to have only weak control over the audit process and to fail to transmit their requirements to individual auditors in time. Digitization of audit fieldwork is absolutely necessary to avoid these drawbacks. Therefore, leaders and chief auditors should be able to handle the IT audit and manage the audit teams effectively under the condition of informatization. The auditors should be able to handle the IT audit and to audit by virtue of the Auditor Office (AO) consciously and skillfully to meet the managerial requirements of the audit project. Meanwhile, audit institutions should arrange and adopt Office Automation (OA) and be able to interact with the data in the audit fieldwork; standard content and format of digital information should be enforced strictly; audit documents, especially evidence and other unstructured data, and audit archives of the project should be digitalized; leaders' instructions should be related to the audit project, TV, radio, and newspaper reports; and the derived results after the audit results are employed, feedback of cyber-citizens, and other information also should be digitized promptly.

III. FUTURE DEVELOPMENT IDEAS ABOUT AUDIT INFORMATIZATION

(1) Development Environment of Future Informatization

The development environment of future informatization involves:

Data centralization. With the rapid development of informatization, financial, communication, and national taxation departments as well as customs, public security, electricity departments, and others have accelerated the establishment of their respective national centralized informatization systems with a unified framework and overall linkage. At present, the data is generally concentrated in the headquarters and under the strategy of "Two Sites and Three Centers"—namely, a data center, backup center, and disaster recovery center. The high concentration, correlation, and calculation of the data have laid a foundation for centralized management and control, classification authority, comprehensive management, and real-time analysis. For instance, the Industrial and Commercial Bank of China (ICBC) has been developing a national unified information system independently since 2000. Every day, billions of records are gathered at the head office data center through tangible outlets and virtual online banks in different parts of the country in real time, realizing full-caliber management, full-range calculation, and full-process management and control within the ICBC, which greatly enhance its core competitiveness.

High concentration. Current "big data" consists not only of traditional structured information but also of nonstructured information. In the face of a vast amount of various data types, dazzling data tables, all kinds of complicated information, and bewildering processing technologies, a data centralized mode is adopted to realize the unification and sharing of national data. The explosive growth in a geometrical progression can be demonstrated by the daily number of transactional data of individual savings in the ICBC reaching over X hundred million, the daily volume of transactions in the online, electronic, and mobile power banks reaching over Y hundred million, the number of single individual transaction data tables reaching hundreds of billions, and the amount of the stored data reaching Z thousand TB; this is replicated in other industries. The data, information, and processing amounts are increasing greatly. The data in many industries will be calculated with PB as the unit. The storage amount of the integrated data of several industries is unimaginably huge.

Massive sharing. As the data is centralized, national data sharing is realized, destroying the idea that sharing is hard because of different systems and structures, as in the past. The high centralization of data overcomes the obstacle of restricting information sharing within departments and forms a unified interface standard, code rule, code meaning, and business process within the system, laying a foundation for realizing the integration of various data. For example, China Construction Bank is developing a new generation of core systems, which is able to realize not only the sharing and interaction of all information in the banking sector but also real-time docking of the data and information transmission with the police and the administration for industry and commerce, achieving extensive sharing and expansion in a preliminary way.

Integration of sharing. Since many auditees have achieved data concentration, each department has its own "data rivers." In the information era, it is rather important to reconstruct waterways connecting various "data rivers" to form a "data sea" in which information can be seamlessly connected. The existence of the "data sea," the most remarkable feature of informatization, means information can be not only shared and gathered but also mined and integrated. For example, the credit investigation system built by the People's Bank of China sorts and integrates the data from industry, commerce, transportation, public security, finance, and other fields to form organizational and individual credit investigation information, thus integrating and utilizing data on a shared basis.

Detailed integration. Currently, attention is paid not only to data centralization but also to the search for detailed data. A variety of data analysis tools are applied to explore and analyze. Modern high-tech analytical tools are applied to find the treasure hidden below the surface of the data. For example, after national auditing integrates data from finance, banking, enterprise, administrative affairs, social security, and other industries, the data sea of auditing will be formed. This is likely to become the information hub of all auditees. In this hub, high-tech methods can be used to carry out real-time, comprehensive, accurate, and true analysis of the economy and finance, banking, national security, and other industries, giving early warning of various types of risks so policy recommendations can be made, thus improving efficiency and promoting the audit institutions' ability to serve the national governance.

(2) Opportunities Created by the Information Environment for Audit Informatization

The information era of sweeping changes, opportunities, and big data is also an era of sharing. For national audit institutions, this is an opportunity for further development in the command system, data reconstruction, mode transformation, business reconstruction, protection system, and other aspects. Only by seizing the opportunity can national auditing make a difference.

(a) Opportunities for the Command System

Big data is not only the sea of data but also the basis for sound decision making. It is both the starting point and the end point of information. It embodies the tracking of information and retains its displacement distance. Therefore, the key point in any audit can be decided in the shortest possible time, and audit clues can be recognized in the most accurate way by analyzing massive data. Multidimensional analysis, multi-angled integration, multifield evaluation, and multilevel screening can be achieved by integrating and analyzing data, which undoubtedly creates conditions for remote command, remote analysis, and remote verification. More importantly, it can ensure that scientific, systematic, and standardized decisions are available to form a new command system with the information analysis platform as the base, remote verification as the approach, high-tech analysis as the core, and high-quality achievements as the objective.

(b) Opportunities for Data Reconstruction

In the information era, complete and accurate data are the basis for good auditing. To properly integrate information in the data sea, the existing data rivers and pools in various departments must be dredged and connected to each other to form the data seas and oceans; the existing fragmented river distribution pattern must be changed into a continuous ocean distribution pattern; the existing spotted distribution pattern must be changed into a single entity; and the existing stationary sources of information must be converted to mobile data sources. These approaches can effectively integrate the data of different industries based on reconstruction. Only in this way can complete informational analysis create conditions for the five transition periods of auditing.

(c) Opportunities for Mode Transformation

The information era has created favorable conditions for the mode transformation of audit, thus easing monetary conditions. This transformation is the requirement and the natural result of data sharing in the information era. Under the unified organizational project structure, business is centralized collectively, data is analyzed collectively, and the mode is transformed collectively. To realize the transformation of the audit mode, various organizational modes must be explored to form corresponding systems, fixed operational processes, corresponding management practices, an advanced approach to obtain evidence, and a complete team management mode based on exploration.

(d) Opportunities for Business Construction

With a unified hub for information analysis, full-coverage of a business has been achieved, which provides an endogenous dynamic impetus for its reconstruction. In the information era, scientific planning of audit objectives provides a rare opportunity to implement business construction. In particular, reengineering achieves mutual interchange and promotion, and inheritance and abandonment, under the condition of informatization.

(e) Opportunities for the Protection System

Informatization involves the collection and integration of data, equipment, personnel, operations, processes, and systems. Technological development, however, imposes higher requirements on system construction, especially an efficient protection system. System construction plays an important role in scientific management of auditing and creates conditions for promoting overall audit construction.

(3) Future Development Objectives of Audit Informatization

In the future, relying on big data, the national audit institutions should establish a new audit mode based on integration of the audit command, audit data, audit business, audit mode, audit system, and audit logistics to protect the country, serve national macroregulation, and prevent economic risk.

(a) Integration of the Audit Command

Integration of the audit command means applying an advanced decision-making and analysis system to command remotely, and make decisions and analyze based on big data. Specifically, the principle of integration of the audit command is "relying on the platform, connecting the National Audit Office with local audit offices and the analyzing mode." Relying on the platform means to analyze data in depth based on the big data platform. Connecting the National Audit Office with local audit institutions means to form a multicommand system for interaction between them. The analyzing mode means to apply analytical platforms to calculate the corresponding analytical results of different projects and compare results with the established indicators and draw objective analytical conclusions. The objective of integration of the audit command is "remote implementation, efficient unification, and scientific decision-making." Remote implementation means linking audit tasks around the country in various ways to achieve a national command system. Efficient unification means to effectively allocate, utilize, and combine national resources through a unified national command system. Scientific decision making means that the system makes quantitative and qualitative calculations to provide quality evidence for scientific decision making. Integration of the audit command includes big data analysis platforms and the construction of the command system. Big data analysis platforms can analyze information from finance, banking, enterprises, and other industries for real-time analysis. Based on the results, the command system makes judgments by virtue of scientific optimum computing methods, so as to provide an informational platform for overall decision making. The structural design of integration of the audit command includes metadata at the bottom, a standards layer in the middle, and an application layer at the top. Raw data from various industries are stored at the bottom; unified and standard data sources for sharing are formed in the middle; the audit mode is applied and used at the top; and integration of the audit command applies concurrent auditing techniques and interface connections. Information connection and function can be achieved by establishing interfaces between big data analysis platforms and the command system. Centralized management and multi-authorization are the management modes reflecting integration of the audit command. While centralizing the data, multi-authorization is provided by assigning data management authority, so as to ensure security and prevent leaks. By the aforementioned methods, full coverage of the audit command can undoubtedly be achieved in the big data era.

(b) Integration of Audit Data

Integration of the audit data, which is based on the existing audit mode with business as its main line, reflects the integration of business and financial data from the financial sector (also including the tax and customs sectors, etc.), state-owned banking institutions (including commercial banks, trust, insurance, securities, funds, finance companies, etc.), large state-owned enterprises, and other sectors. Specifically, the principle of data integration of the audit is summed up by "unified planning, separate implementation, key advance, and interconnection." Unified planning refers to the fact that audit data reflects the properties of the relevant industries; "separate implementation" means to implement the audit by industry audit departments in different stages according to the development of each sector; "key advance" means to promote the healthy development of key industries; and "interconnection" means to break the current closed status so as to share and integrate data. The objective of integration of audit data is to achieve "virtual centralization and decentralized sharing." It means that, after the audit data of industries has undergone deep-processing, virtual centralization is achieved by accessing the auditee's own database; "decentralized sharing" means to share and analyze data through authorization based on the audit objectives and tasks. Integration of audit data means the integration of fiscal, banking, and enterprise data and that of other industries. In the integration process, each industry's business properties, including business categories and the corresponding business contents, should be closely determined. The structural design of audit data integration, based on the data structure of each industry, involves planning the overall data structure and sharing standards and implementation strategies of data. Integration of the audit data can be achieved by identifying the path and technical methods required according to the specific circumstances of each industry. It is implemented step by step according to priority. The management mode of integration of the audit data includes two aspects. First, it is necessary to establish a comprehensively unified data management standard on how to keep secret, process, and withdraw data and to ensure authenticity and integrity of data. Second, it is necessary to set the management standards, working content, and the implementation process for the data maintenance team of the auditees to achieve full audit coverage through integration of the audit data.

(c) Integration of the Audit Practice

Integration of the audit practice is based on the existing business lines. To scientifically assess the implementation results of macropolicies, audit contents of multiple business fields need to be effectively integrated. With one or more important audit objectives, it will then be possible to complete the audit under the overall plan. It is necessary to fully share and absorb the audit results of each business line in order to achieve the combination of point, group, and the entirety. We have to scientifically assess the difficulties and challenges encountered in the implementation of a certain policy to provide precise support for macro-decision making. Specifically, the principle of integration of the audit business involves "subject planning, integrating various industries, studying questions in depth, and focusing on practical effectiveness." "Subject planning" means to establish and carry out significant audit work related to the national economy and people's livelihoods to safeguard national economic security and serve national governance. "Integrating various industries" means to integrate the audit contents of finance, banking, enterprises in general, and various other sectors as required by the tasks set in order to analyze cross-industrial and cross-sector data and carry out extended verification on such a basis. "Studying questions in depth" means to study the questions raised by an audit from both the micro- and macro-aspects. While summarizing and abstracting questions, an audit institution needs to submit high-quality analysis reports to the authorities to serve the major national policies. "Focusing on practical effectiveness" means that the refined audit results must be effective, forward-looking, and with overall coverage, so they can play an important role in improving national institutional mechanisms, evaluate the implementation effect of major national economic policies, and serve the national governance. Integration of audit business involves key sectors such as finance, banking, and enterprises in general. Each sector should be studied for its business type in order to create a hierarchy of audit importance in order to provide the main method of business integration. The structure of integrating audit business is the overall business structure of integrating finance, banking, and enterprises. Links are forged when each key business has undergone the key audit based on the comprehensive plan. The management mode of audit business integration, with establishing uniform business integration standards as the main aim, puts forward clear audit objectives, key points, tasks, and implementation plans.

(d) Integration of the Audit Mode

This means to integrate the audit power of finance, banking, enterprises, and other sectors to realize great integration, organization, and penetration with one common objective in the information era, seeking to efficiently allocate audit organizations and personnel to the main tasks, integrate the audit power of each business line, give full play to their strengths, improve audit efficiency, and achieve scientific and efficient audit evaluation under the existing organizational structure and conditions of human resources. Specifically, the principle of integration of the audit mode is "overall analysis, recognition of questionable points, verification dispersion, and system research." "Overall analysis" refers to the fact that, after comprehensively analyzing all the data, auditors find obvious problems affecting the development of the national economy, thus determining the key audit subjects to more closely examine. "Recognition of questionable points" then focuses on the key subjects. With scientific and rational division of labor, the audit team determines the people directly dealing with the subjects under review and compiles an implementation plan. The team carries out data analysis to look for clues according to the implementation plans. "Verification dispersion" refers to the fact that, having identified various clues, the auditors then seek an extended audit, compiling a verification assignment book for the "extended verification" teams. Each team carries out the work by issuing requisition forms to the auditee, confiscating materials, analyzing data, conducting on-site inspection, and so forth. "System research" refers to the fact that verification teams deliver the extended results to the lead group for further analysis and then develop the specific framework and contents for reporting information. The objective of integration of the audit mode is "establish a special operations team to achieve maximum efficiency and high-end results." The "special operations team" refers to the personnel who will be equipped with whatever is needed when carrying out special audit tasks. That is, the audit office organizes backbone staff from different fields according to the required tasks so as to achieve the highest efficiency. This is reflected in the phrase "maximum efficiency," which means to get the best examination results with the lowest human cost to achieve an optimal cost-effectiveness ratio. "High-end results" refer to the fact that during the determination of the audit tasks, the highest standards, the most stringent requirements, and the best achievements form the ultimate objectives, and the organizational mode should well serve the audit objectives. Integration of the audit mode includes standard modes, principles of team division, and ways of implementation involving the processes of finance, banking, enterprises, and key industries. The structural design of audit organizational integration is to put forward the organizational framework, connecting mode, organizational processes, and operational mechanism of finance, banking, enterprises, and other key industries to achieve efficient operation through comprehensive planning. Management of the integration of the audit mode calls for establishment of a regular audit mode with strong scientific underpinnings.

(e) Integration of the Audit Logistics

Integration of the audit logistics refers to the relevant supporting measures used to ensure the integration of audit command, data, business, and mode based on informatization, so as to realize full-process management and control, full-caliber management, and all-around support for audit work. Specifically, the principle of integration of the audit logistics is "process management, system guarantee, and specific implementation." "Process management" involves sorting out and remolding the execution process of the audit as necessary to fully meet overall goals. "System guarantee" means to formulate rules corresponding to the five integration items to guarantee sufficient and timely supply of human resources, software and hardware, and supporting resources. "Specific implementation" calls for specific approaches to implement the five integration items according to work requirements. Among them, the requirement and goal in the integration of the audit logistics are "timely supply, efficient operation, and seamless connection." "Timely supply" means to solidly guarantee the integration with all-around support in manpower, materials, and finance. "Efficient operation" means to organize exclusive groups to carry out the integration of the audit logistics, thus ensuring the efficient operation of the whole process. "Seamless connection" means that all the logistics work must be connected effectively and seamlessly in order to offer proper support instead of excessive intervention and promote steady progress in the work rather than delaying it. The contents of the integration of the audit logistics include manpower, finance, equipment, and system. Integration of the audit logistics stems from good planning and implementation in all the work and precise distribution of all resources, full-access management and control, and all-around logistics. The approach to the integration of the audit logistics requires giving priority to the system, selecting key audit projects for practice, and then summing up the experience to work out a management system and methods for all-around practice. The management mode of the integration of the audit logistics has the logistics group as the core, and the information measures for the proper deployment of the recourses, the continuous improvement of the system and the extension of the field, and the final realization of the full-coverage logistics.

(4) Future Development Approaches to Audit Informatization

Seeking innovation in audit informatization to promote the revolution in audit modes reflects a new development trend. Audit modes vary with the level of informatization. Given new historical conditions, we must combine this with innovation in the modes of carrying out audits through "overall analysis, recognition of questionable points, verification dispersion, and system research." The approach to realize this is "operating big projects, connecting the five centers, and motivating all layers." Operating the big projects requires close cooperation, distribution of responsibilities, and seamless connection among various offices, businesses, and organizations—namely, the best management mechanism to serve the purpose of establishing a new audit mode so as to achieve the optimal audit results and goals. Connecting five centers requires us to establish the command and decision center, advice and execution center, central verification center, task execution center, and information processing center to meet the demands of "overall analysis, recognition of questionable points, verification dispersion, and system research." The command and decision center equates to the headquarters that takes charge of general decision making and overall command. The advice and execution center is mainly responsible for the plan, audit objective, progress, and implementation of the task assigned by the command and decision center. The central verification center, like the special force that executes tasks and analyzes information involved in them, seeks audit clues and accomplishment of extended verification of special and significant tasks according to the work requirements from the advice and execution center. The task execution center, like a field force, primarily carries out the extended verification of the analysis results offered by the central verification center and closely assists that entity in extended verification of special and significant tasks. The information processing center is chiefly in charge of deep processing, summarization, and extraction of verified audit information suitable for reporting to relevant departments. Motivating all layers means that we must follow the requirements from the audit projects to adopt a decentralized management system in all audit groups. The groups can be divided into three layers led by the National Audit Office, the Resident Audit Office, and the Provincial Audit Office. Each layer manages its own work according to the overall requirements, thus forming effective linkages.

The combination of audit informatization and the management mode will raise the management level. Audit informatization is the development trend, and it should be equipped with a corresponding management style. In the new development stage, we must seek this unity via "system implementation, process control, and hierarchy system, as well as authorization management." "System implementation" means to implement informatization management within the audit site and the office internal system via management software, thus making a breakthrough based on high efficiency. "Process control" means optimizing audit management by simplifying and smoothing its processes to meet the development demand of audit informatization. The "hierarchy system" is the informationalized and effective classification and grading of managers based on their roles and responsibilities. "Authorization management," based on the administration authority and range, requires strict authorization under scientific control in accordance with managers' different responsibilities and authority. To implement this, we must resort to a "horizontal matrix, vertical grid, and overall integration." "Horizontal matrix" is a management style applied to audit groups belonging to different institutions yet part of the same hierarchy, thus realizing the unification of tasks and distribution of responsibilities among different institutions. "Vertical grid" is a vertical management style implemented within the internal system of big audit groups. It's a vertically meshing and dynamic management mode formed by scientific and reasonable arrangement and deployment of resources according to the importance of the audit tasks. Overall integration requires the National Audit Office and its subordinate offices to realize unity of command, planning, arrangement, implementation, and management via informatization means to form an integrated audit mode during their execution of audit tasks.

The integration of the audit date can be promoted through the combination of audit informatization and data application. The audit informatization is the inevitable result of the development of big data and the development requirements of informatization. Development measures vary with development requirements. Facing new development requirements, we must closely link audit informatization and data application to reach the goal of "comprehensive consideration, separate implementation, and integration and sharing." "Comprehensive consideration" means researching and analyzing audit data with an entire industry as the reference. "Separate implementation" means to develop the reconstruction of audit information in key industries based on their characteristics. "Integration and sharing" refers to the realization of information sharing through department data integration within key industries. To realize the reconstruction of audit information, we should adopt the strategies of "key advance, overall centralization, complete auditing, and deep mining." "Key advance" requires us to focus on the data of key industries, such as finance, banking, enterprises, administrative affairs, social security, customs, and real estate, as well as industry and commerce to set up a standard data structure and database of each industry and realize data association analysis among different industries. "Overall centralization" means that, in order to ensure the integrity and sharing of data, we must gather the overall audit data of key industries and upload them to the data center of the National Audit Office to contribute to national data centralization. Complete auditing refers to auditing assisted by exclusive business offices in charge of projects such as national informatization engineering, national information security, and national electronic investment. "Deep mining" means high-end data analysis by virtue of advanced data mining tools to serve the purpose of maintaining national governance and security, uncovering risks in economic operations, and cracking down on illegal activities.

Joining audit informatization and result improvement will lead to improved national governance. Audit informatization is the corollary of overall informatization development and audit achievement. An audit achievement needs a corresponding audit perspective. Facing a new development pattern, we must strengthen the close integration of audit informatization and improved results through "researching subjects, studying questions in depth, and highlighting practical effectiveness." Researching subjects means to research hot audit subjects to meet the demands of state economic security and national governance. Studying questions in depth is to deeply and widely explore the problems found in auditing, which represents a breakthrough in the contents of the subjects both horizontally and vertically, and to produce high-quality analysis to serve major national policy making. Highlighting practical effectiveness means that the audit result must be really effective, insightful, and comprehensive so that it can play a role in improving national governance, macroregulation, evaluation of significant national economic policies, and so forth. To implement integration of audit business, we should concentrate on key fields and start with key businesses, such as finance, banking, and enterprises, researching ways to realize their integration and propose corresponding technologies and strategies.

(5) Combining Audit Informatization with Team Building Will Produce Top Talent

The development of audit informatization must rely on a strong informatization team, along with a correspondingly good data analysis team. Facing a new development opportunity, we must work to link audit informatization and data team building and enhance cooperation via "the combination of business and data, centralization and decentralization, and scientific research and practice." To combine business and data, the team must consist of versatile members who understand information-based analysis and audit business. In this way, more personnel can be trained to master audit skills for the execution of special audit tasks. To combine centralization and decentralization, major problems must be tackled via face-to-face discussion and cooperation—namely, the collective seminar—according to the requirements of the tasks. Decentralization refers to a remote, interactive way via information media. To combine scientific research and practice, theories must be applied to practice to realize a two-way interaction to further improve the business capabilities of the team. To realize the three foregoing combinations, the way of "three systems, three platforms, and three supports" must be adopted. The "three systems" are the informationalized-team management system, the informationalized-analysis management system, and the informationalized-confidentiality management system. Among them, the informationalized-team management system includes developing the principles and organizational modes of the team, management modes, system of rewards and penalties, and so on; the informationalized-analysis management system contains modes and processes of data analysis, authorization management, data transmission, and so forth; and the informationalized-confidentiality management system consists of confidentiality procedures, specific classifications of breaches of confidentiality, confidentiality undertaking ways, the penalty system, and other contents. The three platforms refer to the practice platform, scientific research platform, and training platform. Among them, the practice platform is where the data analysis team manages big audit projects through audit informatization methods so as to get practical training; the scientific research platform is where scientific research projects are set up to improve the abilities of the data analysis team according to their characteristics, and finally lay a foundation for better practice; and the training platform is where top-notch experts carry out training to improve the business capabilities of the data analysis team in the minimum period based on the knowledge structure of the team. The three supports are "data auditing, follow-up auditing, and network-based auditing." Data auditing is full-coverage auditing based on the national audit data center and the data of the auditees. Follow-up auditing means carrying out continuous political follow-up auditing to serve national governance and the execution of policies. Network-based auditing refers to long-distance informatization auditing via cloud computing in different places.

BIBLIOGRAPHY

Department of Monetary Audit of National Audit Office of the People's Republic of China. *Commercial Bank Audit Manual*. Beijing: China Financial Publishing House, 2003.

Dong, Dasheng, Chief Editor, and others. *Chinese Government Auditing*. Beijing: China Modern Economic Publishing House, 2009.

Li, Jinhua, Chief Editor. *Review of 25 Years of Audit Work in China and Prospect.* Beijing: People's Publishing House, 2008.

Liu, Jiayi. *Speed Up the Audit Informatization to Comprehensively Enhance Audit Capabilities and Technologies.* Speech at the State Audit Work Forum, July 10, 2012.

Liu, Ruzhuo. *Recognition of Characteristics of Audit Clues.* Beijing: Tsinghua University Press, 2009.

Liu, Ruzhuo, and others. *Multidimensional Analysis Techniques of the Audit Data.* Beijing: Tsinghua University Press, 2006.

Shi, Aizhong, and Sun Jian. Preliminary Interpretation of the Data Auditing Mode. *Auditing Research* 2005 (4).

Yuan, Ye, Liu Xing, Chief Editors, and others. *Systematic Research on Computer Auditing of Commercial Banks.* Beijing: China Modern Economic Publishing House, 2011.

 NOTES

1. Office Automation (OA).
2. The English name of the on-site audit system is Auditor Officer (AO).
3. Aizhong Shi and Sun Jian. Preliminary Interpretation of the Data Auditing Mode. *Auditing Research*, 2005 (4).
4. Deshan Zhang, Overview of Audit Software. China Essay League, www.lwlm .com.

9

Audit Culture

A UDIT CULTURE IS AN IMPORTANT part of socialist culture, and
also the moral basis, spiritual pillar, and power source for guaranteeing the development of the audit cause. By deepening understanding
of the audit culture and establishing and carrying forward auditors' core values, we can improve moral integrity and the sense of professional honor, and
enhance the cohesion and solidarity of the audit team.

 ## I. CONCEPT AND FUNCTION OF AUDIT CULTURE

(1) Meaning of Culture

Culture is a phenomenon of historical inheritance; as a social ideology, it reflects
a certain level of social, political, and economic development. Research shows
the word "culture" has existed in the Chinese language system since ancient
times, while its current concept can be traced back to the end of the nineteenth
century. Chinese scholars translated the English word "culture" as "wen hua,"
enjoying wide usage. In the *American Heritage Dictionary*, the original meaning
of "culture" is the summation of a code of conduct, beliefs, institutions, and all

other products of human work and thoughts extensively inherited. Culture has both broad and narrow senses. In a broad sense, it refers to the summation of the material and ideological wealth created in the process of human social practice. In a narrow sense, it refers to the form of social consciousness of human works, such as natural science and technology and social ideology. Culture as a historical phenomenon embraces inheritance; as a social ideology, it reflects a certain level of social, political, and economic progress. It has so far become a multidimensional concept with rich connotations and broad extension. It is generally accepted as the summation of the material and ideological wealth created during human social and historical development, especially ideological wealth, which means the ideology, concepts, behavior, customs, and habits formed in a certain period within a specified group (whether a nation, a company, or a family) and all activities in extension generated by the overall awareness of this group.

The historical heritage of culture is shown by the fact that the origin, evolution, and development of each branch have their own trajectory and context. The formation of culture in a society is a very complex process resulting from long-term accumulation, promotion, and extension in human history and economic and social development. Culture is also permeable—it expands and permeates constantly, and keeps trying to invade surrounding subcultures. To some extent, audit culture, as a subculture, is the result of cultural expansion.[1]

(2) Concept of Audit Culture

The concept of audit culture has its own broad and narrow senses. Broadly, it refers to the summation of the material and ideological wealth created in audit activities, comprising audit material culture, institutional culture, and ideological culture, with the latter as the core. In a narrow sense, it refers only to audit ideological culture, such as the core values of auditors, audit concepts, audit spirit, audit ethics, audit psychology, audit image, audit style, and so forth. Due to the rarity of exclusive material elements, audit culture gives priority to ideological elements.[2] The audit culture of this study focuses on the ideological ideas reflected in audit practice. Therefore, the concept of audit culture can be summarized as follows: the audit community gradually forms values and ideological pursuits in long-term audit practice that can be commonly recognized and followed.

Regarding the concept of audit culture, there are three dimensions. First, it is reflected in audit practice, including the vision and mission, values, ethics, professional habits, and so on, so it should be understood with audit practice as the basis. Secondly, audit culture reflects a snapshot of accumulated national, ethnic, and historical and cultural deposits, and should be analyzed and viewed by fully taking into account the sociocultural background of auditing. Thirdly, lying at the heart of audit culture, the core values of auditors are not only the concentrated reflection of the sense of trust, sense of belonging, and sense of honor reflected in the audit profession, but also the ideological pursuit commonly recognized and consciously practiced by auditors.

In a word, audit culture is generated, developed, and continuously accumulated and enriched along with the audit system. Meanwhile, as the extension and reflection of culture in a general sense in the auditing field, the formation and development of audit culture will inevitably be affected by traditional culture, the economic base existing in a certain period, socioeconomic relationships, and other aspects, which reflect the spirit of the times.[3] Audit culture also has continuity in time and space. In different times and in different regions, audit culture has been continually developed and improved via interconnections, reference, and inheritance.

(3) Function of Audit Culture

Audit culture totally permeates the whole auditing process, influencing the thinking and behavior of auditors. It has many functions, such as guiding, gathering, motivating, restricting, and cultivating auditors, and plays a positive role in promoting their development.

Guidance: Leading the healthy development of the audit cause. Audit culture can provide audit offices and individual auditors with guidance on value orientation and play a due role in edification, enlightenment, and establishment of precepts. It may transform and remove all kinds of adverse factors in the audit environment, which helps auditors form a positive ideology, such as probity, selfless devotion, honesty, and so forth, so as to guarantee the healthy development of the auditing profession; it may integrate the individual goals of auditors into the overall goals of the sector, so that auditors can voluntarily and imperceptibly take development of the audit cause as their own ideal and pursuit.

Cohesion: Gathering the wisdom and strength of auditors. Audit culture can effectively concentrate auditors' wisdom and strength and enhance their sense of identity, sense of belonging, and sense of honor. It can closely connect the emotional ends, ideological pursuits, and sense of destiny of auditors with the overall audit cause. It can create unity, reduce conflicts and internal strife, and contribute to auditors' mutual recognition, support, and cooperation to create synergy for the achievement of audit objectives.

Motivation: Strengthening the internal power of the audit cause. Audit culture can stimulate the enthusiasm and potential for work by giving full play to the initiative and creativity of individual auditors and audit groups. It allows auditors to maximize their intelligence and builds execution and cohesion for the team to strive to achieve audit objectives. It encourages auditors to conceive a healthy mood and enterprising spirit from the bottom of their hearts, so as to form positive overall strength and possess lasting driving force. Thus, by continuously enhancing self-motivation and mutual encouragement as well as integrating the achievement of individual values into the overall audit results, auditors can continually promote development of the audit cause.

Restriction: Regulating the behavior of audit offices and auditors. Audit culture can harmonize audit thinking and behavior in a consistent way through the establishment of a sound tangible or intangible restrictive mechanism. This can come not only through "tough constraints"—for example, the code of professional ethics and "Eight Restrictions" for Audit—but also through "soft restriction" on auditors' psychology and behavior originating from various features of audit culture—namely, fulfilling responsibilities, exercising caution, following the norms, and maintaining integrity and devotion. Auditors can therefore be encouraged to consciously correct their behavior, improve their work style, and develop and exert self-control, which helps overcome reverse psychology and resistance caused by a rigid system, and thus achieves long-lasting restrictive effects.

TERMINOLOGY: THE "EIGHT RESTRICTIONS" FOR AUDITING

The "Eight Restrictions" for auditing (issued by the National Audit Office of China in 2000 and revised in 2008):

1. Auditors are not allowed to ask any audited entity to pay for or to subsidize accommodation and meal fees.

2. Auditors are not allowed to use vehicles and communication tools of any audited entity to handle matters irrelevant to the audit.

3. Auditors are not allowed to participate in activities arranged by any audited entity, such as banquets, travelling, entertainment, and social gatherings.

4. Auditors are not allowed to accept any souvenirs, gifts, cash, consumer cards, and securities from any audited entity.

5. Auditors are not allowed to seek reimbursement for any public and private fees at any audited entity.

6. Auditors are not allowed to sell goods or to introduce business to any audited entity.

7. Auditors are not allowed to use the audit authority or knowledge of trade secrets and inside information related to any audited entity to make profits for themselves and others.

8. Auditors are not allowed to impose any requirements irrelevant to the audit. ▪

Cultivation: Establishing the image of the audit offices and auditors. The function of audit culture to establishment image aims at showing a value orientation and ideological pursuit of auditors and establishing a good image among audited entities and the public at large. It can win the understanding, recognition, and respect of people from all walks of life for the audit process through establishing an image of being daring, rigorous, uncompromising, truthful, dedicated, and so forth. It can promote communications and interaction with other professional cultures and cultural fields as well as society at large, enrich, improve, and develop the audit culture, and constantly enhance the public image of audit offices and auditors.

II. CORE OF AUDIT CULTURE

The core socialist value system is at the heart of socialist culture. While inheriting and developing traditional culture, China has put forward its core socialist values—namely, prosperity, democracy, civility, harmony, freedom, equality, justice, rule of law, patriotism, dedication, integrity, and friendship. In regard to the formation and development of the audit culture, the core values of auditors were formed gradually in audit practice through accumulation and further deepened in different historical periods. After years of discussion, it has been agreed that the core audit values are responsibility, loyalty, integrity, legality, independence, and devotion.

TERMINOLOGY: SOCIALIST CORE VALUES

Socialist core values are the concentrated expression of the socialist core value system, reflecting its fundamental nature and basic characteristics, rich connotations, and practical requirements. The 18th CPC Congress advocated prosperity, democracy, civility, harmony, freedom, equality, justice, rule of law, patriotism, dedication, integrity, and friendship as the ultimate goals of socialist practice. Prosperity, democracy, civility, and harmony are values at the national level; freedom, equality, justice, and rule of law are social values; patriotism, dedication, integrity, and friendship are values to be embraced by the individual citizen. Together, they form the basic content of socialist core values. In December 2013, the General Office of the CPC Central Committee distributed the *Opinions on Cultivating and Practicing the Core Values of Socialism*, setting out the requirements for the development of socialism with Chinese characteristics, inheriting the excellent Chinese traditional culture and the outstanding achievements of human civilization, and reflecting the common value of the whole Party and society. ■

From the perspective of the inheritance source of audit culture, the core values of responsibility, loyalty, integrity, legality, independence, and dedication retain a strong link with traditional Chinese culture, of which Confucian culture is the most influential, most basic, and most fundamental aspect. The core is "the Four Principles and Eight Virtues"[4]—namely, "propriety, justice, honesty, and honor" and "loyalty, filial piety, benevolence, love, integrity, righteousness, harmony, and peace." Traditional Chinese culture highlighted "righteousness" and "justice" rather than "benefit" and "desire," advocating justice, honesty, benevolence, loyalty, practice, tolerance, unbiasedness, steadfastness, and avoidance of evil, which constitute the basic features of the Chinese national spirit with patriotism at the core. Core values for auditors contain the essence of Chinese traditional culture: "responsibility" stems from "filial piety" and "love"; "loyalty" stems from "loyalty" and "integrity"; "integrity" stems from "integrity" and "honor"; "legality" stems from "propriety"; "independence" stems from "righteousness"; and "dedication" stems from "due diligence." Traditional Confucian culture advocates "correct mind, self-cultivation, family management, national governance, and universal peace in succession,"[5] whereas the core values for auditors are upholding themselves and shouldering responsibilities.

The core values of auditors (responsibility, loyalty, integrity, legality, independence, and devotion) have highly summarized the long-term audit practice and reflected the occupational characteristics of government auditing as well as the ideological pursuit and values of audit offices and individual auditors. They can inspire and guide all auditors to do a better job and improve themselves. The current audit culture connotation and ideals are defining responsibility, maintaining loyalty, upholding integrity, emphasizing legality, adhering to independence, and staying devoted.

(1) Responsibility

Responsibility means doing what should be done, including completing tasks and performing duties, and so on. It also means avoiding wrongdoing and bearing the consequences if we stray. As for audit, responsibility means effectively performing the duties entrusted by the Constitution and relevant laws, devoting oneself to the audit, finishing tasks in accordance with orders and requirements, giving full play to the functions of auditing as an "immune system," acting as the guardian of public finances, earnestly safeguarding public interests and national security, promoting national governance, guaranteeing a sound economy and society, and being accountable for any errors during auditing. "Responsibility is a kind of love, a filial duty, an obligation, an ideal and one's personal goal. An auditors' responsibility as entrusted by the law is to fulfill duties, protect the interests of the country and the people, investigate and punish those who damage these interests."[6] With the rapid development of the economy and society and increasing demand for auditing, auditors should further enhance their sense of responsibility and mission and strive to effectively monitor the due processes of the economy and society, so as to fully supervise and promote each cause, provide constructive criticism, and guarantee scientific development of the economy and society. A well-established and enhanced sense of responsibility in auditing can provide strong ideological support for auditors to devote themselves to the work and excel in audit missions, thus providing a strong impetus for the scientific development of the audit cause.

(2) Loyalty

Loyalty means someone is sincere, respectful, obedient, and honest to a particular object. In terms of auditing, loyalty means loving the country and the people, believing in the great ideal of communism, respecting laws and regulations, upholding truth and justice, and devoting oneself to the cause of socialist auditing. Currently, as China is experiencing a special period of economic transition and social transformation, social conflicts occur frequently and abruptly. People are under the influence of all kinds of ideas and concepts. Under these conditions, it is rather important to advocate loyalty. Guided by core socialist values, all auditors should uphold loyalty, be responsible to the country, people, history, and society, devote themselves to auditing with high morale and spirit in order to effectively perform their duties entrusted by laws, and strive for the Chinese audit cause.

(3) Integrity

Integrity means that one should not take advantage of one's powers to gain any kind of personal or group interests in official activities. In terms of auditing, integrity means vigilance, self-reflection, and self-discipline. Auditors should firmly build awareness as civil servants and auditors, strive to strengthen self-cultivation, and consciously resist all kinds of benefit enticements. They must earnestly follow the Eight Restrictions for auditing and other integrity regulations, strictly regulate thinking and behavior, seek no personal gain, and work and live honestly. As auditors do not live in a vacuum, they will meet many enticements in audit work. Only by sticking to integrity can auditors truly be selfless, objective, impartial, rigorous, and prudent and effectively fulfill their statutory duty of supervision through auditing, so that the audit can be successfully carried out and good results can be achieved. Meanwhile, auditors can effectively resist enticements, prevent themselves from breaking laws and regulations, and maintain the good image of their audit offices and auditors. Integrity means auditors must be clean, respectable, and free from corruption and bribery, regulating their thinking and behavior while leading by example.

(4) Legality

Legality means handling business in accordance with the laws, rules, and regulations. Law-based auditing requires auditors to carry out audits according to laws and regulations, adhere to the principle of taking facts as the bases and laws as the criteria, judge and deal with audit subject matters in accordance with laws and regulations, and defend the dignity of the law to ensure that laws are observed and strictly enforced and law-breakers are prosecuted. Law-based auditing is necessary and is important for the rule of law and the construction of a law-based government and a socialist harmonious society. As the fundamental principle for audit offices and auditors, it is crucial for implementing scientific auditing and improving national governance. As the legal basis for the auditing profession and practice, legality deeply influences auditors' way of thinking, criteria, and behavior. The audit must be carried out in accordance with the provisions and requirements of the laws. Auditors must perform their supervision function by legal means within the legal mandate. Auditors should advocate, respect, lay emphasis on laws, and consciously regulate their own words and deeds to be law-abiding models.

(5) Independence

Independence is a state free from external forces, restraint, and interference. In terms of auditing, it means auditors shall be fair, impartial, and free from external pressures and influences when dealing with audit items. Auditors must avoid any potential interference in organizations, personnel, and funds, stick to principles, and work impartially and objectively. As an important part of professional audit ethics, independence is considered the soul of auditing. Auditors must consciously overcome the adverse impact of external factors, resist the enticements of improper benefits, fight against lawbreakers, and not be afraid to give offense during the audit. Unless they can remain free from external interference, manipulation, and the fetters of desires, they cannot effectively perform their supervisory function and conduct the audit smoothly to achieve results. With the current development of the economy and society, independent auditing has a new meaning. To independently exercise supervisory powers and effectively perform legally entrusted duties, auditors should have independent personalities and thinking and always be enterprising, so as to continuously innovate in audit systems, concepts, organization, and methodologies.

(6) Devotion

Devotion means that people serve and contribute to the specific objects willingly regardless of the return. In terms of auditing, devotion means that auditors have a high sense of historical mission, a strong sense of social responsibility, and a noble professional spirit, work diligently and scrupulously without complaint or regret, give full play to their subjective initiative to overcome all kinds of difficulties and pressure, work hard, and devote themselves to development of the audit cause. Devotion is advocated to motivate and inspire the auditors' sense of honor, belonging, and achievement. They will always strive to achieve the audit objectives, promote the development of the audit cause, and integrate the realization of the auditors' individual and collective values with that of the audit's contributions to the country, people, and society. Devotion requires auditors to improve their political and ideological pursuit constantly, cultivate a good moral character, temper a tough work style, improve their professional qualities and work abilities, and regulate their behavior in order to continuously enhance the audit's quality and results. Under the influence of devotion, auditors can not only strive for achievements enthusiastically but also better realize individual development and self-accomplishment.

Thus, the core values of auditors—namely, responsibility, loyalty, integrity, legality, independence and devotion—which reflect the current objectives, missions, value orientations, ethics, and professional habits of the audit culture, represent auditors' ideals, beliefs, codes of conduct, and ideological pursuits. It is safe to say that the core values of auditors take responsibility as the lead, loyalty as the cornerstone, integrity as the guarantee, legality as the premise, independence as the pursuit, and devotion as the destination. The auditors' core values are present throughout the whole process of audit practice and activities, reflecting the career, life, self-cultivation, and other aspects of the individual auditor.

 ## III. CHARACTERISTICS OF AUDIT CULTURE

As a professional culture, audit culture has rather obvious characteristics, as shown in seven aspects.

(1) Maintain Order, Rights, and Interests

According to the provisions of the Audit Law, audit offices should "strengthen state supervision through auditing, maintain the fiscal and economic order of the country, improve the efficiency in the use of government funds, promote the building of a clean government, and ensure the sound development of the national economy and society." They should supervise the truthfulness, compliance, and performance of fiscal and financial revenues and expenditures, preserve order in politics, economy, management, and so on, including the correct implementation of laws, regulations, and provisions as well as related policies and measures, maintain fiscal and economic order, seek to wipe out corruption, and so forth. Auditing mainly aims at maintaining economic and social security, efficiency, and fairness. On the one hand, it maintains the fiscal and economic order of the country, safeguards national economic security, protects public interests from infringement, and upholds the legal rights and interests of the relevant departments and units through compliance audit; on the other hand, it promotes and improves the efficiency in the use of fiscal funds, improves management, reduces losses and waste in the audited entities through performance auditing, and enhances the reasonable appreciation of funds and assets. Therefore, the maintenance of order, rights, and interests is the lawful duty and most important task of the audit and the main content of supervision through auditing. Meanwhile, it is also an important mission of audit offices and individual auditors and a vital feature of the audit culture.

(2) Keep Independent and Objective

As the most important ideological element of the audit culture, independence can best reflect the essential characteristics of audit work as widely recognized and accepted by the people. The various laws and regulations specify that auditing must be independent. Without this feature, audits cannot be judged and evaluated fairly and impartially, and the realization of audit objectives will be hampered. This means that audit offices and individual auditors must retain an objective and impartial attitude, but never yield to external pressures. In audit practice, audit offices and individual auditors should regard the discipline against corruption as "a high voltage cable." They must vigorously advocate honesty and self-discipline and guarantee and promote audit independence.

Objectivity is a built-in necessity for auditing. As the audit process is full of uncertainties, auditors often need to make experiential judgments and subjective conjectures, which, despite their importance, may sometimes be biased or mistaken for a variety of reasons. Therefore, in accordance with the objective requirements, auditors must respect facts and history conscientiously, make comprehensive judgments, and carry out the audit with an objective, neutral, and realistic attitude.

(3) Advocate Rationality and Evidences

In order to achieve audit objectives, audit offices and individual auditors must always seek authentic and reliable evidence through scientific methods, and adopt correct logical thinking to judge, reason, and evaluate according to statutory or accepted standards in order to produce audit results. Rationality, not arbitrariness, is needed in implementing an audit, and no random judgment, evaluation, or opinion should be made. "Being realistic and pragmatic," an audit policy proposed by the CNAO, is a requirement for the rationality of audit work. Evidence is critical to good auditing. For example, to formulate an audit plan, auditors must determine the types of the evidence they need to collect and the means of collection according to the audit objectives, whereas to prepare an audit report, auditors must reach conclusions and express opinions after sorting out and summing up the audit evidence. Especially for field auditing, auditors must make specific judgments after analyzing evidence and reaching conclusions. All judgments, evaluations, and opinions in the audit must be based on evidence. Without evidence, the audit loses its credibility. In long-term practice, according to the internal requirements for the rationality of the audit, audit offices and individual auditors must adopt standard and scientific audit technologies and methods, comply with laws, regulations, policies, and provisions as well as industrial standards or conventions, and obtain conclusions based on clear evidence, including facts and data, in order to establish the professional image of all auditors as being reasonable, evidence-oriented, fair, and objective.

(4) Remain Rigorous and Cautious

In the audit process, a great deal of highly professional, rigorous, and logical work needs to be done, such as obtaining evidence, reasoning, judging, and evaluating; the audit results have a major influence on the audited entities, related departments, and even other stakeholders. Therefore, audit offices and individual auditors must always be prudent, rigorous, meticulous, realistic, objective, fair, and accurate to ensure the quality of their work. In audit practice, audit offices advocate a rigorous and meticulous working style. For instance, the CNAO has put forward the requirement of "being realistic and pragmatic," "seeking high standards," "developing and innovating unceasingly," "implementing the audit under strict management," and "always being rigorous and cautious." Audit offices at all levels have made strict provisions for auditors' professional behavior, thinking mode, working attitude, and other aspects, and implemented a series of mechanisms, such as audit quality control, assurance review, and audit accountability, which have ensured audit quality effectively and established the image of auditors as being rigorous, cautious, self-disciplined, and pragmatic.

(5) Follow Standards and Procedures

As the audit is statutory supervision, audit offices and individual auditors must carry it out according to the Constitution, the Audit Law, and other relevant laws and regulations. Also, as the audit is highly professional with established norms and standards, auditors must carry it out according to the relevant laws, regulations, norms, and standards to ensure its smooth implementation and expected results. The Audit Law and its Implementing Regulations, the National Auditing Standards, and other relevant normative documents specify the responsibilities and authority as well as procedures and methods of the audit. For instance, an audit is divided into three phases—namely, pre-audit planning, on-site implementation, and audit reporting; the methods and requirements of obtaining evidence, the format of the audit report, and other aspects are also standardized. Professional ethics and standards apply to all who engage in audit work. These provisions and requirements can restrain audit professional behavior, prevent negligence, reduce audit risks, and guarantee audit quality effectively. In early 2007, the former prime minister Wen Jiabao put forward the concept of "civilized auditing." To be exact, it includes "legality, procedural compliance, quality, and civility," with the first two requirements as the core and the premise. Civilized auditing fully demonstrates the importance of complying with standards and procedures, which is also part of the ethics and code of conduct for auditors. According to this requirement, audit offices of all levels as well as individual auditors must pay attention to standardized operation and process control when scheduling audit work plans, preparing audit schemes, implementing field auditing, and producing and using audit results, so as to contribute to a professional image of "carrying out the audit in compliance with standards and procedures in a civilized way."

(6) Encourage Innovation and Development

With the continuous development of the economy and society and the changing audit environment, requirements for work are constantly raising. Hence, the audit must adapt itself to these objective requirements and continuously make innovations and develop. For example, the rapid development of the economy and society, deepened reform, and the complicated international economic situation impose new and higher requirements for the objectives, priorities, methods, and other aspects of the audit. Meanwhile, with broader IT application in the whole society, many audited entities have fully adopted computerized accounting and some have begun to use ERP systems, office automation platforms, and data management systems. Hence, the informatization and digitization of the audit must be accelerated overall. Innovation and development are necessary not only for audit offices to continuously improve their performance and ensure audit effectiveness, but also for auditors to develop their own career paths and realize their values. Therefore, audit offices at all levels have vigorously carried out systematic activities, including education and training, theoretical research, practical mentor systems, and so forth. For instance, the CNAO has set up the CNAO Continuing Education School for Auditors to promote audit case studies, build computer simulation laboratories, and actively promote the establishment of a master's degree in auditing at universities in order to promote the overall quality of auditors as well as audit operational capacity.

CASE 9.1: **STRIVE TO BE "MASTERS IN FOUR ASPECTS"**

To strengthen the building of audit professional teams, the CNAO has implemented a training project for leading auditors and key auditors. In November 2007, Jiayi Liu, auditor general of China, first explicitly proposed the strategic objective of training "Masters in Four Aspects."

This refers to being masters in problem checking, analysis and research, computer application, and internal management.

The project of training "Masters in Four Aspects" is a major initiative begun by the CNAO to promote personnel development and capacity building, which has greatly stimulated the enthusiasm of auditors and improved their learning ability, creativity, and work style.

(7) Focus on Unity and Cooperation

Covering a wide range of industries, auditing has high professional requirements and detailed business divisions. Hence, only by cooperation and teamwork can auditors complete projects. Given the demands for enhanced objectivity, audit quality control, and honest administration, audits are generally carried out by many people with multiple controls under relevant rules and standards. In audit practice, field audits are carried out by audit teams as the basic unit, which undergo a number of double-checks and assurance reviews. The audit report has to be checked at the auditing business meeting and audit subject matters reviewed at three levels. By implementing these provisions and practices, auditors can fully embrace team spirit. At present, field auditing is still the main way of carrying out audits. In most cases, auditors need to stay away from the audit offices for extended periods and travel frequently. Working on the same team, individual auditors need to have a strong sense of teamwork, respect collectivism, and focus on unity and cooperation.

The inherent relationship between core values of auditors and characteristics of the audit culture is rather close. For example, responsibility and loyalty provide the backing for "preserving the order, rights, and interests," "remaining rigorous and cautious," and "encouraging innovation and development"; legality is the basis of "advocating rationality and evidence" and "following standards and procedures"; integrity and independence are the direct embodiment of "observing independence and objectivity" and "following standards and procedures" and the inherent requirement for "remaining rigorous and cautious"; devotion is the sublimation and destination of "observing independence and objectivity" and "encouraging innovation and development"; and so on.

IV. AUDIT CULTURAL DEVELOPMENT

Strengthening audit cultural development is an important foundation for advancing the audit cause. At present, it has become one of the essential activities in audit offices. It includes the following aspects.

(1) Follow the Basic Principles of Audit Cultural Development

Be guided by core socialist values. The core socialist values represent the essence of socialist ideology. As part of the socialist cause, Chinese auditing should always be guided by core socialist values and adhere to the theoretical system of socialism with Chinese characteristics. Thus, all auditors, indeed all civil servants, must master the Marxist viewpoint and methodology. The construction of the core socialist value system should be carried out during team building and the entire process of auditing, so as to help auditors carry forward the core values, enhance their professional qualities, standardize auditing behavior, shape a good image, cultivate noble sentiments, and consolidate common ideological foundations.

 Serve the overall development of the audit cause. The construction of socialist culture should serve economic and social development. Likewise, audit cultural development should serve the overall development of the audit cause. In the current situation, audit cultural development should aim at channeling auditors' career ambition and promoting scientific development of the audit cause, and tightly combine audit cultural development with audit practice so as to firmly establish scientific auditing, improve the overall capacity of the audit team, and give full play to the audit function. Audit offices and individual auditors should enrich the connotations of audit culture so as to constantly expand the ways and available space for audit culture. Auditors should strengthen their professional convictions, stick to professional ethics, carry forward the core values, improve their professional capacities, and standardize professional behavior so as to continuously promote the image of the profession.

 Advocate inheritance and innovation. Cultural development is closely related to historical inheritance and continuity. The Chinese nation has long been known as a country of ceremonies (rites). Many aspects of audit culture originate from traditional Chinese culture. The connotations of the traditional culture have all kinds of linkages with the auditors' core values, such as responsibility, loyalty, integrity, and devotion. Understanding the traditional culture from which the audit culture originates can help auditors comprehend the connotations and historical development of the audit culture more clearly, which has important theoretical and practical significance. Audit cultural development should also be carried out in association with the economic, social, and cultural characteristics in various regions. Therefore, during audit cultural development, audit offices and individual auditors should adhere to inheritance and innovation, absorb anything and everything, vigorously carry forward the excellent traditional culture of the Chinese nation, learn from the useful experience of various sectors at home and abroad, and keep pace with economic and social development. With absorption and development during the process of inheritance and learning, auditors should continuously innovate in their work and associated mechanisms, personally develop effective audit cultural activities with rich content and diverse forms, actively summarize and disseminate good methods and experiences during audit cultural development, and constantly improve its quality.

Put people first and emphasize the central role of auditors. People are the most important and positive factor for cultural construction. Audit cultural development requires every auditor to analyze and study the cultural accumulation in China's audit development history, forge close links to audit practices, and grasp the basic rules, methods, and approaches of audit cultural development. Audit cultural development should fully mobilize various human factors to enable auditors to carry out their work in a good mental state so as to standardize auditing behavior and enhance audit capabilities. Auditors' comprehensive growth needs should be taken as the basis, to put auditors first and put them in the central role. It is the starting point and focus to care about people, love people, understand people, respect people, cultivate people, help people, and fulfill people. Together with a good working environment and cultural atmosphere, there should be full respect and accommodation of auditors' needs for self-development, participation, and individual accomplishment so as to mobilize their initiative and unleash their potential. Audit culture can ensure that all auditors get educated in a good cultural atmosphere and embrace correct values, which can effectively improve the audit team's cohesion, creativity, and execution and promote scientific development of the audit cause.

(2) Grasp the Core of Audit Cultural Development

The core values of auditors—namely, responsibility, loyalty, integrity, legality, independence, and devotion—the heart and soul of audit culture, reflect the excellent Chinese traditional culture, distinctive spirit of the times, and behavioral characteristics of government auditing, which have been widely recognized by all sectors of society. At the present stage, the core of audit cultural development is to vigorously carry forward and cultivate auditors' core values.

Establishing and promoting responsibility, loyalty, integrity, legality, independence, and devotion, the core values of auditors, should be combined with audit practice. We should further strengthen the study of the core values, expound scientific connotations, significance, and practical requirements, and incorporate them into the training programs to enable all auditors to keep the core values in mind and put them into practice.

Establishing and promoting responsibility, loyalty, integrity, legality, independence, and devotion should achieve harmony and unity of morality and legality. To keep the core values in mind means auditors take them to heart as universal values and rules. Therefore, auditors must firmly grasp the moral spirit and the spirit of legality to establish concepts combining morals and legality. On the one hand, we should conscientiously implement the policy of ruling the country by virtue, vigorously strengthen socialist ideals and beliefs, audit professional ethics, social ethics, and family virtues, so as to cultivate people with advanced morals, enable auditors to enrich the ideological connotation, and improve the ideological and moral realm; on the other hand, we should conscientiously implement the rule of law, further improve codes of conduct, such as legality and honesty under the socialist market economy, enhance publicity and education to enhance legal, democratic, and civic awareness, arm auditors with advanced legal concepts, and guide their operations and overall behavior. In short, virtue and law should be closely combined to comprehensively promote audit culture.

(3) Further the Contents of Audit Cultural Development

To strengthen audit cultural development, its contents must be further enhanced. We should adopt flexible and diverse forms and practical measures to mobilize all available positive factors, and constantly enhance the penetration and influence of audit culture.

Strengthen ideological and moral construction. The ideological and moral construction of auditors is the primary task of audit culture. We should vigorously promote the construction of a core socialist value system, focus on the establishment and practice of the socialist concept of honor and disgrace, conduct various education activities about patriotism, collectivism, and socialism, carry forward the national spirit, traditional morality, and spirit of the times, and improve the political and ideological quality of the audit team. We should firmly establish the scientific outlook on auditing and constantly deepen understanding of the laws of audit development. All auditors need to fully understand the nature, fundamental objectives, primary tasks, and basic policies of government auditing and strengthen their sense of political responsibility and historical mission. We should further improve the professional ethics system and carry out related education and promotion to strengthen the implementation of professional ethics as genuine guidance for auditing. Taking the core values of auditors—namely, responsibility, loyalty, integrity, legality, independence and devotion—as the guide, we need to firmly strengthen beliefs, respect the law, adhere to principles, work hard, be selfless, practical, innovative, and uphold the professional ethical qualities of probity and civilization. In this way, auditors can be law-abiding, upright, frank, objective, impartial, and diligent, keep secrets, and constantly improve their ideological and moral standards.

Reinforce audit professional ability. Auditors' professional ability is the key factor to perform supervision through auditing according to the law and promote scientific development of the audit cause. Moreover, it plays an important role in the development of audit culture. We should further strengthen the construction of a learning organization, urge auditors to never stop seeking new knowledge, establish a long-term learning mechanism, actively create a strong learning atmosphere, and educate and guide auditors to establish scientific audit concepts, fulfill their duties, and continuously improve their professional abilities. We should further strengthen the professionalization of auditors, establish a training system for auditors' vocational education, and give priority to practical exercises. We must pay attention to improving the abilities of thinking and judgment, study and practice, abiding by the law, scientific management, and innovation, to create a professional audit team that can adapt to the requirements of the times. The auditors' team-building mechanism, which embraces characteristics of auditing and can guarantee the sustainable development of the audit team, should be promoted to create an environment where excellent auditors stand out, grow, and maximize their abilities. We should pay special attention to the construction of audit leadership, audit professionals, and audit management experts, build a high-quality team of leading auditors and key auditors, and actively cultivate a group of masters in problem checking, analysis and research, computer application, and internal management. By building a strong professional audit team, we can ensure the role of auditing as an "immune system" and a "guardian" of public finance, providing intellectual and personnel support for the promotion and improvement of national governance.

Boost the audit work style and anticorruption campaign. Strengthening discipline and work style and carrying out an intensive anticorruption drive is of great importance in audit cultural development. We should conscientiously implement the work style requirements of being realistic and pragmatic, seeking high standards, developing and innovating unceasingly, implementing the audit under strict management, and always being rigorous and cautious, ensure that the spirit of dedication and pragmatic devotion can be reflected in every piece of work, and actively create a good working atmosphere with devotion, due diligence, and excellence. We should get rid of "Yong Lan San" (mediocrity, laziness, and desultoriness) and "Jiao Jiao Mu" (delicacy, pretension, and the lack of energy). We should manage disciplines strictly, remedy bad ethos, sharpen the will, and boost the spirit. We should uphold the correct view of achievements and interests. By learning from the people and the things happening around us, we can create a good atmosphere where the main emphasis is on contribution and results. We should further strengthen anticorruption education, which should run through the whole process of auditors' training, management, and utilization. Furthermore, we should extensively carry out anticorruption education at both formal and informal levels (an example of the latter being to enlist family help), to effectively help auditors to resist corruption. We should strictly abide by the audit disciplines and self-discipline regulations with the "Eight Restrictions" for auditing as the core. We must establish sound and effective supervision and restriction mechanisms, and strengthen daily supervision and inspection of audit projects. We have to further strengthen the prevention of integrity risks and pay attention to the effectiveness of the construction of an honest and clean audit office.

TERMINOLOGY: "YONG LAN SAN" AND "JIAO JIAO MU"

"Yong Lan San" and "Jiao Jiao Mu": in English, "Yong" refers to mediocrity and inaction; "Lan" refers to laziness without diligence; "San" refers to no restriction and desultoriness; "Jiao" (the first one) refers to delicacy and weak will; "Jiao" (the second one) refers to pretension and arrogance; and "Mu" refers to lack of energy and gloom. ■

Thoroughly carry out audit culture building activities. Audit culture building is an important part of audit cultural development. Combined with the actual audit, it should be promoted with the audit team as the unit, which shall include colorful and healthy cultural activities in sports, entertainment, training, seminars, essay writing, speech, calligraphy, and painting, so as to further improve the audit team's solidarity and cohesion. We should encourage auditors to actively participate in various cultural activities in their spare time and create conditions for them to do so. Through these activities, they can enhance their ideological and cultural literacy, strive to cultivate an excellent lifestyle with healthy life interests, and remain vibrant and enthusiastic. We should promote audit literary creation, strengthen communication with culture circles, and vigorously promote the construction of audit fine arts, so as to create various outstanding audit literary works with distinctive themes, profound meaning, new forms, and strong appeal, such as poems, essays, novels, movies, and TV series reflecting the work, study, and true feelings of the auditors in life, and to form a mainstream that shapes people with noble spirits and inspiration to vigorously carry forward the audit culture.

Strive to improve the audit image. The audit image is the external manifestation of audit culture. It can be best promoted by improving audit culture, especially by strengthening the audit work style. Therefore, great attention should be paid to the formation of a good cultural atmosphere inside audit institutions—for example, making use of historical data related to the audit, to reflect audit achievements, the vigor of auditors, results and experiences of audit cultural development, and its profound connotations. This can be done by the introduction of publicity columns, preparation of special programs, establishment of an audit honors room, composition of audit logs, and so forth, so as to stimulate auditors' sense of vocational mission, honor, and belonging. Auditors should adhere to legality as well as civility, strictly regulate their audit behavior, uphold principles, and speak the truth. We should strive to objectively and impartially handle problems in accordance with laws and procedures and give priority to quality. We must convince people with principles and facts, treat people equally, speak kindly, never talk big, and always behave in a civilized manner. Be modest and prudent, pay attention to public opinion expressed on the Internet, respect and listen carefully to opinions and suggestions from all social circles, including the audited entities, so as to further establish and consolidate the trust basis of the audit, and establish and maintain an audit image of being impartial, honest, independent, objective, legal, professional, and reliable.

(4) Strengthen the Guidance and Build Mechanisms of Audit Cultural Development

Strengthen overall planning and guidance. Audit cultural development involves all aspects of the audit, so it must be carefully organized, led, and planned. Firstly, it must be well planned. This means including audit cultural development in the overall deployment of the audit, including audit development plans and annual plans, so that audit cultural development and audit business are arranged, implemented, and checked at the same time. We must earnestly implement the accountability system to form a working pattern where the leadership guides and all auditors participate with clear responsibilities. Secondly, we must strengthen the guidance of audit cultural development and define goals, contents, priorities, and specific steps to avoid creating false "castles in the air" or "being in a state of disunity." We have to effectively integrate audit cultural development into audit practice to achieve substantial results. Thirdly, we must fully combine audit cultural development with the progress of culture and ideals, political and ideological education, and daily cultural and sports activities.

Improve mechanisms and institutions. Audit cultural development requires a strong mechanism and system as its guarantee. Therefore, audit offices should make clear the competent organ for audit cultural development and its functions, implement relevant responsibilities, powers, and benefits, prepare a plan of audit cultural development, and define the tasks and requirements clearly. Besides strengthening the internal management of audit offices, they should establish and improve the relevant working mechanisms related to audit cultural development and explore new contents, forms, and methods actively to ensure substantive content of the work; audit offices should establish efficient and smooth information and communication channels, establish and implement systems linking leading cadres and auditors, such as regular contacts and daily communication, grasp the auditors' ideological trends in time, pay attention to humanistic care, help auditors solve the actual difficulties in their work and life, strengthen their psychological health and counseling, and positively create harmonious and healthy interpersonal relationships and working atmosphere. Audit offices should establish effective systems of objective management, examination, evaluation, encouragement, restrictions, and so on, evaluate and examine the activities of the audit culture, examine the fulfillment of objectives, sum up experiences, and encourage further advances to ensure audit cultural development is effective and ongoing.

Strengthen team building in audit cultural development. Audit cultural development is consolidated by strengthening the team building of auditors, which comprises three aspects. First, fully mobilize auditors' initiative and creativity in strengthening audit cultural development and form a macrosituation involving all auditors. Second, through strengthening the management of audit newspapers, press, colleges, universities, museums, and other audit culture units, improve the qualities and abilities of auditors in these units constantly and make them an important force to spread the audit culture and carry forward the audit spirit. Third, exploit and make full use of the audit culture resources in the engaged systems, departments, and units and organize the staff that are well versed in audit culture and enthusiastic to promote the great cause.

BIBLIOGRAPHY

Chen, Chenzhao. "Scientific Development and Government Auditing," *Auditing Research*, 2007 (5).

Gui, Jianping, and Ni Aiguo. *Theory and Practice of Audit Culture*. Beijing: China Modern Economic Publishing House, 2006.

The Institute of Internal Auditors. *Practice of Internal Auditing Standards— Professional Practice Framework*. Beijing: China Modern Economic Publishing House, 2004.

Liu, Yinglai. "Symposium Overview of Audit Cultural Development." *Auditing Research*, 2005 (1).

Shi, Aizhong. "Probe into Audit Culture." *Auditing Research*, 2005 (1).

Xu, Yanfu. "Brief Introduction to Audit Culture." *Auditing Research*, 2005 (5).

Zhang, Yikuan. "On Morality and Code of Ethics of Audit." *Guangdong Audit*, 2002 (2).

NOTES

1. Wan Jifeng, "Between Auditing and Culture," *Auditing and Finance*, 2003 (6).
2. Aizhong Shi, "Observations on Audit Culture," *Auditing Research*, 2005 (1).
3. Zhao Gang, "Constructing A New Audit Culture," *Journal of Audit and Economics*, 2001 (2).
4. In China's traditional concept of values, the "Four Principles and Eight Virtues" have always been taken as the most important moral norms. The Four Principles originated in Guan Zi, a masterpiece by Guan Zhong, a thinker in the Spring and Autumn Period, which says, "What are the Four Principles? The first principle is propriety, the second is justice, the third is honesty, and the fourth is shame. With propriety, rules will not be violated; righteousness

prevents arrogance; honesty forbids the concealing of mistakes; and, the sense of shame averts submission to the evil. . . . If the Four Principles are not upheld, the nation is doomed to perish." The Eight Virtues are the embodiment of the core values of the traditional Confucian culture. During the Song Dynasty, there were the Eight Virtues, referring to "filial piety, fraternal love, loyalty, integrity, propriety, righteousness, honesty and shame," which resumed the Four Principles of "propriety, justice, honesty and shame" as put forward by Guan Zhong, took away "benevolence," and added "loyalty" and "fraternal love," putting family morals first. In his *Nationalism in the Three Principles of the People*, Sun Yat-sen said that the morality inherent to China is "loyalty and filial piety" first, "benevolence and love" second, "integrity and righteousness" after that, and then "harmony and peace."

5. *The Book of Rites: The Great Learning*: "To show virtue and morality to the world, one needs to manage a country well; to run a country well, one must maintain a good family; to have a good family, one must well cultivate one-self in terms of morality; to cultivate oneself well, one must enhance one's knowledge . . . Enhanced knowledge helps cultivate one's morality; cultivated morality facilitates the maintenance of a good family; with the backing of a good family, one is likely to govern a country well; and, well-run countries contribute to world peace."

6. Jiayi Liu, "Speech on the Inspection of the Guangzhou Resident Office of the National Audit Office of China," November 2010.

Index

Note: Page references in *italics* refer to illustrations.